DF Kelly
Dogma

CONTEMPORARY
CATHOLIC THEOLOGY

CONTEMPORARY CATHOLIC THEOLOGY

An Introduction

John Tully Carmody
and Denise Lardner Carmody

1817

Harper & Row, Publishers, San Francisco
Cambridge, Hagerstown, Philadelphia, New York
London, Mexico City, São Paulo, Sydney

FIRST EDITION

Designed by Jim Mennick

Library of Congress Cataloging in Publication Data

Carmody, John Tully, 1939–
    Contemporary Catholic theology.

    Includes bibliographies and index.
    1. Theology, Catholic—History—20th century.
2. Theology, Doctrinal—History—20th century.
I. Carmody, Denise Lardner, 1935– joint author.
II. Title.
BX1747.C35 1980   230'.2   80–7743
ISBN 0–06–061317–3

80 81 82 83 84 10 9 8 7 6 5 4 3 2 1

For Jim and Sheila Lardner, Nancy and Rich Thesing,
who have given us a taste of having six kids

Contents

Preface

The aim of this book is to organize the traditional themes of Catholic doctrine into a unified contemporary statement. It derives its central inspiration from the writings of Karl Rahner, and the audience we have in mind is educated laity, college students, and clergy and religious interested in a new view of the whole.

We owe debts to several people who forwarded the book's progress and would like to acknowledge them here: John Loudon of Harper & Row sponsored the book and oversaw it editorially; Larry Cunningham of Florida State University read the first draft with a Catholic Studies teacher's eye; and Karla Kraft of Wichita State University's Religion Department typed the text expertly. Our sincere thanks to them, and to the many friends who taught us the Catholic tradition.

The Current Challenge to 1
Catholic Theology

OVERVIEW

A book such as this does well to begin by taking cognizance of the current situation. In the case of American Catholicism, the current situation might be called a lively discord between liberals and conservatives that is largely based on their different readings of the Second Vatican Council. Much of this discord, however, bypasses middle-range, "ordinary" Catholics, who are more interested in family issues. By one sociological tally, such family issues have severely eroded the church's traditional teaching authority. In the future, other issues, such as women's rights, are bound to challenge Catholic theology even more.

In Karl Rahner's work we find a theology that might meet this challenge by supplying a revision of Catholic faith both broad and deep. From the mystery that welds human beings to God, through the theology of Jesus, to the church and concrete Christian living, Rahner brings his venerable tradition to new life. This book would serve such a renewed traditional theology to any persons interested in Catholicism, be they insiders or watchers from without. By so doing, it would hope to advance the ecumenical day when the separate Christian theologies more clearly bow to the one Jesus who prayed for their unity.

THE CATHOLIC CHURCH IN THE 1980s

Every book begins from a definite place on the map of space and time, and often it is good for authors of a book that has existential—concretely personal—implications to acknowledge where they begin. We begin in the United States of the last fifth of the twentieth century. While many of the topics we treat have guided Christians since the beginning, they resonate differently today than they did in biblical or medieval times. For instance, the Pope who today has visited Mexico, Ireland, the United States, Turkey, and Africa was in biblical times a quite circumscribed local bishop. In medieval times he resembled a secular prince, but again his world was quite circumscribed: He knew nothing of the Western Hemisphere, East Asia and Africa were beyond his pale. Thus, even if a Pope such as John Paul II claims today to be teaching what the apostle Peter or the medieval Pope Gregory the Great taught, his words ring with different overtones. A book such as ours misfires from the beginning it if ignores this basic fact.

The overtones that mark the tunes of the contemporary American Catholic church are, to say the least, discordant. The liberal press (e.g., *The National Catholic Reporter*) is full of the crackdown on theologians such as Hans Küng and Edward Schillebeeckx, who have been trying to update traditional doctrines. In the liberal press's view, the Vatican does not understand the value of such theologians' academic freedom. For, if in rethinking the doctrine that the Holy Spirit secures the Church in Christ's truth, Küng comes up with a rejection of papal infallibility, he is simply publishing the fruits of his research. Other scholars may disagree with him, and when they publish the fruits of their research the resulting conflict will sharpen the issues involved in both "securement by the Holy Spirit" and "papal infallibility." This process is how scholars, serious students of serious issues, collectively advance our understanding. It is how scientists advance our understanding of nature, historians advance our understanding of the past, sociologists advance our understanding of group interactions. If theology is to be a respectable intellectual enterprise, it too must proceed in this "dialectical," assertion and counter-assertion way. Thus, forbidding a theologian to publish his or her scholarly opinions runs counter to the very dynamics by which humanity has in the last four hundred years or so extended its knowledge so many fold. It revives the ghost of the Spanish Inquisition that persecuted "deviants" in the sixteenth century, the ghost of Galileo who suffered in the seventeenth century because he saw the earth move around the sun.

The conservative press (e.g., *Twin Circle*) sees things differently. In its view the Catholic church has since Vatican II (1962–1965) muddled things badly. Prior to Pope John XXIII's unfortunate brainstorm in thinking up Vatican II, the church had for centuries known exactly what it was, what it believed. But the Second Vatican Council "Protestantized" the Catholic church. It brought new emphases on scripture, individual rights, and the laity that echoed themes of the sixteenth-century Protestant reformers. By moving in their direction, the Catholic church changed its agelong character. No longer could one go into a Catholic church anyplace in the world and hear Mass in Latin. No longer were the clergy clearly the leaders and the laity clearly the followers. Especially in sexual matters, all sorts of confusion broke loose. Divorce, homosexuality, contraception, priestly celibacy, even abortion were discussed as though traditional morality could change.

Even worse, theologians overly responsive to Protestant colleagues or overly concerned to make sense of Catholic faith to the "world" deemphasized the church's privileges, deemphasized even Christ's divinity. Confused, they made theology another academic discipline subject to the common rules of intellectual research and debate. In so doing, they forgot that theology is *sacred* science, knowledge whose control God has entrusted only to the church's teaching authority, only to the "magisterium" of the Pope and the bishops. It's about time, then, that we got a strong man at the helm, a real leader courageous enough to maintain control. It's about time we stopped the mush-minded liberals who disturb ordinary people's faith.

In simple sketch, or even caricature, the two presses, liberal and conservative, go at one another in such terms. But what about the vast middle range of Catholic believers? If the American priest-sociologist Andrew Greeley is correct, they are largely unmoved by this sort of war. Neither what the liberal intellectuals say nor what the conservative church leaders say is likely to direct their thinking. The bread-and-butter issues of ordinary Catholics' faith are things that make a difference in their own households and neighborhoods: the quality of the local school, the sort of counseling available in the local parish, the human warmth shown or not shown by their local fellow believers. Above all, Greeley found that domestic peace, accord with one's spouse, most influenced the ordinary American's religious affiliation and life.

In that context, the Catholic church's teachings on sexual morality, which its ordinary faithful largely reject (three-fifths of the most pious— those who receive Communion every week and pray every day—approve of divorce and three-quarters approve of birth control), loom very large. Indeed, since Pope Paul VI's encyclical *Humanae Vitae* (1968), which reaffirmed the traditional ban on artificial contraception, Catholic church authority has come into genuine crisis. Presently, eighty-five percent of American Catholics reject the church's right to teach (to bind consciences) on either racial integration or birth control. In the fifteen-year period 1963–1977, the percentage of Catholic adults who attended

Mass once a week declined from seventy-two to forty-two. Even the bread-and-butter issues, then, have made it a new ball game. In the foreseeable future that the 1980s begin, the Catholic tradition will likely be a lively battleground.

To illustrate this just a little further, let us refer to the issue of women's rights in the Catholic church. The issue came to special prominence during John Paul II's visit to the United States in 1979, when a representative of female religious ("nuns") petitioned him to give women who feel they are called to the priesthood a fair hearing. The Pope's stony silence made it clear that the tradition that says only males may be ordained Roman Catholic priests will get strong support during his pontificate.

It is not clear how the middle range of American Catholics feel about the possibility of women priests, but it appears that the tide is running toward greater acceptance of it. What is clear is that enough theologians now see the Catholic church as significantly sexist to ensure that in the near future it will find its scripture and faith quoted against itself. Few such theologians are more sensitive to the roots Christianity has in the biblical prophets' concern for justice—especially for justice toward society's marginalized peoples—than Rosemary Radford Ruether. In a recent article, she put pungently the sort of thinking feminists presently have about Catholic Christianity:

> Although it may not be true, in terms of strict theological tradition, that maleness can be literally ascribed to God or regarded as *essential* to the incarnation of God in Christ, operationally the psychic identification between these figures and male identity is very deep. So much so that when the very idea of severing the connection between the two is suggested, we witness, again and again, what amounts to a public "freak-out" by church leaders and teachers. After a couple of encounters with this kind of behavior, it is not surprising when some women conclude that they ought to clear out of the church (or the synagogue) and find a women's religion. [Ruether, p. 308*]

To be sure, there are alternate views of women's possibilities within the church, and following Ruether's piece in this journal is an interview with Giglia Tedesco, an Italian woman who is a mother, a Communist, a senator, and a Catholic. No stereotypes, then, do justice in this presently volatile area. Nonetheless, the issue of women's rights in the church represents the sort of challenge Christianity is sure to face in the decades ahead. Politically, ecologically, economically, it is sure to be challenged to show how Christ fulfills our best human intuitions of the ways to build a better world. It will be legitimate to answer this challenge rather paradoxically. That is, it will be legitimate to draw on the obvious New

---

* The bibliography following each chapter provides full publication information for works referred to in text.

Testament fact that Jesus of Nazareth did not conceive human "fulfill-ment" as secularists of his time, or of any other time, conceived it. On the other hand, it will not be legitimate to avoid the challenge of relating Jesus of Nazareth—his person, teaching, death, and resurrec-tion—to the task of coexisting with nature and other human beings justly, lovingly.

To women of any gumption, certainly, it will not be legitimate for the church to ignore what feminists consider a long neglect, a present injustice, or even a call from God. To citizens of any ecological sanity, it will not be legitimate for the church to ignore lethal contamination such as that perpetrated by the Hooker Chemical Company on the people of Niagara Falls and its Love Canal. Many of the most dedicated political activists of Latin America will not countenance the church's neglect of Marxist class analyses that reveal massive social injustice there. Many of the most sensitive readers of the New Testament will continue to ask how the church can seek fellowship with Wall Street and Capitol Hill when Jesus clearly rejected wealth and power.

In the future that stretches before the Catholic theological tradition, acute challenges like these should force a reappropriation of its old core insights. The church will either rethink its charter from Jesus, retrieve its saints' best understandings of the Spirit's liberating love, or it will totter to the sidelines. That means that theologians like ourselves, who want to communicate the Catholic tradition popularly because they find it rich and deep, have to try to repenetrate its heart. Fortunately, the movements of the last twenty-five years, in the midst of which stands Vatican II, give us considerable help. A great many other Catholic theolo-gians have been struggling to reinvigorate their faith and church, and a good deal of our work here will be just to present their findings. In that way, we may be able to suggest the full future the Catholic church could have.

THE PREMIER RE-VISION: KARL RAHNER

Just about a century ago (August 4, 1879), Pope Leo XIII's encyclical *Aeterni Patris* inaugurated a renewal of Thomistic studies. From that time until Vatican II, the philosophy and theology of St. Thomas Aqui-nas (1225–1274) had a privileged place in Roman Catholic priests' educa-tion. Other theological movements of the late nineteenth and early twen-tieth century paved the way for the biblical, liturgical, historical, and ecumenical studies that finally gained official promulgation at Vatican II, but the core reconception of Catholic theology that the Council popu-larized came from what a number of gifted philosophical theologians did with Leo XIII's motto, "to augment and perfect the old by the new."

For instance, in the theory of knowledge, the Canadian Jesuit Bernard Lonergan correlated Aquinas's basic insights with modern physics and statistics. In the area of political science, the American Jesuit John Courtney Murray reread medieval theories of church and state to shed light on the function of religious liberty in a pluralistic society. The European Dominican theologians Yves Congar and Edward Schillebeeckx updated Aquinas's theories of the church and the sacraments. The Swiss theologian Hans Küng launched a career in ecumenical theology by comparing Protestant theologian Karl Barth's theories of grace and justification with those of the Catholic tradition and Aquinas.

All these theologians, and many more, extended, amplified, and enriched the scholastic heritage they had appropriated by studying Aquinas. But one other Neo-Thomist, by the extent and depth of his redoing of Aquinas, furnished the whole skeleton of a new Catholic theology. He was a German Jesuit named Karl Rahner.

The extent of Rahner's output is overwhelming: more than three thousand books and articles. Its depth is daunting: He goes to the bedrock of both Christian faith and human experience. Nonetheless, we plan to make special use of Rahner here, because his theology, more than that of any other recent Catholic theologian, has the prime qualities we hope to convey. It is traditional, in the sense that it has studied the past carefully and builds on it. It is contemporary, in the sense that it listens for new questions and does not assume that old answers are adequate. Because Rahner is passionately (not fanatically) religious, his theology usually has personal or affective undertones—usually clearly reflects his prayer. Because he has a systematic mind, his treatment of a given topic usually opens onto the others that it immediately implies. For instance, when Rahner treats baptism he shows how it depends on the primordial sacramentality of the church and Jesus. When he treats grace he shows how faith is a share in the trinitarian God's own love-life. To read Karl Rahner, then, is to journey through the whole kingdom of Christian wisdom. That is exciting, and we write in good measure to help you share such excitement.

Karl Rahner was born in Bavaria in 1904. His parents and family were sturdy traditional Catholics (his mother recently celebrated her one-hundredth birthday), and he went off to a Jesuit seminary, following an older brother, when he was seventeen. The course of studies that the Jesuits set for young men in those days included two years of noviciate, where they learned the traditions of the Society of Jesus and the rudiments of the spiritual life; two years of classical studies and literature; three years of philosophy; three years or so for practical experience, such as teaching in a Jesuit high school; four years of theology; another year of spiritual exercises like those of the noviciate; and finally, for certain gifted members, doctoral studies at a secular university. Out of that lengthy preparation came, at least for the hardy, an unusual breadth of intellectual background and an unusual self-discipline.

In person Rahner is small, round, and serious. Those who attended his courses at Innsbruck, Munich, or Münster in the 1950s and 1960s used to describe how he would pace back and forth, hands behind his back, spinning out staggeringly complex reasonings in Latin or German. His written style in German tends to very long sentences full of subordinate clauses on occasion taking up an entire page. (Rahner folklore has the story that his older brother Hugo, who also became a well-known Jesuit theologian, would not read Karl's books until they had been translated into French.) More historically, we have seen him approach an American lectern, read a few sentences of his prepared text in halting English, and then retire to the back of the stage to say his Rosary (and fall asleep) while a stand-in read the rest of his text.

For all the efforts of Rahner lovers to reduce his formidability, though, he remains a serious, sober man. Perhaps that is a legacy from his years under Hitler and war. Perhaps it results from long meditation on human waywardness. Whatever, under the human traits of a simple piety and a fascination with toys, one finds a complete absorption with God's holy mystery. More and more through the years, Rahner has come to center in precisely divine mystery. One glimpses this early on in *Foundations of Christian Faith:*

> For a Christian, his Christian existence is ultimately the totality of his existence. This totality opens out into the dark abysses of the wilderness which we call God. When one undertakes something like this, he stands before the great thinkers, the saints, and finally Jesus Christ. The abyss of existence opens up in front of him. He knows that he has not thought enough, has not loved enough, and has not suffered enough. [Rahner, *Foundations of Christian Faith*, p. 2]

Rudolf Otto, a pioneer in comparative religious studies, once defined the holy as "the mystery that is both tremendous and fascinating." In its Latin roots, "tremendous" does not mean huge or gigantic, as popular American usage now has it. Rather it means "fear-inducing" or "awe-inspiring." Through human history, to meet the holy, the sacred, the divine has been a matter of chills down the spine, hair standing on end. It has also been a matter of ardent, we might even say erotic, response to splendor and beauty. Today, in industrialized societies such as ours, it is hard to accredit this raw religious core experience. We have so tamed the natural world, so laid things out in concrete and neon, that the primitive be-ing of things little shocks us. Unlike prehistoric or ancient peoples, we do not find sun and storm nearly incredible marvels. Unlike medieval or fourth-world peoples, we do not meet death as a near certainty by age thirty-five. Rahner's "mystery," then, is for most of us a wilderness first glimpsed within. It is the fathomless depth, the foundation out of sight, that we start to suspect whenever we begin to ponder the way things are.

Mystery links God and human beings, because our natural, inbuilt sense of "God" makes him (or her*) the origin and goal of the totality of things (which is too immense for us to grasp). It also links them because having this sense, wondering about the origin and goal of the totality of things, is essential to what we mean by "humanity." We human beings are the species that raises questions. There is no science, no art, no philosophy or theology in a pride of lions or a gaggle of geese. By focusing so resolutely on mystery, Rahner therefore joins God and human beings inseparably. Human beings are the only creatures who fashion theo-logies. By keeping to their specific distinction of asking why, they inevitably come to "God." Even "primitive" peoples, whom Westerners long despised, come to "God," for, as Mircea Eliade has shown, their concern with the sacred is a quest for the *really* real—for the ultimate power on which one can fully depend, from whose assurance one can finally feel secure.

Mystery alone, however, would make Rahner only a philosopher of religion. It is one thing to say that human beings raise questions, or even to interpret their raising of questions as a listening for revelation. It is another thing to describe reality through faith that revelation has occurred, that divine mystery has shed its veil of obscurity and vouchsafed a word. What makes Karl Rahner fully a Christian theologian is his complete embrace of the traditional faith that God did in Jesus Christ vouchsafe a privileged, definitive word. There the mystery that our questioning human constitution always implicitly pursues gave flesh to its self-expression. There the human questioning stuff and the divine answering stuff met in a full symbolization of both what God is most like and what human beings are best called to become. Karl Rahner is a thoroughly Christian thinker because faith in Jesus' utter centrality motivates all the analyses in his system. Insofar as such a faith is both "traditional" (long handed down) and "catholic" (universal, proper to Christians everywhere), it makes him riveted to the common core.

Behind Rahner's probing analyses of how human beings strive toward divine mystery stands the existential philosophy of Martin Heidegger, one of his teachers at the University of Freiburg. Behind his final understanding of both human nature and divine reality stands the Christian tradition. Neither of these background influences, however, explains the creativity by which Rahner has reworked Christian theology. Ultimately, of course, that creativity is as inexplicable as the creativity of

---

* In fidelity to the traditional notion that God is beyond gender, we use either the masculine or the feminine pronoun.

an Einstein or a Picasso. One senses an important part of its dynamics in Rahner, though, when one reflects on how his faith in Jesus comes to color his "God."

In the quotation cited above, Rahner is saying, in effect, that faith in Jesus does not remove God's mysteriousness. No matter how strongly we cling to the Christian center, we still know dark abysses of noncomprehension. Indeed, in an article on Thomas Aquinas for the University of Chicago's celebration of his seven-hundredth birthday, Rahner has recalled and made his own Aquinas's view that even the beatific vision of God that constitutes "heaven" does not remove the divine mystery. Nonetheless, despite all this "negative" stress on God's intrinsic exceeding of our capacity to understand, Rahner's most basic inference from faith in Jesus is that God has once and for all shown the divine mystery to be pure love.

We shall have full occasion to develop this theme, and to show how it recasts the traditional doctrines of grace, the trinity, salvation, and more. Here the point is simply to introduce a few leitmotifs from the mastersinger who will be our main guide. For Karl Rahner God the mysterious is finally a creative love more intimate than we are to ourselves. If Dante was taken by the love that moves the stars, Karl Rahner is taken by the love that keeps the human heart from the hell of self-absorption. By the warrant of Jesus' life, death, and resurrection, Christians can call the dark wilderness of their lives' ultimacy "Abba"—"Father," or even "Daddy." That is what Jesus called God. It is what Paul heard the Spirit groan in his depths (Rom. 8:15–16). We hope to show, in full concreteness and leisure, how such grace is no palaver, no cheap emotion, but rather the one energy that makes life good.

THIS BOOK

The mystery into which all reflection on human performance leads; the light on such mystery that Jesus sheds; the community and personal life that Jesus' light forecasts—these are principal topics that a Catholic theology derived from Karl Rahner or a synthesis of the past tradition will develop. Therefore, they chart our way here. Following this introduction, we embark on what we hope is a thoughtful consideration of "the human quest." Misused, that title could serve a noon-hour soap opera. But taken judiciously, as a cue to consider not so much what human beings say as what they do, it may make mystery the near silence and darkness we all know in our bones.

"Man fragt," the Germans observe. Human beings ask questions. At core, human beings *are* questions—opennesses, capacities—for meaning. Sensitive scholars such as Michael Polanyi have rung many changes on "meaning." In science, art, or just ordinary intercourse, they show

that we know more than we can say, that we are always probing the world, both its outside and its in. "God" most really, most genuinely emerges from such probing, for "God" is the light, the illumination that lures it. Similarly, "God" is the love that lures the probing of our hearts, the sense we have that a quality of goodness most situations lack just "has" sometime, somewhere, to burst forth for our fulfillment.

Biblically and traditionally, Catholic theology finds Jesus' meaning and love its interpretational key. Jesus so fits the mystery of God that faith in him swings open the treasure house of Father-Son-Spirit. Father-Son-Spirit is so rich a symbolization of meaning and love that Pauline hope starts to become credible. In the wake of Jesus, it does indeed seem possible that where sin abounded grace abounds more. If so, the theology of Jesus is the nub of the theology of revelation and salvation too. Evolutionary science asks whether Jesus can center the eons of the universe, and some Catholic theology answers yes: In the revelation, salvation, person of Jesus stands clear the intimacy with God for which *all* creation groans.

These topics will take us three full chapters to develop. By that time, though, we will have pondered rather thoroughly what Rahner calls the three "cardinal" mysteries of Catholic faith: Incarnation, Trinity, and Grace. On that foundation, we can build a chapter called "Christian Realism." It will be a pause to refresh our sense of the whole—especially our sense of what core Catholic faith gives as an orientation in reality. For instance, ought we more to trust our spontaneous instincts or distrust them? Is the nature we see in Yosemite Valley, or from the heights of Big Sur, or in the sere winter grasses of Kansas—is that nature like a good mother or a demon? More interiorly, does the rush of desire a man feels for a ripe woman carry God's voice or the devil's?

Reformation theology has bequeathed us the solid wisdom that we are both "just" (right before God) and sinners. Catholic theology traditionally has added the slight wrinkle that grace perfects a nature already good. It is true that many a Catholic moral theologian (both the professional kind who dominates a classroom and the practical kind who dominates a confessional) has seemed not to know this tradition. It is true that a solid Catholic school thought all sexual matters intrinsically grave. One of our small pleasures in representing the high Catholic tradition will be to skewer such aberrations. In the high Catholic tradition, one shows "sinfulness," or felt need of God, not by thundering about human corruption but by encouraging the best human drives to see what they do indeed reveal. This can make a wry theology of hope (not optimism), quite a salty religion of good tears.

Christian theology and religion (response to God) occur of course in the "church." The church is the community of Jesus' followers, the organic body that Jesus heads. In the best tradition, the authority of the church comes from the genuineness of its religion and shows itself a service. For the church as a whole, honesty and love make a mission that "the world" cannot overcome. Recently, that sort of mission won Mother Teresa of Calcutta the Nobel Peace Prize. "Simply" by giving her life for the most wretched poor, she both testifies to God's intimate character and convicts "the world" of stupid heartlessness. Such heroic charity seems to be beyond the rest of us. Nonetheless, were we but honest in our work and kind in our human interactions we too would missionize the world. Being the church is not mainly a matter of heroism, as it is not mainly a matter of brains. Being the church is mainly a matter of trying, day in and day out, to follow Jesus' very plain rule: "You will love the Lord your God with all your mind, all your heart, all your soul, all your strength, and you will love your neighbor as yourself." That is the law and the prophets. That is the church's constitution. All church office subserves such love. All church arrogance, or pomp, or pretense disserves it. The church, then, is impossibly simple. It merely gathers people to remember Jesus and become as good as his God.

In the chapters that follow the church, we will try to concretize a program for personal and social living. What does Jesus' love entail for prayer, personal life, family life, ecology, work, and the like? What does it reveal about politics, social justice, the economy of oil, the hopes of the Green Revolution? Do women and minorities have a special place in a Catholic social action really up to its founder's mark? Are the liberation theologians right when they make the poor the apple of God's eye? Such questions are not easy, but they are full of life. If Catholic religion—the actual daily living of Catholic Christian faith—cannot be sexy, creative, joyous, long-suffering, on the side that's right, what healthy person wants it? The grandeur of the tradition is that it *can* be all these good things—that it *can* shout with Irenaeus, "God's glory is human beings fully alive."

This book concludes with some reflections on the future of Catholic theology strictly so called, a summary, and two appendices. By Catholic theology strictly so called we mean the professional discipline of trained theologians. In effect, the issue here is methodology. Recently, there have arisen a number of important works on how to conceive theology itself, and they suggest what future shape Catholic reflection should assume. Methodology can be a deadly affair, so we have postponed its treatment to the end. By that time, we hope to have interested the reader enough in the theological enterprise—to have shown winsomely enough how it is simply disciplined reflection on faith—to have her find the conception of Catholic theology's future a matter of some personal interest.

The summary is an effort to render the heart of Catholic faith's matter in several "short formulas." Rahner has pioneered the use of such formulas, and we find them more than useful for pastoral work. In addition, the summary will try to suggest how the ordinary believer has a right to theologize, and how exercising that right can become a framework for his or her ongoing maturation. The appendices offer a brief history of Catholic theology and an even briefer estimate of the theology of the man who bids to play a dominant role in the Catholic church's future, Pope John Paul II.

Since we have chosen to structure the major portion of our book topically, under the conviction that such a structure is likely to prove most apt for the audience we envision, the historical flow of Catholic reflection is present only obliquely. The appendix on the history of Catholic theology is therefore an attempt to redress any imbalance the major focus causes, by offering at least a beginning sense of how this tradition got from Jesus to contemporary visions such as Rahner's. In treating Pope John Paul II, we shall give an interpretation of several of his writings, trying to gather from them a first impression of what his liberal social views and conservative doctrinal views imply for the next phase of Catholic faith's self-understanding.

By now this word "Catholic" has appeared almost too frequently, and we wish to close our introduction with the hope that before long it can fade to some subordinate place. The major scandal of Christianity is the division in its own household. Because of that division, "Catholic," "Protestant," and "Orthodox" theologies all leave a somewhat sour taste. It distorts reality to ignore the differences for which they stand, but it equally distorts the clear prayer of the Johannine Jesus (17:20ff.) to make them permanent or crucial. What all Christians hold in common by staking their lives on Jesus renders what they hold apart relatively trivial. In no way do we want to distract from what is common, or to promote what is trivial.

Having been raised in Roman Catholic Christianity, we feel competent to offer an inside view of its configuration and how it feels. As several articles in the *Bulletin* of the Council on the Study of Religion recently have shown, there is an interest nowadays in Catholic studies, and a need for good texts. So, for all students of Catholicism, committed and uncommitted alike, we offer this contribution. If it shows anything of how our tradition has rendered something of Jesus Christ, whom Paul unforgettably called God's power and wisdom, we will be content. If it does for our tradition anything of what our teacher Robert McAfee Brown's *The Spirit of Protestantism* did for his, we will feel it has repaid a little of a big ecumenical debt.

BIBLIOGRAPHY

Brown, Michael H., "Love Canal and the Poisoning of America," *The Atlantic Monthly*, 244/6 (December 1979), 33–47.

Brown, Robert McAfee. *The Spirit of Protestantism*. New York: Oxford University Press, 1965.

Cunningham, Lawrence S. "On Teaching Catholicism to Undergraduates," *Bulletin of the Council on the Study of Religion*, 10/2 (April 1979), 43–45.

Eliade, Mircea. *The Sacred and the Profane*. New York: Harcourt Brace Jovanovich, 1959.

Greeley, Andrew. *Crisis in the Church*. Chicago: Thomas More, 1979.

O'Donovan, Leo, ed. "Living into Mystery: Karl Rahner's Reflections at 75," *America* 140/9 (March 10, 1979), 177–180.

Polanyi, Michael and Prosch, Harry. *Meaning*. Chicago: University of Chicago Press, 1975.

Rahner, Karl. *Foundations of Christian Faith*. New York: Seabury, 1978.

Rahner, Karl. "Thomas Aquinas on the Incomprehensibility of God," *The Journal of Religion*, 58/Supplement (1978), S107–125.

Ruether, Rosemary. "A Religion for Women: Sources and Strategies," *Christianity and Crisis*, 39/19 (December 10, 1979), 307–311.

Swidler, Leonard, ed. "Woman and Communist, Senator and Catholic: A Discussion with Giglia Tedesco," *Christianity and Crisis*, 39/19 (December 10, 1979), 311–315.

Terrien, Samuel. "Progress and Regress Among Roman Catholics," *Religion in Life*, XLVIII/4 (Winter 1979), 400–412.

The Human Quest 2

OVERVIEW

The human quest is a search through daily life for a true, mysterious God. Catholic theology has in recent years focused its understanding of human nature in this way, by analyzing our drive for understanding, our drive for love, and our responses to personal or social disorder. In analyzing our drive for understanding, recent Catholic theology has solidly affirmed the rights of the mind, and so closed the gap between the church and modernity. If we follow them, the dynamics of the mind lead to an ultimate meaning that correlates well with God. So too with the postulates of our love. Be they the artist's need for beauty and creation, or an adolescent's sexual yearnings, the postulates of love show an ardent hope for goodness and intimacy that also conjure God. From their experiences of breakdown or dysfunction, human beings are equally primed for religion. In ways both formal and very humble, we all try to get a handle on injustice, to make some compromise with our pain. So doing, we all open to the issue of God.

Religion, East and West, has traditionally organized these drives and experiences for people. The serious times in the average person's life continue to point toward religion, as do even the wandery philosophizings of the local bar and grill. For religion is "but" the search for ultimate, stabilizing meaning. And the God of such omnipresent religion? God ordinarily appears as mystery—as the ungraspable ultimate into which all our strivings and times lead. Consequently, the real God requires a certain contemplation. We will only mature to the measure of our own defining drives if we let God become as real as the mysterious source of everything we know, love, or hope.

THE CENTRALITY OF QUESTIONING

In our introductory chapter, we suggested that a major force behind the reformulation of Catholic theology that occurred in Vatican II was the work of Neo-Thomists. Perhaps their strongest wing was what came to be called "transcendental Thomism." It derived from the research of European Catholics, many of them at the University of Louvain in Belgium, who tried to reconcile the philosophies of Thomas Aquinas and such modern thinkers as Kant and Hegel. The focal point in that enterprise was the dynamics of the human spirit, especially of the human intellect. By a careful study of how our subjectivity stretches toward reality, wants to know more broadly and more deeply, Neo-Thomists such as Joseph Maréchal gave new precision and cogency to the old scholastic dictum that the human mind is able to "make" and "become" all things.

Potentially, through its abilities to imagine and conceive, the human mind rises to the horizon of all reality. In principle, it is convinced that it is proportioned to anything that exists, for to be (to exist) is to be intelligible, understandable. Because of this quality, the Neo-Thomists called the human spirit "transcendent." It is always "going beyond" (that is what transcendent means in its roots) present achievements, always stretching out to "more." Indeed, if we prescind from the mortality that stops this process, we can say that the human spirit is equal to the entire universe.

Now it may seem a far journey from this rather abstract analysis of human intelligence to the *aggiornamento* (bringing-up-to-date) that John XXIII hoped Vatican II would achieve, but in reality it is not. The conflict "modernity" had brought between the Catholic church and European culture, the gap it had created, largely pivoted on the rights of human intelligence. In the Enlightenment, of which Kant was an especially prominent representative, European intellectuals had proclaimed their independence of external, what they called "heteronomous," authority. It was their own reason that would form their consciences, would delineate their world. The spectacular successes of this attitude in the physical sciences, above all in the work of Galileo, Copernicus, and Newton, made autonomous human reason modernity's prize. Any church wishing to be up to date, up to the measure of the best human aspirations, had to contend with autonomous human reason.

Rather belatedly, Catholic thinkers took up this challenge. As we show below, they pointed to the limits of human reason (which today's scientists are more willing to admit than post-Enlightenment scientists were). But more importantly, they accepted the positive values of modernity's experiences and strove to find the human drive to understand good. Aquinas was a great help in this, for he had seen the value of

Aristotle's highly positive interpretation of human reason and brought it into his own theological system. Before long the Neo-Thomists were going beyond Aquinas, learning what they could from Kant, Hegel, Darwin, Einstein, Freud, Marx, and other pioneer explorers of consciousness.

This process was by no means a smooth one, and it continues today. Nonetheless, the spirit of renovating the Catholic intellectual tradition by a vote of confidence in humanity's God-given powers drove those who prepared Vatican II's innovations. As late as 1950, Pope Pius XII was still casting a jaundiced eye on evolution and existentialism. However, priests such as Teilhard de Chardin and laity such as Gabriel Marcel had used evolutionary and existential insights to such good effect that only repression, or simple dishonesty, could deny the rightful impact of such insights on contemporary Catholic faith.

Perhaps a few concrete examples will sharpen the issue here. Consider, for instance, the modern scientific laboratory. Having worked in one, I (John) can report that there is much to admire—much to admire on precisely theological grounds. The Worcester Foundation for Experimental Biology, where I worked in the mid-1950s, was already acquiring a fine reputation for research on such disparate phenomena as cancer and schizophrenia. It made its biggest popular splash, though, in developing an oral contraceptive—"the pill." Ironically enough (for a Catholic school kid), I served the development of this contraceptive, by systematically frustrating a cluster of laboratory rats. (The chairman of the biology department at Holy Cross College had opined that such work would not be "immoral.")

Despite the cheerful atheism of most of the scientists I encountered, and despite the use they made of poor women in Puerto Rico, or indeed of all sorts of women, who in some sense were chemical guinea pigs, the work of the Foundation was at its center a very moral, high-minded affair. Essentially, the people assembled there were highly intelligent, highly trained persons dedicated to understanding. What Neo-Thomist Bernard Lonergan's book *Insight* calls "the pure desire to know" was basic in their motivation. Further, they set their striving to know in the service of what they considered human betterment. That is, they strove to know the dysfunction of cells so as to cure cancer, to know the chemical imbalances of schizophrenics so as to cure mental disease, to know the intricacies of female hormones so as to give people control over their own fertility.

In hundreds of laboratories, where science is both pure and applied, this sort of mentality prevails. This mentality does not necessarily remove arrogance, egotism, or even the desire for money. Neither does it exhaust the ways the human spirit can be great. But it does manifest something so human, so representative of men and women at their best, that it conjures up the Genesis story of God making men and women in the divine image. Indeed, the creativity of a Linus Pauling or a Max Planck reflects the Johannine God in whom there is no darkness at all. Moreover, the very structure of science—its central gamble that human light can illumine physical data—seems to the religious observer a vote of confidence in God. Whether churchpeople see it or not, scientists assume, stake their every day, on God's having done good work—good work in the universe, good work in their own minds. Stanley Jaki has recently shown the correlation between the rise of Western science and faith in the world's intelligibility, and while not all his fellow historians of science accept his theological inferences, the data that he assembles and the light that his theory sheds are impressive.

What Jaki and the Neo-Thomists share is a willingness to look beyond scientists' words and investigate their concrete assumptions. Albert Einstein agreed with this attitude, for he counseled those who would understand scientific creativity to study what scientists do more than what they say. Many scientists, as many people in other kinds of work, are poor philosophers of their own activity, indeed of their own lives. There is often a great gap between what we "know," in a tacit or intuitive way, and what we can express conceptually. There is, in other words, a whole realm of preconceptual knowledge. As Michael Polanyi has shown in the case of physical science, the best way to get access to this sort of knowledge, to learn the creative intuitions and techniques by which productive research actually proceeds, is to apprentice oneself to a master. As common experience tells each of us ten times a week, there are things we "know" about a friend or spouse long before they come to conceptual focus in conversation or reflective analysis. To anticipate a bit, it is a cardinal principle of the transcendental Thomists' analysis of God's presence to us human beings that we "know" divinity preconceptually, recognize the Spirit intuitively, long before any formal theology gives us the "right" words.

Therefore, from our ordinary questioning, our quite commonplace efforts to get a better handle on the world around us, there arises the issue of "God." Probe any of the implicit or explicit moves of human intelligence, look for its assumptions and implications, and the issue of a final cause, an original source, or a guarantor of meaningfulness will emerge. Bernard Lonergan has put this issue of God very precisely, linking it with his careful analysis of human knowing. From our ability to *understand*, to have insights, there arises a confidence that the universe is intelligible, and from that confidence there arises the question whether the universe could be intelligible unless it had an intelligible ground. From our ability to *judge*, to weigh evidence and conclude that something is or is not so, there arises an awareness of necessity and non-necessity, and from that awareness there comes the question whether a non-necessary world could exist without a necessary source. Finally, from our ability to *decide* between the worthwhile and the trashy, to love things that are good and hate things that are evil, there arises a sense of moral calling. But that moral calling becomes a cruel deception, a destructive revelation of absurdity, unless there is a guarantor of the lovable and a judge of the hateful—unless an imperishable goodness finally holds the world.

The preceding is a full, slightly technical elaboration of the preconceptual assumptions people make as they go about the business of living. It is clearest in those people whose living depends on a vigorous exercise of their wits, such as scientists, judges, and mothers of six, but it can be teased from the humdrum life of John Q. Public. The drives to know, to make, to be fair—they all assume that intelligence, reasonableness, and justice are worthwhile. The teacher assumes that it is worth long years of schooling to master a body of knowledge and the skills to communicate it. Moreover, the "worth while" in the teacher's case is not the paycheck or the social status. Rather it is the experience itself of understanding, the experience itself of helping another to understand. We do not mean that all teachers are so idealistic, so realistic about the genuine heart of their matter. But we do mean that the good teachers, those who show what the profession ought to be (and so in a directive sense "is"), are idealistic/realistic in this way. To teach with any élan, success, manifestation of real humanity, one has to assume that things can be understood, people can understand, understanding is worthwhile. One has to assume that the light that flashes when a math problem is solved, the light that flashes when a child says "Wow!"—that this light is a nearly pure treasure, a nearly sure index of what we are made for.

One could write a similar analysis for doctors, lawyers, engineers. Good police work contrasted with bad, good politics opposed to shabby— these too would show what decent human being entails, assumes, postulates. Why bother to raise children, if the world is the tale of an idiot? Why feel any outrage about pollution, government corruption, inner-city crime? Racism or sexism are but indifferent evolutionary accidents, if the world has no constitutive judge. Constitutional rights, international law—they are but frangible conventions. The alternative to faith, hope, and love of a world that ultimately reposes on light and love is cynicism so sheer most of us have never seen it, the monstrosity of people so self-destroyed that their own lies and lovelessness no longer pain them.

Perhaps a Hitler or a Stalin achieved this difficult end. Perhaps the Vietcong who drove chopsticks through children's eardrums achieved it. But even they had to appeal to the world's sense of "right," "justice," and the like to give their causes some decency. National Socialism, Stalinist Communism, and Vietnamese Communism all had to present themselves as systems that would advance reason and goodness. None could blatantly sell sheer cynicism or evil, for the majority of even their own followers knew from within that human life concretely is "made" to move toward being rather than non-being, the intelligent rather than the stupid, what makes for justice rather than what makes for disorder. If "God" be the term of all the positive options in these sets, then "God" clearly is nothing extrinsic to human living. Rather God is its very soul.

THE POSTULATES OF LOVE

So far, then, we have tried to show how the dynamics of the human mind, the postulates of the human orientation toward meaning, inevitably place the question of God. In this section we focus on the dynamics and postulates of the human heart. Of course, no sensible anthropology (analysis of human nature) dichotomizes the mind from the heart. When Pascal (1623–1662) spoke of the reasons of the heart that the mind may not know, he reminded a rather rationalistic time of a truth common sense has always held. One place where mind and heart frequently hold together to lovely effect is the artistic spirit. There, mediated by imagination, they concentrate a whole human person on creative work. Since all of us have to work, if we are either to survive or to prosper, and since creative work is the happiest version of this necessity, perhaps a little reflection on the implications of artistic spirituality will serve our present purpose well.

We don't personally know a first-rank artist well enough to discourse on how such a person actually proceeds. However, in the Australian Nobel Laureate Patrick White's remarkable novel *The Vivesector* one can find a splendid literary account. Hurtle Duffield, the main character of this novel, was to the artistic manner born. From the dawn of his reflective intelligence, he realized that he had to draw and paint. A dazzling chandelier, the dance of the sun on clear waters—all species of radiance absorbed him. So, he became a pure case of someone called to a life of art, a life of fresh seeing. To be sure, such pure cases are easier to find in novels than in real life. Nonetheless, we can find the living historical entity in the child prodigy, such as Picasso, who picks up crayons at the tenderest age and only lays them down after seventy, eighty, or even ninety years of pursuing new forms and radiance each day.

What is fascinating to the religious observer of Hurtle Duffield is the way his art completely dominates his time. As soon as he can, he frees himself from home and school, in order to get into his work full-time. The early years are hard going, both financially and psychologically. Though his childhood was a romance with light, early adulthood

is a harsh initiation in human darkness. It is not that Hurtle himself
is especially mistreated or abused. His own direct bruises are rather
slight. But he sees the torpor, the economic depression, the boundedness
in which most of the people of his city live. The person who summarizes
much of this lesson is a young prostitute, whom White only slightly
romanticizes. She stands for the dozens of ways in which people who
are neither heroic, nor gifted with genius, nor wealthy—the majority
of us—get cabined into squalor. It may be the squalor of a low-rent
part of the city, or the squalor of a spirit with no transom for light.
Either way, it makes an impact on sensitive observers. If they are politically minded, it probably makes them socialists of some stripe. If they
are artists like Hurtle Duffield, it keeps them probing human darkness
in search of ultimate light.

For his grave, brooding, twisted depictions of human sufferers, Hurtle wins a small initial notice. That gets him money enough to purchase
a house (which he comes to share with a dotty sister-by-adoption) and
so mold a regime to his work that he becomes increasingly eccentric
to ordinary society. White emphasizes this eccentricity through a variety
of tragi-comic social encounters that Hurtle has through his middle
years. He is always discovering, through some faux pas, that normal
society considers him an outsider. The most penetrating examples are
his several love affairs, where his foreignness defeats even taste and
touch. There is no other half for his artistic self, no shared sleep to
reknit his care. Slowly, Hurtle realizes that he himself is partly to blame
for this. His true spouse is his work. So much of his self-expression
goes into the only semi-human materiality of forms and colors that he
has few of the notions or words by which ordinary people render love
doable, manageable.

At the end of his career, Hurtle's work takes him directly into mystery. To adopt the language of the mystic's journey, he has walked
the purgative way of identifying with human limitation, walked the
illuminative way of realizing his own peculiar character, and now he
must walk through a dark night toward union. So his final canvasses
are huge dark "indigo" paintings. Reversing the biblical adage, he proceeds from lights to shadows and barest imagery. As a counterpoint,
to keep the landscape somewhat familiar, White shows us Hurtle's increasing critical acclaim—and the bemusement this brings him. Critics
prate about his native Australian genius, museums hold special exhi-
bitions of his work, and he walks through it all with egg on his coat.
But now he is resigned to the egg, and resigned to the craziness of
"ordinary" life, of what the world calls sane and well appareled. For
he "knows," in a very preconceptual way, that the full light for which
his creative heart hungers is too bright for human bearing. To creatures
in skins and heads like his, it must appear pitch blackness. At his very

end, jumbled by a stroke, he teeters between despair and purest love's surrender: "Too tired too end-less obvi indi-ggoddd."

Of course, we choose Hurtle Duffield because he serves our purposes well. Patrick White so reads the human quest that it comes to term at "ggoddd." Were he to write Hurtle a wake, as James Joyce, whom the jumbled language recalls, wrote a wake for Finnegan, it probably would mock a good deal of Christian religion. But it would be untrue to the dynamics of Hurtle's story if it mocked that, or any religion's real God. For any religion's real God is inseparable from the light and darkness, the chiaroscuro that frightens its best artists and fascinates them. Like science, art seeks a fresh way of seeing the real, and all the really real is the holy. Because art separates emotion and reason less than science, its intentions of the holy more clearly nourish the heart. Nonetheless, significant art is as religious in its tacit assumptions as significant science. If there is no secure beauty, no fully satisfying light, its vitality stands unexplained. The peaceful pauses that creativity experiences, its joy in giving birth, harbinger God's glory. For God the primal creator (full faith finds) takes glory in our dappled things, in beauty that is pied.

The heart of an artist such as Hurtle Duffield wants a love affair that renders experience orderly, fruitful, beautiful. It searches a love that postulates good work. But even nonartists, persons who consider themselves uncreative, persons whom society considers drones—even this great mass of the rest of us have hearts of lonely hunters. What do our hearts, our capacities for love, postulate? Do we too restlessly search after God?

It is easy enough to say that we do, and hard enough to show convincingly how. Human passions and affections are so tangled a skein that few "proofs" of their Godwardness are smooth. Still, it does not seem overreaching to say that human passions and affections more imply a mystery of holiness, more hope after God, than they imply or hope after a void. Let us try to show this in the case of sexual love, where traditional Catholic theology often has felt uneasy.

In its 1979 Christmas issue (December 21), *The National Catholic Reporter* published several articles on teenagers' sexual experience. Their general drift was grim: poor information, skewed first experiences, unwanted pregnancies and abortions. Persons physically competent for sexual relations, physically able to reproduce, were in most cases still children, still far from ready emotionally to handle their sex. Since some of the cases dealt with young people only thirteen or fourteen, that is hardly surprising. In our complicated society, thirteen or fourteen years is hardly time enough to learn the rudiments of what one's body is for. But, as the droves of troubled teenagers testify, it is time enough to wonder painfully how that body's desires and needs can make sense.

If we translate that a bit, it seems to say, first, that even the youngest loves ask protection against abuse. It may be the abuse of being treated as just a thing, an instrument of pleasure. Or it may be the abuse of being frustrated by elders who have forgotten their own early needs. Either way, even the youngest loves cry for understanding, peace, and fulfillment. They say, with considerable confusion, that having this welter of wants and hopes and angers and fears is a painful way to have to live. If there is no achievement of intimacy and integration, adolescent longing writes teenagers' first creeds in blots and scratches. So even the early teens are years when the scheme of things comes in for intense scrutiny. The scheme of things that parents and teachers propose may seem thoroughly ill-fitting. The scheme of things that peers mumble forth may seem equally inapt. And living between the two, sailing back and forth, is like Odysseus trying not to founder. Between the rock of official "morality" and the soft place of quick comfort, the young person worries sorely tried.

There is a wholesale therapy postulated by such an early striving for love, and perhaps a retail redoing of our ethics. On the therapeutic side, Catholic theology could bring forward, in quite concrete ways, the element of suffering that love constantly reveals. For ancient peoples, the rites of passage into adulthood often took the form of physical suffering. Adulthood meant having to endure the jungle hunt or the arctic cold, and sterner tribes sometimes taught such truth by knocking out a tooth or lopping off a finger. That does not mean the Catholic ceremony of Confirmation should include lopping off a finger. It could mean that when people come of age to reproduce themselves they become candidates, catechumens, for straight talk about ordinary suffering. To follow Christ is to take up his cross. To gain adulthood is to fight for it. It might clear the air and delineate the real situation, to put such things on the line.

Of course, doing so would implicate the whole suffering or nonsuffering, maturity or immaturity, of Christian adults. To be credible to well-roiled adolescents, adults preaching sacrifice would have to show it. Further, they would have to show, to evidence by the total configuration of their own sex, love, and work, that their real sacrifices subserved real fruitfulness and joy. With such demonstrations, and the kindly suffering-with that humility about them could carry, fewer adolescents would feel bereft of a world view, a community, a band of fellow sufferers who understood.

On the ethical side, a hard look at the heart of the Christian matter might show us that God is less nervous about sex than we. Cultures past have arranged for love's sexual postulates less repressively than American Catholicism has. They have also been more savage. But the full experience of human societies, for all its consensus that sexual love needs control for the common good, shows considerable creativity.

Though early marriage has usually proved quite harmful, as was the case for Gandhi and other Eastern masters, forms of engagement that allowed sexual relations seem often to have worked fairly well. The translation to our time is not certain, but it suggests that we might relax our fears about adolescent eros, realizing that its vitality is in fact hunger for a beautiful, incarnational god.

The point is not to make ethical pronouncements. It is not to slice away traditional identification of the self with its body that the apostle Paul wrote into a high case against fornication. Rather, the point is to describe a real aspect of the heart's drives and confusions enough to show that tussling with them calls for an ultimate religious view. To say that past ages vetoed premarital intercourse does not secure the ethical case against it. Few past ages have kept their own sayings immaculately. One only gets to the heart of the issue of premarital intercourse, as one only gets to the heart of marital contraception, when one appeals to "the way things ought to be"—to the divine order human love postulates.

Those arguing against premarital intercourse argue that the human person is such that sexual intimacy without marital commitment violates or devalues it. Those arguing against marital contraception by "artificial" means argue that the human person is such that intervening in its reproductive processes violates or devalues it. Behind both arguments is an order of things, and giver of things' order, that thinks it understands the person and its morality quite exactly. That is a certain kind of religion and a certain kind of God. Behind the opposing arguments of those who see circumstances in which premarital intercourse and marital artificial contraception could be good is a conception of the order of things, and a conception of such things' orderer that sees the person and its morality as a matter of our own human responsibility. Either viewpoint, pushed to its limit, comes up with an assumption about the nature of the world and the human person. Either viewpoint suggests (does not prove) that the heart's loves reveal a lot about ultimacy, and so about God.

PERSONAL AND SOCIAL DYSFUNCTION

We have been considering the implications of the preeminent human drives, those of knowing and loving. In the main, our analysis has been positive. People do pursue truth, people do want to love well. It is characteristic of the Catholic view of human nature, in opposition to the pejorative view that some followers of John Calvin developed, to take this positive position. That does not mean, however, that any sane view of human history—Catholic, Protestant, or Zulu—can dismiss the tragically full bins of evidence that personal and social life often misfires.

At the end of a long life spent studying human history, Arnold Toynbee wrote what was for him a "short" narrative (600 pages) of the whole. It is mainly wars and rumors of wars. Toward the end of an energetic career spent studying human fulfillment, psychologist Abraham Maslow estimated that only about one percent of the population realize a significant amount of their potential. From the sorry story of the outside of things, theologians have long discoursed on original sin. From the personal experience of inner division, their early captain and poet, the apostle Paul, cried out to God for release. There is nothing in the current headlines, nothing in the average personality one meets, to let us judge that Toynbee, Maslow, the theologians or their captain describe a reality we have outgrown.

In the earliest days of the 1980s Americans watched the ordeal of their compatriots held hostage by Iranian students. Night after night, the television news reported this drama, well beyond the limits of easy patience. Germinally, it revealed the massive dysfunction of the prevailing world political and economic order. Part of the dysfunction was rooted in opposing legitimate claims. America wanted its relatively innocent embassy personnel to receive the civil treatment that international law and solid custom guaranteed them. Iran wanted recompense for its suffering under the Shah. Minimally, then, social interactions run the risk of running aground on legitimately conflicting claims.

Maximally, social interactions reveal a deep disorder in the interactors. The United States presence in Iran had been for decades a thing self-serving and impure. The Shi'ite Muslim revolution that gave the students their chance showed many signs of fanaticism, ruthlessness, and a leader more megalomaniac than his predecessor the Shah. Thus, the innocent parties to this stalemate were few and far between. Western allies who rushed to the United States' support kept an eye on their own fuel reserves. Russian invaders of neighboring Afghanistan did their best to profit from the confusion. For far too long, the world has enjoyed the spectacle of its own uncivility. After nearly half a billion years of experience, we human species have not learned how to share the pie. By any reckoning, that shows a pretty low intelligence quotient.

So low has been our practical intelligence, in fact, that deeper analysts have called for our species' remaking. Thus, in many traditional societies one finds a ritual pattern of death and rebirth. The classical Siberian shaman, for instance, dies, is transported to the gods, receives from the gods new perceptual organs, and revives as a fresh holy being. The modern purveyors of technology, if one reads between the lines of their ads, see themselves as providing equally new organs. By probing the world of business with new computers, the world of weekends with new sports equipment, one will rise above the present debilities to snatch gusto and new good life.

Christianity has its own view of dysfunction, analogous to those cited above. It speaks of dying to sin and rising to Christ, of new faculties come from the Spirit. But it also speaks programmatically of human impotence to sustain moral development, human impotence to be human without God. In other words, it reads the disorder we all know and lament as most revealing. Left to themselves, without clear direction and new motivation, human beings largely make a mess. Generation after generation, we birth children into a game we ourselves received tilted. Year after year, we persist in our personal vice. Unhappy people that we are, who will rescue us from this bondage? "Liberation" is such rescue, and it has become a major theme of our theological time.

We shall study this theme at some length in the chapter on social justice. Here we need only note that analysts of the human situation in Europe, the United States, and Latin America see so much dysfunction, so much injustice, that they search desperately for a faith that could rework the whole social condition. In Europe this search has gone under the name of "political theology," and it has raised the hackles of traditional Europeans. In the United States it has dominated black theologians, and more recently women. It has raised the hackles of traditional Americans as well. In many countries of Latin America, liberation theology has tried to fuse Marxist analyses of class oppositions to Christian sources of renewal. There it has both raised the hackles of repressive governments and become the crisis issue of such meetings as the Puebla Conference to which John Paul II hastened in the fall of 1979.

Put rather simplistically, these and other examinations of the human social condition find that wealth and power regularly corrupt it. For instance, in Brazil during the period 1960 to 1970 the top 5 percent of wage earners increased their share of the national income from 27.4 to 36.3 percent, while the bottom 80 percent saw their share decrease from 45.5 to 36.8 percent. The Southern Hemisphere of the world now accounts for about 80 percent of humanity's poverty, most of it among rural peoples. Those peoples have the highest birth rates, and about 40 percent of their population are under 15 years old. From figures such as these economists predict that by the year 2000 the earth will have about 6 billion people, 1.5 billion of whom will not be able to earn enough to live.

Nor are the figures comforting at home. The millions of Americans who live below the poverty level, the gross percentage of black youth who are unemployed, the number of women who are paid less than comparable men—they too witness that present society malfunctions. It is more unequal, more unjust, more causative of suffering than it has any right to be.

Such a judgment carries potent implications. One may be that human beings are so equal in their basic natures that they render the present

American use of the world's raw materials obscene (we, 6 percent of the world's population, consume about 40 percent of its resources). Is this implication foolish or deeply wise? Do Americans, who use about nine times the resources per capita that people of India use, justify this disproportion by some greater intrinsic worth, or some greater service to the world community, or some special election from God that Indians do not have? A few analysts of the situation, such as the American oil companies, imply that it is simply a survival of the fittest. In their lexicon, no profit is "obscene," because part of any profit fattens the Gross National Product. The Gross National Product says something (a rather vague something) about jobs, bank accounts, consumption— about the quantities of an economic life. That it says little about the quality of a spiritual life goes by the oil companies like a greyhound.

The above may seem a liberal or radical view of the implications of economic disproportions, but it has impressive conservative credentials. In the Catholic tradition, socio-economic dysfunction is an index of human disorder, human greed, for which "sin" is a proper name. From Leo XIII to John Paul II, with high points in John XXIII's *Pacem in Terris* and Paul VI's *Populorum Progressio*, the writers of papal encyclicals have hammered this judgment home. Their God made the world for *all* human beings, and a radically imbalanced use of the world's goods violates their God's creative intentions. In other words, they see a direct link between social order or disorder and "God," the world's origin and end. Insisting on the dignity of all human persons, they call the profiteering of some persons on the flesh of others an insult to the holy.

All sorts of persons do not accept this connection, but few of them do not raise it in their lifestyles. How a woman in Japan reacts to the male chauvinism (in Western terms) of her economy and culture, what a Chicano child thinks when she compares her migrant life to that of the large-scale grower—these are exercises in theology. More precisely, they are exercises in theodicy—the search to find a meaning deeper than the world's manifest injustice. From the side of the less oppressed, or even of the oppressors, thoughts and actions that bear on the socio-economic set of equations are similarly freighted. During one Barbara Walters special we watched four interviewees describe their living quarters. They were all currently hot properties in show business, and the least expensive of their houses went for three-quarters of a million dollars. That two people would have to work full-time to use a thirty room house seemed to escape all these luminaries. That their lifestyles contradicted all the masters of humanity's past was never even hinted. What must the world be, for such things to happen? How must "God" and "humanity" be related? Does inequality sing forth that our basic law is from the jungle? Or does inequality sing, by the suffering it causes, that the hot dog of today fries in hell tomorrow?

We could continue this sort of inferring, puzzling, drawing of lines, using more personal disorders. If a child is brain-damaged, or a teenager overdoses, or a good father ruins himself with alcohol, or a good mother has terminal cancer—if these disorders and evils are questioned, what do they say about "life"? At the least, they say it is painfully trying. At the most acute, they say it subserves a pattern we cannot comprehend or simply is without meaning. Either way, they push our hearts and minds beyond mere food and clothing. Either way, they fuel a search that soon becomes religion.

RELIGION

"Religion" conjures up ceremonies, churches, and interior acts such as prayer, but its core is being "bound" *(religatus)* to the holy, the mysterious source of meaning. In terms of the dysfunction that we have been discussing, a clear case of profound religion shines forth in the life and teaching of the Buddha. Raised to wealth and security, the legendary sources say, the Buddha became serious and sad when he discovered old age, sickness, and death. After trying various regimes that purported to solve this composite problem, he found light and peace in an experience of illumination whose conceptual expression is the "four noble truths." Together, the four noble truths explain the cause of suffering and the way to overcome it. First, there is the bedrock fact-truth: "All life is suffering." Second, there is its source: "The cause of suffering is desire." Third, with the active acceptance of this causality a therapeutic program comes into view: "The removal of desire removes suffering." And fourth, the way to remove desire is to follow the eightfold path of right views, right intention, right speech, right action, right livelihood, right effort, right mindfulness, and right concentration. Thus, from personal combat with dysfunction and the suffering it causes, the Buddha won through to a re-formation of how we view the world—a re-formation that has brought meaning and peace to millions.

We could write similar analyses of the other world religions. Unless they face the problem of suffering and offer a plausible solution for it, they do not survive or prosper. Equally, unless they show themselves compatible with the tendency of the mind to keep raising questions, and the tendency of the heart to keep seeking a stable love, they win no great adherence. It may be that they reset the terms of those tendencies, as Zen Buddhism does in trying to undercut discursive thinking, or as Christianity does in elaborating "faith." But to serve any significant number of human beings at the level of deep significance, a religion has to illumine and guide our questioning, postulates of the heart, and grappling with widespread dysfunction.

Indeed, before the rise of Western modernity, which first cast the world in a secular or nonreligious horizon, the general population of all societies lived in religious culture. Actually, there was no distinction between their general culture and their religion, for the whole culture quite directly tied to the peoples' common view of ultimate meaning. That was true in ancient or "traditional" societies of Africans, Australians, American Indians, and Eskimos. It was true in Hindu India, Confucian China, the Muslim Middle East. Christian Europe made no great schism between its culture and its religion, nor did its scattered Jewish ghettoes. To be a people was to live with a common set of values that quite directly folded into a common mythology or world view based on the gods, or the scriptures, or the ancestors' traditions about the "way." The human quest, through both prehistory and most of its recorded story, took direction from privileged tales or seers who formed a common culture around the way holy being gave the world meaningful patterns.

Today civil religion—culture formed around a common consensus about the holy—is a more complicated affair. The societies that call themselves "advanced" tend to be pluralistic. As well, they tend to be secularist—to deny the cultural significance of the holy. It is not our desire or competence to analyze this newer phenomenon, which sociologists still struggle to unravel. We merely point to the view of theoreticians such as Max Weber, Edward Shils, and Clifford Geertz that societies continue de facto to depend on charismatic personalities. John F. Kennedy, Martin Luther King, Jr. and Pope John XXIII come to mind. They, along with effective symbol systems, provide at least a minimal sense of being consonant with a cosmic order. The alternative would be such massive lack of norms that social transactions would grind to a halt. Thus, the traditional social functions of "religion" continue powerfully today, even when some of their traditional forms have fallen by the way. Similarly, we may not be fully satisfied with our Memorial Day and Fourth of July, but we still feel the need to celebrate.

Discourse about society in general, however, tends to be unsatisfying. "Society" is such an inclusive term that few of its phenomena are clearcut. Of course, the "individual" is a concept almost as variable, in that all of us realize it differently. However, at least there is a definite personal reality to which any reader can refer it—him- or herself. Let us therefore try to bring this reflection on how human orientation to meaning and human suffering from dysfunction correlate with religion to bear on the individual human person.

For a society such as the current American, it is not clear that most individuals understand themselves as religious, at least in the most common traditional senses. True, better than 90 percent report some of the traditional marks of religion, such as a belief in a supreme being or a final order to things. This sort of report, along with the evidence that a solid majority of Americans occasionally pray, gives the lie to an easy reading of American secularism as irreligion. But neither church attendance nor firm commitment to a full program of religiously based morality seems to dominate the average American's daily life. Rather, an unanalyzed mixture of hope, comfort-seeking, ambition and fear shepherds most of us along. In no clear way does the average undergraduate in a large public American university rivet each day's time on the question of God. In no clear way does the average businessperson place his or her work in the horizon of a golden rule such as Confucius', a twofold commandment such as Jesus', a passionate hope for the Messiah such as that of premodern Jews. At best, their reliance on religion is tacit or implicit.

On the other hand, we do not know the core motivations of most people very well, including perhaps ourselves. The things going on inside the "average" person are so complex that it is legitimate, even wise, not to pass judgment too quickly. Thus, there is the folk wisdom that the typical young buck becomes quite quiet after sowing his wild oats. Who would have thought that Bill Walton, the superb and radical basketball star, would take to vests and three-button suits before he hit thirty? And, along the same line, there is the stereotype that the wild filly will become quite the madonna when she nurses her first child. The life cycle has a certain gravity toward responsibility. Becoming accountable at a job or accountable for children tends to increase one's respect for the laws and intuitions of order that one's elders have developed. They do not immediately make one religious, in any sense that a Catholicism close to Jesus wants unreservedly to applaud, but they do make one serious.

Being serious is half of religion. It is not the same as being grim, and it does not supply the other half of religion, which is free-spirited and close to play. But being serious does express the tie to ultimacy, the drive to fit oneself to a larger pattern, that all the religions have seen as an energy close to their cores. If so, part of the question whether God is relevant to a given individual's life pivots on his or her seriousness. Is this person someone who thinks, at least now and then, about how "it all hangs together"? Is he or she constrained by some sense of obligation to use time well, to treat other people fairly, to take care of the goods of the earth? When we answer yes to such questions, as we would in a majority of cases, the "religiousness" of the average person becomes considerably more impressive. For all its neglect of deeper things, all its mediocrity and worship of mammon, Western society shows more to admire in the case of the average individual than secularism really explains. There is a seriousness, a regular if not steady move toward

basics, that confutes "eat, drink, and be merry." Both students and shop-
keepers feel the tugs, the attractions, of more.

Sometimes we bolster a commonsense, descriptive argument such
as this if we take on the least promising cases. For some commentators,
the hellish shouting of the Chicago Commodity Exchange, or the queer
emotionalism of the Super Bowl, are quite unpromising cases. We do
not find them so, because the Commodity Exchange seems clearly to
be religious (ultimate) passion set towards the false god of profit, while
the Super Bowl seems to be but new myth, ritual, and distraction. Much
less promising as cases for religious analysis, religious arguing that the
human person is set for God, are the brutish types on whom ultimate
things make virtually no impact. Gross in their pleasures, such persons
show so little humanity, so little soul, that evolution seems on them
wasted. Enough for them would be troughs for eating, trees for swinging,
red rumps for reproduction.

One of the early films that established the Italian director Federico
Fellini's reputation was a modest production called *La Strada*. It featured
a very brutish circus performer who went through life in a haze of
lust and alcohol. He had little redeeming social value. He gave considerable pain and took away considerable decent pleasure. If ever one followed
an unpromising candidate for religion, one did so through most of *La
Strada*. At the film's end, however, things changed rather revealingly.
Finally disgusted by his own torpor, finally reached by the pain he
had caused an innocent woman to suffer, the man (who made his
wretched living by displays of strength) was brought to his knees by
an idea. On the beach it struck this brute that not even a pebble, a
senseless bit of sand, could *be* without some meaning. Not even the
lowest bit of creation could lie there except mysteriously. Reeling with
this perception, the strong man turned his eyes toward the sky. If the
pebble cried out for explanation, how much more so did he. If the
pebble's dirty being-there was a pledge that there could be more, how
much more was his own dirty being-there an invitation to seek after.

There aren't many films that can manage to make metaphysics from
a pebble, and Fellini's presentation, though it does much better than
our skeletal sketch can suggest, is less than fully convincing. Still, one
knows that even the people of the Gong Show have pains and struggle
to soothe them. Even Joe's bar on the corner, or Marie's kaffee-klatch,
buzzes with low-grade metaphysics. In a half-serious, half-time wasting
way, the places we congregate show us turning over the order of things.
We may more gossip than philosophize but we seek some sense of resolution, even if it is only the resolution, the diminishing of upsets and
conflicts, that comes from realizing that others share our pains. Thus,
in suburban stereotype, women become friends by sharing confidences.

Each has a clear enough window on the other's life, maybe even on the other's bedroom, to feel both compassion and nakedness.

Men tend to be less self-revealing, at least without alcohol, but they too work into their conversation considerable rumination. About two-thirds of the time we've traveled on airplanes we've been unwilling overhearers of time-killing conversations. Beneath their pomposity and drone, they've shown businessmen groping after order. More than their manifest efforts to impress one another, or their attempts to appear wise and grave, the interlocutors have been seeking some confirmation that another person finds life sane. Enough of business, let alone international politics, is insane to make such a search both reasonable and touching.

At core, then, religion is the search for ultimate, stabilizing meaning. Its fringes may show hysteria or boredom, revolutionary newness or conservative mold. But its core is the search after ultimate meaning. In ecstatic mystical fulfillment, or plodding daily pain, religious people answer the call of their bones to find and make the world good. Conveniently (for our purposes) but nonetheless really, religion therefore turns out to be the centerpiece of being human. Whoever has a heart restless for more being, more explanation, more love is by our definition religious. Whoever is seriously irreligious is seriously inhuman. Such restlessness can derail badly, as it has in many Nazis and many followers of Marx. It can also overturn our easy cataloguing of personalities, and thereby cause salutary confusion. For instance, it can suggest that "atheist" Albert Camus was more religious than Cardinal Cooke, Billy Graham, Jimmy Carter, or others born again, who do not manifest his passion for full meaning. Thus, our definition has the utility of riveting the question of God or ultimacy to the dynamics of being human. God and genuine religion are nothing apart from our struggle to endure and grow. Rather, they are those stuggles' most revealing inner foci.

GOD AS MYSTERY

In Karl Rahner's summary reading of the human situation, we who quest after meaning and love soon run into an undeniable mystery. Wherever we go in our search, the totality of things escapes us. For the astrophysicist who studies the stars, the totality of the universe remains a thing between brackets. For the microphysicist who studies subatomic particles, the end of the infinitesimal still dances well out of sight. Within the realm of natural biology, staggering numbers keep full comprehension at bay. Annie Dillard, for instance, reports that a single grass plant of winter rye sends forth 378 miles of roots with 14 billion root hairs. One cubic inch of its soil contains 6000 miles of root hairs. That sort of power or creativity is staggering. It tells us very clearly that behind the world is a force far greater than we.

"Mystery," then, is not the same as "problem," as Catholic philosopher Gabriel Marcel has explained. A problem is something we do not understand presently but have good grounds for expecting to understand in the future. "Mystery," as Rahner and other theologians employ it, is intrinsically beyond us. No matter how much further information we obtain, we will not penetrate its core. It has a fullness of being or light or love or power that simply goes beyond our human limitation. To think of grasping it, comprehending it, is like thinking of carrying the ocean in a glass. Consequently, we better deal with mystery, better "understand" God, by simple acts of contemplation. If we open our "hearts," by which both the Bible and common usage often mean our integral summary selves, and somewhat disregard our discursive, step-by-step minds, we can appreciate things really beyond us.

This is a rather important point, so we beg patience to pursue it. To have experience of the real God, to locate divinity in one's own present time, normally requires some contemplation. God can step in and knock any of us over, as the story in Acts has Christ knock over Paul. But that is not how it usually happens. Usually, we get our intimations of God in moments that show us a mysterious "more." For ancient peoples, sunrise and sunset were two such regular moments, and sometimes they can be mysterious even for city dwellers of today. If you think a little about the total darkness that would come over the desert, when in the writer of John's time the desert had no artificial lighting, you may be able to imagine how he could make "light" a primary designation for God: "The light shone in the darkness, and the darkness did not overcome it" (John 1:5).

Other mysterious moments occur in interpersonal relations. Romantic moments, for instance, when one swells with feelings of love. They bring a fullness, a rightness, a harmony with the order of things that tend to make us grow quiet and wonder. Just being with another person, in full silent accord, is a primal experience our little analytic minds will never come near to mastering. The sexual expression of such romance longs to give it joined bodies. It succeeds about as often as the free, gratuitous swell of love itself flows through us, but that is enough. It shows us what sexually different bodies are for, and why marriage was for Paul a great mystery.

We could give other examples of peak experiences, and they all would flow out to mystery that involves us personally. The aesthetic experience of overwhelming beauty, the intellectual experience of leaping to a higher viewpoint, the communal experience of real teamwork, the ecclesial experience of union in the Spirit—all are exactly mysterious. So, in a reverse way, are the valley experiences of failure, of bereavement, of brokenness—the times when the world seems flat and barren. The strain they put on us, the depression they threaten, suggest that two-dimensional, mystery-less living is the frustration of our spirit. Not to live toward a "more," not to stretch out in hope, is a retrenchment to telltale sadness. By speech no linguist can fully fathom, it tells us things should be different. If we listen, we hear a counsel to make a change, get some help, rest the body and ease the mind. If we listen, we get our first lesson in what the saints call the discernment of spirits.

One of the most famous cases of the discernment of spirits involved the founder of the Society of Jesus, Ignatius Loyola (1491–1556). Wounded in battle by a cannon ball, he sought to relieve his recuperation by some interesting reading. The library available to him had mainly romances and lives of the saints. He alternated between them, and before long he noticed a significant difference. The romances he took up with anticipation and lay down with a certain unease or sadness. The lives of the saints he took up rather reluctantly and lay down with a sense of peace, even an eagerness to do like deeds. That experience was the germ for Ignatius's famous and very influential *Spiritual Exercises.* Following the way to peace, reading out the alternation between what he came to call "consolation" and "desolation," he stripped away vainglorious ambitions and came to make such evangelical ones as poverty and humility the stuff of his spirit's nurture.

We live in a different time, and most of us have vocations different than Ignatius's. Nonetheless, we can learn a great deal from reports such as his, because they greatly illumine the processes of any deep personal maturation. To grow mature, we all have to move beyond what Freud called the pleasure principle and come to accept reality as it is. By the common report of persons most societies call holy or wise, reality as it is asks us to die to mere sensual gratification and ego. That sounds harsh, so the majority of us run away and block our ears. However, bit by bit, the years themselves etch in the message. If it does not carry much weight when we are twenty, or even when we are forty-four, it probably makes some sense by the time we are sixty. For by the time we are sixty we know in our bones, and not just in our minds, that we are soon to die. Clearly enough, there will die with us all the sensual pleasures we spontaneously pursue. Neither the good meal, nor the comfortable coat, nor the wavy orgasm stays with us very permanently. On the other hand, the way we change through creative work, the way we change through creative love seem to go to our marrow. Whatever of "us," of our "spirit," survives the grave is more likely to be colored by them than by our sensual pleasures.

In the Catholic contemplative tradition, these homely little lessons take sharp focus. For an Ignatius Loyola or a John of the Cross, who had extraordinary interior experience, God lures us through our sadnesses and joys to grow in religious understanding. So grown, we begin to deal with God not as a projection of our needs, not as a great father figure, but as he really is: mysterious, other, too bright for our minds. Such influential modern antireligionists as Feuerbach and Freud criticized Christianity (and religion generally) for what was essentially its immaturity. They had eyes to see, and all around them was wish-fulfillment. Living in fantasies of "heaven" and "hell," distracted from both self and the earth, religious people seemed like children. By Freud's criteria of good psychic health—the ability to love and the ability to work—few religionists were healthy. Rather, their religion seemed a symptom, even a cause, of widespread neurosis. As Michael Buckley has recently shown, contemplative Catholicism largely seconds this diagnosis. John of the Cross and Ignatius Loyola are more kindly than Feuerbach or Freud, but they too want fantasy to yield to sober realism.

That is the point to such close analyses of interior experience as those developed by John of the Cross as the "dark night of the senses" and the "dark night of the soul." The real God must wean us away from the images (often quite self-serving) that we interpose between ourselves and her. Slowly, in the Spirit's good time, we must come to real-ize, to recognize experientially, the conciliar Catholic faith that no matter what we say about God he is more unlike than like our description. In Thomas Aquinas's terms, that comes out as a teaching that while we can know *that* God exists we cannot know *what* God is (precisely how God exists). And even this revered teaching is but a small diminishment of God's mystery, for though the First Vatican Council (1869–1870) taught the natural capacity of the human mind to know God's existence, it neither affirmed that particular individuals achieve this knowledge nor separated it in fact from the work of God's grace—from God's own activity of revelation.

But how does all this "mystery" work out concretely? Rather consolingly, we believe. First it suggests that none of us human beings has a handle on the full plan of things, and so none of us has a diploma boldly to pontificate on God's inner doings. God is not a King who has made certain human beings his privy counselors. We are all in the dark, and the sufficient light that God gives us all, through either conscience or tradition, is a thing so modest we can trust it. Probably the most trustworthy catechetical volume of the recent Catholic past was the Dutch bishops' *New Catechism*. It begins with the human orientation to mystery and maintains throughout that faith is a wonder-ful way to respond to the otherness of God, a way both humble and joyous. Equal in our being unequal to God, all of us stand needy. As the medieval artists saw it, we all are led by death to dance the same measures. King or jester, peasant or pope, none of us has ever seen God.

Second, however, most of us have felt God—have received some intuition. We may have been little schooled to appreciate what we've felt, but our daily lives have borne us the divine. If only in small groups, we have had our version of T. S. Eliot's moments in the rose garden, in the draughty church at "smokefall," when a stillness brought us God's "more." Or we've learned a little wisdom through suffering. Detached by some pain, we've taken a fresh look at our time and resolved to get its next acts together. The mysterious, real God is the fullness into which our best moments go, the limitation on the world shown by most suffering. Close as the pulse at our throat, mystery lets all our being be. The most basic question in philosphy is, "Why is there something and not nothing?" The most difficult question in most people's lives is, "Why are my hopes so often thwarted?" However these questions play for a given person, they suggest in religious perspective that God is as objective, as ready-to-hand, as the most ordinary local pebble. Similarly, God is as integral in one's life as the most ordinary daily frustration. The pebble is not God, the frustration is not pure revelation. Catholicism teaches neither pantheism nor magical divination. But it does teach that, in Augustine's phrase, God is more intimate to us than we are to ourselves. Today, we suggest, the most real way to summarize this notion is to accredit the mystery into which *all* human experience leads. Quite literally, we are nothing without God—we do not exist. And quite playfully, God is no thing, but rather a fullness of a different order.

None of this analysis, rhetoric, or playfulness, we conclude by saying, is *proof* that the human quest intends or attains God. At best it is persuasive indication or suggestion. But it gathers together a group of experiences that surely keep God's possibility open. As full religion finally is an option of faith that goes beyond experience through personal commitment, so full atheism finally is an option of faith that does very much the same. The question for Jesus, then, is how persuasively he makes the mystery a saving parental love.

BIBLIOGRAPHY

Buckley, Michael. "Atheism and Contemplation," *Theological Studies*, 40/4 (December 1979), 680–699.

Carmody, Denise Lardner and Carmody, John Tully. *Ways to the Center: An Introduction to the World Religions.* Belmont, Ca.: Wadsworth, 1980.

Dillard, Annie, *Pilgrim at Tinker Creek.* New York: Harper's Magazine Press, 1974.

Donceel, Joseph, ed. *A Maréchal Reader.* New York: Herder and Herder, 1970.

Dutch Bishops, The. *A New Catechism.* New York: Herder and Herder, 1970.

Geertz, Clifford. *The Interpretation of Cultures.* New York: Basic Books, 1973.

Jaki, Stanley. *The Road of Science and the Ways to God*. Chicago: University of Chicago Press, 1978.

Lonergan, Bernard. *Insight: A Study of Human Understanding*. New York: Harper & Row, 1957, 1978.

Marcel, Gabriel. *The Mystery of Being*. Chicago: Regnery, 1950.

Maslow, Abraham. *Toward A Psychology of Being*, Second Edition. New York: Van Nostrand, 1968.

Polanyi, Michael. *Personal Knowledge*. New York: Harper & Row, 1964.

Rabut, Olivier, *L'expérience Religieuse Fondamentale*. Tournai: Casterman, 1969.

Rahner, Karl. "The Concept of Mystery in Catholic Theology," *Theological Investigations, IV*. Baltimore: Helicon, 1966, 36–73.

Rahner, Karl. "Science as a Confession," *Theological Investigations, III*. Baltimore: Helicon, 1967, 385–400.

Rahner, Karl. *Spirit in the World*. New York: Herder and Herder, 1968.

Shils, Edward. *The Center and the Periphery*. Chicago: University of Chicago Press, 1975.

Toynbee, Arnold. *Mankind and Mother Earth*. New York: Oxford, 1976.

Weber, Max. *The Sociology of Religion*. Boston: Beacon, 1963.

White, Patrick. *The Vivesector*. New York: Viking, 1970.

Jesus Christ 3

OVERVIEW

The warrant for the Christian view of God and human destiny is Jesus Christ alone. To begin to assess this warrant (who soon turns and begins to assess us), we take up the biblical theology of Jesus—how he appears in the New Testament. There we find innovations on the contemporary Jewish religion and a remarkable personal authority that together make Jesus remarkable, singular and intriguing. Indeed, so intriguing and powerful did Jesus' early followers find him that before long they read his unique degree of humanity into a case for divinity. A man so charged with the grandeur of God, a man resurrected by God—he must be God's very son. Rendering the conjoint truths of Jesus' full humanity and filial divinity has never been easy, but it has become especially difficult in modern times. Today Catholic theologians prefer to begin with Jesus' humanity, letting the awe it provoked lead them to faith-language about divinity.

Modernity asks how Jesus can be central to an evolutionary world and incarnational Christology answers in terms of God's desire to communicate divine life to creation. Insofar as Jesus is the omega or realization point of this desire, he both centers evolution and stands as the personal symbol of God's eschatological (definitive and final) will to save. Salvation implies giving sense, completion, and release from sin. Jesus models this divine intent (which works in all persons' lives) so he clarifies the destiny even of non-Christians. When we take salvation concretely, both non-Christians and Christians show ambiguities. When we take salvation concretely, we ask Jesus to enable forces of liberation and justice all around. Thus, the practical Christology that comes from following Jesus involves us in a pro-grammatic commitment to justice. For all doers of justice, Christian or non-Christian, Jesus' blessing is rich.

THE BIBLICAL THEOLOGY OF JESUS

At the end of the last chapter, we said that the question for Jesus—the question we ought to put to his religion or theology—is whether he makes the mystery into which our lives lead a saving parental love. That question squares with a straightforward reading of the biblical story of Jesus. As the gospel writers present him, Jesus did not primarily preach or promote himself. Rather, he primarily preached and promoted a God whom he called "Abba": "Father" or "Daddy." This God Jesus identified with the God of his people's past—the God of Abraham, Isaac, and Jacob. However, on the basis of his own experience, Jesus spoke more intimately about his God than his people's past had, and more insistently. For whereas the scriptural tradition had passages, such as those in the writings of the prophet Hosea, that depicted God intimately as a suffering spouse, in Jesus' time the God of the fathers was mediated by *Torah:* traditional guidance, "Law." Because of that mediation, most of the Jewish religious establishment did not take kindly to Jesus, for Jesus insisted God cared little about past moral performance. Breaking into history to cure its disorders, God wanted wholehearted conversion.

We have packed a great deal into one simple paragraph, so it will be wise to step back and unpack the above at some length. Doing so we note, first, that all present-day New Testament theology assumes Jesus' Jewishness. Jesus of Nazareth was a man of his times, as we are men and women of our times. He inherited a language and culture that shaped his thought, and he could only communicate his thought to his contemporaries in terms of that language and culture. Even to begin to understand him or his message, then, we have to grasp at least the rudiments of his cultural situation. Of primary importance, for instance, was the influence of Torah. On the basis of what they took to be God's revelation to Moses, Jews of the centuries preceding Jesus had elaborated a full program for religious living. Religious living meant being "clean" in one's dealings and so worthy of the holy God who had made a covenant, a quasi-contractual relationship, with the Jewish people. To have such cleanliness or purity, the good Jew would refrain from work on the Sabbath, refrain from unclean food such as pork, stay far from pagan idols and licentious games.

The people to whom Jesus preached his new conception of God, and his new sense that God's rule was rushing in, were trying to live a Torah-directed life in rather trying circumstances. Politically, they were not a sovereign people but subject to Roman authorities. Culturally, the Greek language, art, philosophy, physical nurture (gymnasiums, games), and the like—which comprise what scholars call "Hellenism"—dominated the Mediterranean world. This culture was greatly at odds with traditional Jewish ideals. Religiously, various cults from Greece and the Near East offered alternatives to the traditions of Torah. It is not surprising, then, that many of Jesus' contemporaries were confused. Some retreated to a stubborn conservatism and refused to have anything to do with "foreign" elements. Harkening back to a solution hammered out during the Babylonian exile, they kept to themselves and pivoted the community's whole life on the synagogue, where Jews could pray, study scripture and Torah, while supporting one another in pure living. Other Jews found foreign notions attractive and so abandoned the traditions of their fathers and mothers. Taking part in Gentile culture, they tried to lessen the strangeness that Gentiles associated with Jews by downplaying dietary laws, Sabbath laws, and the physical mark of circumcision.

To those of Jesus' contemporaries who kept a strong sense of their traditional faith, at least four parties or groups presented different options. The group called Zealots were a politically oriented party dedicated to the overthrow of the Roman occupation, if necessary by force. The group called Essenes were separatists. For them the way out of the current conflicts was to withdraw to remote areas, such as the hills around the Dead Sea, where they could live a religious life of the strictest observance. The group called the Sadducees took a conservative position on Torah and political accommodation. For them only the written law, especially the Pentateuch (first five books of the Bible) comprised the revelation God had given Moses for the community's guidance, and only keeping peace with the Roman authorities could ensure the community's continued survival. The group called the Pharisees were largely laypersons of middle-class status (in contrast to the Sadducees, who tended to be priestly and wealthy). They tended to be zealous for Torah rather than for political opposition to Rome, and to extend Torah beyond scripture, so that it included the interpretations developed by leading rabbis, who had labored since the rise of the synagogue in exilic times to adapt the Law to changed conditions.

Jesus associated himself with none of these groups. Rather, he responded to the appearance of a prophetic figure, John the Baptist, who was preaching a message of repentance in preparation for God's coming judgment. In Jesus' adaptation and development, that message became the centerpiece of the preaching we find in the synoptic gospels (Mark, Matthew, Luke): the Kingdom of God. To one and all, Jesus preached that God was at hand, ready to overturn the present unsatisfactory state of affairs. A whole new order was dawning. With a personal *authority* that his observers found astonishing, Jesus reinterpreted much of the Torah. Where it had been said in the past, an eye for an eye and a tooth for a tooth, Jesus said God is such that we must love our enemies, do good to those who persecute us. Whereas in the past Sabbath was made for God, in the sense that one was to do no worldly work, Jesus said that the Sabbath was made for human beings, in the sense that good deeds such as healing the sick were the genuine religion that God wanted.

In such ways, Jesus more than challenged the conventional understanding of religion. No longer could one feel secure that by keeping the precepts of Torah he or she stood right with God. Much more important than any precept-keeping was love—of God with one's whole mind, heart, soul and strength; of neighbor as oneself. Thus, those who refused to support their parents in their old age, by taking advantage of a law that allowed them to give monies to the service of the temple, did not break a precept of Torah—but they did break the more fundamental duty of loving their parents. In much the same way, those who had the power to cure fellow human beings and refused to do so on the Sabbath were not, in Jesus' eyes, pleasing to God. God was such that laws, "rights," precise calculations of "justice" fell away. The parable of the prodigal son (Luke 15:11–32) put all this indelibly. A son who had brashly demanded his inheritance, and then wasted it in high living, found himself reduced to the disgusting occupation of tending pigs. So he "came to himself" and decided to return home and beg his father's forgiveness. But long before he could recite his little speech, his father spied him and ran out to embrace him. The father ordered rings for his fingers, a feast for his friends. When the son's older brother, a dutiful but cheerless type, grumbled about this celebrating, the father explained the logic of his heart: "This your brother was dead, and is alive again; he was lost, and is found."

The parables are our best indications of how Jesus actually taught, and in this parable he was saying that God is so good, so loving, that he does not hold grudges. His love and concern for us all is such that he runs out to meet us, takes any indication that we have "come to ourselves" as warrant to welcome us back and make merry. There is more joy in heaven over one sinner who repents than over ninety-nine just, because God is heartsore over those who ruin themselves by rejecting his love.

A similar sort of God emerges in another of Jesus' stories. The parable of the good Samaritan (Luke 10:30–37), who takes pity on a man beaten and robbed (after "good Jews" have walked by), shows Jesus' understanding of what sorts of acts imitate God. The judgment that Jesus makes on the Pharisee and the publican (tax collector) who pray to God (Luke 18:10–14) (the one self-righteously, the other very humbly) shows that Jesus' God wants deep honesty. When Jesus consorted with publicans and prostitutes—the ostracized of his society—he made concrete his God's unlimited love. When he told those who brought him a woman caught in adultery, "Let him among you who is without sin cast the first stone" (John 8:7), he showed the nonjudgmental, re-creative side of his God's love.

That love reset all human relationships. In a word, it said we should treat all others as we would have them treat us. We should forgive them, try to understand them, try to love them because this is what our own hearts most deeply crave. Out of our hearts' cravings, we "know" what a genuine, worthy God must be. It was Jesus' amazing gift to have no doubts about this worthy God. Through most of the gospels, Jesus moves with an utter confidence, an utter trust. God his father so centers his whole life, is so overwhelmingly real to him, that he has virtually none of the fears or inhibitions that keep the rest of us from being fully human. He can respond to nature, to fellow men and women, to even the despised rejects of his society—respond lovingly, understandingly, healingly.

It is this startling humanity, this transparent goodness, that rivets most contemporary biblical theologies of Jesus. What he says and does is fresh and challenging after nearly two thousand years. Despite the fact that all the New Testament accounts of Jesus filter the original historical happenings through at least a generation's worth of interpretations, he continues to breathe the dearest freshness. No tidy formulas capture him. No comparison with other world religions founders detracts from his sublimity. Quoting an earlier scholar, the Jewish interpreter Geza Vermes concludes near the end of his study of Jesus: "In his ethical code there is a sublimity, distinctiveness and originality in form unparalleled in any other Hebrew ethical code; neither is there any parallel to the remarkable art of his parables." [Vermes, p. 224]

Fully human, able to get angry at evil and to weep for his friends, Jesus has fascinated not only his contemporaries but all the subsequent generations that have bothered to study him. A spate of literary and musical interpretations shows this fascination continuing today. *Godspell*, for instance, captures the joy and liveliness that Jesus could have shown. *Jesus Christ Superstar* captures the countercultural quality of his mission. Such interpretations, along with the New Testament and any acquaintance with Christian history, show that few past times have understood Jesus very well. All too limited, most times have turned from his originality, his freshness, his challenge and tried to go on doing business as usual. So long as there are copies of the gospels, however, that will never be completely possible, just as so long as there is the Hebrew Bible we will never be able to domesticate God.

For his challenges to the establishment, political and religious alike, Jesus went to his death. His closest disciples deserted him; he was so alone he wondered whether even his God had gone. The first reading of Jesus' story, then, shows us a man faithful unto death. He gambled on God's nearness, God's total goodness, and he lost his very life.

THE THEOLOGY OF THE INCARNATION

But this first reading of Jesus' story is inadequate. There would have been no gosepls, no New Testament, no Christian church had Jesus merely been faithful unto death. The passionate conviction of his first followers was that God resurrected Jesus—took his death up into the divine life and made him present again in their midst. Since the resurrection colored all the New Testament writers' understandings of Jesus, we find in their reminiscences a second story line. Even prior to his resurrection, Jesus was extraordinarily powerful. His cures and "miracles" (calming the storm, changing the water to wine, raising Lazarus) revealed him to be more than just a man. As the Gospel of John put it, before Abraham (the father of the Jews) came to be, Jesus was.

It is a tendency of New Testament scholars today to attribute the first reading to the historical Jesus and the second reading to the early community that came to believe Jesus was still alive. Catholic and Protestant scholars alike share this tendency. They remind us that the earliest portions of the New Testament (in its present form) are the epistles attributed to Paul, and that those epistles focus not on the historical Jesus but on the Christ, the risen Lord. Consequently, all our reading of the New Testament runs into the "hermeneutical circle." Hermeneutics is the study of interpretation—how to determine what a text means. In the New Testament context, it is first of all the matter of gaining critical control of the fact that faith informs all the writers' declarations. None of the writers attempted an objective, detached history or philosophical analysis. All of them wrote "from faith for faith." The way that even the gospel writers who do depict Jesus speaking and acting in historical situations proceeded was determined by their faith, their theological point of view. Matthew, for instance, was a believing Christian, probably of Jewish background and writing for Jewish Christians, who wanted to show how Jesus fulfilled scriptural prophecy and perfected the old dispensation. He cast his materials so that they served this intention.

So too with the other New Testament authors. Each of them had a "Christology," a point of view that assumed Jesus was the decisive revelation of God. In various parts of the New Testament, such Christology reaches beyond titles and symbols to state rather directly that Jesus was the divine Son or Word of God. The beginning of John's gospel, the first chapter of the Epistle to the Colossians, and the first chapter of the Epistle to the Hebrews all exemplify this trend. In their view, Jesus' life represented a great circle. He existed with God before his earthly birth, assumed flesh to serve God's work of salvation, and then returned to God's right hand. Thus, the New Testament itself has a theology of the Incarnation, a conviction that in Jesus God's Word took flesh.

God's "Word" (as God's "Spirit") was a notion available from Jewish scripture. Thus, according to Genesis, God created the world by speaking: "Let there be light." Similarly, it was God's word that came over the prophets, giving them their words of both accusation and comfort. The theologians of the New Testament took this conception and fitted it to the task of interpreting what this exceptional man, Jesus of Nazareth, meant. He was so full of power, so close to God, that he must have been God's very self-expression. From his words, his deeds, his whole bearing, God stood disclosed—made human, come into our terms. Therefore, Jesus was the beginning and the end of God's alphabet— God's alpha and the omega. Therefore, one who saw Jesus saw his Father.

We need to stress that this conviction of Jesus' divinity, which has been central to Catholic faith from the beginning, is precisely an article of *faith*. As such, it is not something that historical data can ever clearly prove. Even if we had pictures of Jesus calming the storm or raising Lazarus, we could not "prove," in a scientific way, that he was divine. We do not understand natural phenomena well enough for that. Rather, we would still have to assent from the heart—go beyond the mind's persuasion to the full acceptance that only love brings. Indeed, Jesus' own sayings—the parts of the gospels that have the best title to be considered historical—make this very point. They do not present his cures, for instance, as displays of divine power he himself possesses. Rather, they ask onlookers to believe in God, his Father, with whom all things are possible. In other words, Jesus almost always points away from himself to his Father. Almost always, it is faith—wholehearted trust—in God's goodness to which he attributes his success. To talk about what Jesus meant, or what Jesus continues to mean today, apart from this context of faith, is almost surely to misfire. Jesus speaks a language of faith, hope, and love. The understanding of Jesus, the estimation of who and what he was, has equally to proceed in faith, hope, and love. It is a dictum of good methodology that one has to fit one's procedures to the tasks at hand. Contemporary study of Jesus' Incarnation often shipwrecks on this dictum, for that study has the very difficult task of trying to extract objective, detached meaning from a wholly subjective, faith-and-love-laden set of reports.

This very difficult task has practical implications or applications at the present time. In early 1980, the bishops of the Dutch church met in Rome with Vatican officials and the Pope to try to solve some deep divisions that troubled their people. Those divisions had many causes and foci, but the one that seemed most to trouble Rome was the Dutch effort to work out a truly contemporary understanding of Jesus' divinity. The progressives among the Dutch theologians wanted to reset the question of Jesus' divinity in the context of faith and love. It is incumbent on us today, they said, to be more sophisticated than Christians have been in the past. Principally, it is incumbent on us to appreciate the results of biblical scholarship, and scholarship on the development of Christian dogma, and so to realize that often past ages underestimated the distinction between objective assertions and assertions of faith. That distinction does not make a complete disjunction (faith depends somewhat on objective reality, and somewhat intends to say "how things are"). It does, however, keep a proper distance between what one does in the laboratory and what one does kneeling in the pews.

Perhaps an analogy will help. At the time of the frightening accident at the nuclear reactor on Three Mile Island, we heard Helen Caldicott, an Australian M.D. who works in Boston, lecture on the medical dangers of radiation. In explaining the breakdown of radioactive materials, their half-lives and particle changes, she was a marvel of objective discourse. However, when she turned to the implications of these objective facts—to the probabilities of wind currents bringing radioactive materials to Boston, where her children presently were—the dispassion ceased. A great deal was at stake, and it clearly colored the "truth" of what had happened at Three Mile Island.

The same sort of bifocal vision occurs in other situations. The surgeon who operates on a cancer victim—for instance, to amputate a leg—has to suppress certain emotions and proceed rather mechanically. This is a rational, necessary choice, based on the judgment that the good of saving the patient's life outweighs the evil of taking a leg and causing great pain. However, if that same surgeon cannot change lenses and later see the patient as a suffering human being rather than a surgical problem, "reality" will be dishonored. The coolness that helps good surgery can ruin a post-operative interview. What the patient wants after the operation is some warmth and understanding. It is not a question of either/or—either competence or warmth. It is a question of both/and. There is a time to be cool and a time to be warm. There is a whole medicine, a complete enterprise of healing, that knows how to treat patients as both objective biological problems and subjective bundles of feelings.

The application to Christology is analogous. As an expression of passionate personal faith, the confession of Jesus' divinity tends to symbolic, or mythological, or poetic discourse—to language that is warm. In both the New Testament and the centuries of subsequent Christian faith, to call Jesus Savior, or Lord, or Son of God was to invest in him the great treasure of one's life. He was such a revelation and powerful realization of the way things ought to be that he was more than ordinarily human. Rather, he was a man singularly connected to the deepest and best power, a man actually identifiable with the creative love that makes all the best things be. Committing one's life to Jesus meant opening to this love. Because the love was so ultimate, it meant being "healed" (the root notion of "salvation"). Because the love was so profound, people could only talk about it rather paradoxically. Being seized by it, one felt that he or she was passing from "death" to "life," from unacceptability before God to acceptability.

That is the way that contemporary theologians such as the Dutch progressives tend to interpret religious discourse about Christ's divinity. They see it as a set of symbols struggling to express the deep impact that the real wonders of Jesus, and his real effects through faith, produced. There is another side to this issue, however, and it has an interesting history. Early in the fourth century, a number of Christians who had been educated in Greek analytic techniques pondered the question of Jesus' relation to the Father. They were of rather speculative temperament, and they wanted to know whether Jesus was of the same stuff (was *homoousios*) as the Father. The most important representative of this group, a priest of Antioch named Arius, put the matter succinctly: was there a time when the Logos (Jesus as the divine Word) did not exist? Arius answered his own question affirmatively: yes, there was a time when the Logos "was not" (did not exist). At the ecumenical Council of Nicea (325), the bishops assembled voted against Arius' position, saying that it did not represent traditional Christian belief. Their champion was Athanasius, who argued that the Logos was indeed of the same stuff as the Father and so existed eternally.

Few contemporary theologians have studied the methodological implications of this bit of dogmatic history (a *dogma* is an article of faith officially defined) more profoundly than Bernard Lonergan. His reading of what happened at the council of Nicea is that there the Church legitimized the rights of the mind to move beyond the horizon of scripture. Arius had raised a legitimate question, one that scripture itself had not posed (in his overtly metaphysical terms). By choosing to respond in Arius's terms, and not simply to repeat the nonmetaphysical language of scripture, the council faced up to the challenge (itself seen by scripture: see 1 Pet. 3:15) of giving an account of its faith that would bring it up to date. The alternative would have been an anti-intellectualism or fideism. It would have been to deny a legitimate question about the divine nature. Slowly and painfully, the councils of Nicea and Chalcedon hammered out the dogmas of Christology. At Chalcedon (451) came the classical definition: there is in Jesus Christ one person and two natures. The one person is that of the Logos; the two natures are those of divinity and humanity. The precise mystery of Jesus' identity lies in the juncture, the "hypostatic union," of the two natures in the one person.

Through the centuries, this classical definition gave rather abstract form to the catholic understanding of Jesus. In the thirteenth century,

Thomas Aquinas argued that we gain some understanding of the hypostatic union if we entertain the hypothesis that what Jesus' human personhood lacks (the reason why there are not two persons) is only and precisely the act of existence *(esse)*. The union of Jesus with God, the identity between Jesus and the eternal Word, is such that Word's act of existence gives Jesus' natures their being.

Now, this sort of scholastic development, which in its own way is a work of genius, has left rather far behind the solid reality of Jesus of Nazareth. For all that it resolutely affirmed Jesus' full humanity, scholastic theology dealt with him so abstractly that it left ordinary readers quite cold. Moreover, since the time of scholasticism speculative thought has moved from metaphysical categories, which give a rather wooden treatment of objects, to categories that derive from the personal intentions of consciousness. Thus, both the needs of ordinary persons' faith and the advances in philosophy conspire at the present time to demand that theology rethink Jesus' reality in more personalist terms.

In part, this demand can be answered by a distinction. We can say that what one preaches on Sunday, or writes in popular books, ought not to proceed in the detached, analytic categories of the professional theologian. The professional theologian is like the surgeon at work. Insofar as his or her goal is the most lucid theoretical understanding, the professional theologian can be coolly objective. But, like the good doctor after the operation, the good theologian who would communicate theology to persons with deep needs and hopes must find a language that is concrete, warm, and personally meaningful.

On the other hand, a vexing problem remains. *What* one communicates, even popularly, ought to be what one holds to be true. Insofar as the dogmas of Nicea and Chalcedon, and the elaborations of those dogmas through subsequent church tradition, represent something that the body of Christians has long believed to be true, we cannot lightly discard them. Insofar as their truth may be merely partial, or may be outmoded in its language, we must in all honesty try to update it. To deny that our understanding of traditional dogmas can, indeed must, develop is to deny that we human beings change—to say we do not live in history, do not have an inbuilt imperative to grow. So, poised amidst all these conflicting claims, the best contemporary theologians struggle mightily to honor all the truth they see. They make clear what the church has taught in the past, what they find permanently true in that teaching, and what they find inadequate or unintelligible by today's religious or intellectual standards.

Religiously, we clearly need a Jesus who is fully human. As Gerald O'Collins's short survey of recent Christology shows, there is a solid consensus on this. Intellectually, by following carefully the great power of Jesus' teaching and person, we may be able to retain his divinity and make it meaningful yet. For instance, if we start from "below," with the manifest humanity in Jesus' speech and then go on to analyze the implications of his singular authority and love, we may discover how all human beings seek union with divinity. In that case, Jesus will be "just" the full, unique realization of something the rest of us partially share. Were we so gifted by God, we too might be amazing expressions of divine love, amazing minatures of God's eternal Word. This approach is rather hypothetical, but Rahner and others have used it to good effect. By showing that we should not assume too quickly that we know precisely what "God" and "man" fully mean, they make us realize our own orientation to divine mystery, our own revealing of God. Then, in the space they have cleared, the possibility that God chose to take one man's capacity or orientation and so fill it that that man uniquely "incarnated" God's self-expression does not seem ludicrous. Indeed, for those who cannot disregard Jesus' singular New Testament portrait, it can become persuasive.

From below, then, we can keep open the possibility that much of what the older Christology, which proceeded from "above" (from the Logos in heaven, who came down to take flesh), really wanted to say. And, to keep that possibility open is all that theology rightly can expect to do. For theology is only faith *seeking understanding.* It can never substitute for faith, for the personal commitment that finds, based on *all* the aspects of the whole situation, that Jesus is the best interpretation of how human beings are called to live. The dogma of the Incarnation is only one of the whole situation's aspects. Equal in importance to it is the dogma of grace: God shows in Jesus that the divine intent is to befriend us in love. If a given person finds the dogma of grace, or other central aspects of the way of life that radiates from Jesus, more helpful or significant at a given time, there is no burdensome obligation to concentrate on less helpful, more problematic areas.

That surely is true in the case of such secondary matters as papal infallibility. It is arguably true even regarding the Incarnation, for what ultimately matters in Christian faith is living as Jesus did, not speaking as Chalcedon did. As Rahner has argued, any person who honestly accepts the challenges that life sets us, especially the challenge of being honest and loving in the horizon of death, is so imitating Jesus that, in the context of a Catholic understanding of grace, that person is very likely a "believer." Essentially, God invites us all through the experiences of every day. Those who respond with love anything like Jesus' make a commitment to God, an ongoing act of trust, that slowly draws their lives to a goodness (and often a suffering) like that of the "God-man." In that sense, all faith has a Chalcedonian "orthodoxy": Those who meet life lovingly continue the Incarnation. For that reason, Christian tradition has long spoken of "the whole Christ"—Jesus joined with his believers.

JESUS IN AN EVOLUTIONARY WORLD

Can we continue to speak of a whole Christ, or a unique Incarnation, or a definitive salvation today, when evolutionary science has so vastly extended our "world" (horizon of reality)? In our contemporary context, many find it difficult to think that the billions of evolutionary years center in Jesus. Yet Colossians 1:17 says: "He is before all things, and in him all things hold together." Is that a woeful anthropomorphism, a relic from benighted ages when people thought the world only a hundred generations old (and soon to come to completion)? Catholic interpretation of Jesus that mounts from his extraordinary humanity to his divinity, and that tries mightily to bring the conciliar traditions up to date, has to investigate this issue fully. In fact, it has to investigate whether one can have either a fully intelligible evolutionary theory or an adequate Christology without placing Jesus Christ at the center of global history.

Let us begin this difficult investigation with a strategic detour. It involves a reconaissance of the thought of Teilhard de Chardin. Time was, not so long ago, when one could assume a general familiarity with Teilhard's main theses, but that no longer seems possible. So we have to note, first, that this quite original thinker was driven to try to synthesize his science (paleontology) and his faith. He suffered for his boldness, in ways quite instructive, for both scientists and theologians took ready aim at him. However, when one considers how the logic of his detractors ran, his intent seems all the more admirable. The logic of his scientific detractors ran to a denial that the biosphere has any finality—any goal or terminal meaning. In many evolutionary scientists' view, it is a system accidental in its beginnings and purposeless in its developments. The logic of Teilhard's theological detractors ran to a denial that science should have any influence on the understanding of faith. If, for instance, paleontology suggests that the first human beings likely arose in several unconnected ancestral pools ("polygenism"), that ought not at all to impinge on the theological position ("monogenism") that all human beings derive from a single set of parents ("Adam and Eve").

Since Teilhard's day, in the years after World War II, considerably more sophisticated positions have arisen, and they mediate between these two logics of detraction. It is clearer now than it was then that the different orders of questions and interests that science and theology represent have to be brought into dialogue, and that with good will and imagination many of their differences can be whittled down. For instance, theologians can learn to appreciate the limits in the scientist's assertion that evolutionary mechanisms have no finality in view, and the reasons why the scientist's proceedings have to screen out the tendency to think that species develop organs (e.g., thumbs) *for* specific reasons (e.g., tool manipulation). On the other hand, scientists can learn why theologians are concerned about the unity of the human species (our solidarity in sin and grace), and their sympathy can help theologians rethink precisely what biblical language is trying to say in its accounts of Adam and Jesus Christ (the new "first man").

We give Teilhard a prophet's honors, then, for being boldly concerned to make Christ relevant to the world of science and evolutionary nature. Influenced by his faith that Jesus is God's supreme revelation, Teilhard tried to look behind the face of things. In the inside of things of nature, he thought he discerned a law of complexity-consciousness. Increased complexity, especially in neural systems concerned with information, seemed to correlate with increased consciousness (self-awareness). By this law, cosmogenesis (the development of the natural world) seemed ordered to noogenesis (the development of thought). That was a rather macroscopic or large-scale inference, but it gave all the data of science and Christian faith a certain coherence. If one cannot speak of finality in individual subhuman agents of evolution, one certainly can speak of finality or design in the prime agent, the divine creator. Everything in the Christian conception of God conspires to make us think that if he made the system we call the universe it was with deliberateness and purpose. Teilhard thought that his law captured, after the fact, some of the coherence that the creator intended in the fact.

Looking from this point of view, one who finds the traditional doctrine of the Logos credible and illuminating will infer that Jesus has an intimate function in the evolutionary process. If that process derives from the divine mind, and Jesus is the very Word of the divine mind, then that process correlates with Jesus from the outset. When God diffuses the divine goodness, so as to create, creation's "logic" partakes of the self-expression that a Father makes in speaking forth a Son. And if the Son be incarnate in the material world of evolutionary processes, then the communication of divinity to humanity in the Son becomes a primary channel or instance of the world's divinization (since the humanity that the Son assumes is not separable from the material world). By rather abstract reasonings such as these, speculative theologians have tried to make sense of the New Testament assertions about the Word's centrality in creation.

For the Eastern church, such reasonings undergirded and derived from the doctrine of the *Pantokrator:* Christ is the ruler of all creation. For the West they combined with Greek science and philosophy to make the world amenable to rational investigation: The world is a product of divine intelligence. For us today, they sharpen the question of evolution's meaningfulness, linking Christ to the current ecological crisis.

In the Christian view of nature, Jesus' full humanity receives the fulfillment for which all creation labors and groans (Rom. 8:19–22). The solid, material flesh that Jesus has from Mary so carries God's life that it becomes "God-with-us (Emmanuel)." For the Hebrew Bible, the God of Israel promised ("made a covenant") to be with his people through history. Indeed, "he" (for Israel God was largely a patriarch) revealed his divine nature in the people's experience of his hidden presence in time: "I am as I shall be with you" (Exod. 3:14). For the New Testament, Jesus was so full a presence of the hidden God that he became the new covenant, new ark, new temple—the redoing of the old symbols of God-with-us. Through his flesh, all the expectation and longing of human hearts for wholeness and death-defeating life finds satisfaction. Through his flesh, the processes that lead up to creatures who can have such expectation and longing also find fulfillment. That is how a contemporary Christology might advance the old theses. Doing so, it assumes that union with God, attainment of God's own life of love and holiness, is the "goal" or "end" not only of human beings, who can think about the implications of their strivings, but also of nonhuman creatures, who strive unawares. If we are indeed convival with natural creation, it makes sense that we read into the "lives" of oceans and mountains, leopards and camels, a striving like to our own. It makes sense, that is, that we take our Christology to ecological conclusions.

The conviviality that human beings have with nonhuman creation has been put in popular, accessible form by such naturalists as Lewis Thomas and Annie Dillard. In his recent *The Medusa and the Snail*, Thomas uses a story that we heard him tell during a lecture at The Pennsylvania State University in 1977. He had a layover in Tucson, and he decided to visit the local zoo. It was a fine day, and as he wandered between the tanks that housed the otters and beavers, admiring the play of the sun on the waters, he was overwhelmed by the "perfection" of these animals' sport. They were larking to the sun and the waters, swimming and diving and turning flips. So wonderfully did they take him out of himself that Thomas knew they were his kin. Like a Saint Francis, who preached to the birds, he felt at one with the whole of animal creation. The same sort of vitality—response to sun and sparkling waters—coursed through his blood as coursed through the otters' and beavers'. Reflecting on this back in his study, Thomas added to the holistic or organismic philosophy that his years as a cytologist (student of cells) had been developing for him. As the inside of human beings shows them to be "colonies" rather than isolated entities, since they house all sorts of viruses and parasites and quasi-independent subsystems, so the outside of human beings shows them to be parts of an organic whole, of a "nature" that is so intimately cross-related it is more than just poetically one.

At her hermitage near Tinker Creek, in Virginia's Blue Ridge Mountains, Annie Dillard, a professional writer, found dazzling variations on this theme. What she and Thomas share is a sense that we human beings cannot divorce our lives and fates from the incredibly energetic, profuse, and beautiful nature that has spawned us. Let "ecology" name this sense of the interdependence of all living things, and the old theses about Christ's pantokratorship become planks for an ecological platform and faith. Through the Incarnation, God has given not just human beings but all of creation a definitive ("eschatological") promise that its processes and labors are not in vain. Where microbiology or molecular biology may see only random reactions, Christian faith "sees" a divine concursus or co-action that carries all that has been made toward the ocean of God's own love-life. If we humans have been saved, our world has been saved with us. The new heaven and new earth that scripture (Rev. 21:1) glimpses express, in anticipatory intuition that never cracks the mystery of *how* God's promises actually will be realized in time, the joyous hope that *all* indeed will be well.

In Teilhard's language, Christ is an omega point of all creation where its fulfillment already stands realized. In more pedestrian speech, the unification of the nations that economic interdependence and communication are achieving, and the unification of material creation that the evolutionary and ecological sciences are discovering, point to a postulate or call for unitary fulfillment that the cosmic Christ, who for Colossians (3:11) is all in all, already has achieved. In a truly evolutionary world, Jesus forces theology to upgrade its appreciation of nature, and forces biology to raise its sights to religion.

HOW DOES JESUS SAVE?

But is all this not impossibly high-flown? What does it *mean* for Jesus to be the nodal point of all humanity, let alone of all creation? How do we bring these soaring assertions and fancies down to solid earth? Primarily, we bring them down to earth by recalling the analyses of human striving on which we labored in the previous chapter, and then by trying carefully, restrainedly, to correlate them with a sober estimate of the Jesus of Christian faith.

The strivings of concrete human living, as we analyzed them in the previous chapter, and as we have extended them analogously to the rest of creation in the present chapter, postulate ("demand") an achievement that will give human living sense and completion. By sense we mean explanation: showing human time to have significant purpose and order. By completion we mean emotional satisfaction: peace and love. To "save" human beings is to furnish them sense and completion. Insofar as we human beings "demand" a sense and completion "right now," in the time before our deaths, salvation has to touch our biology, politics, history and biographies. It has to be a vision and power that can bring us to harmonious relationships with nature, international co-operation, confidence that there is a solid path to the future, confidence that our individual stories report that it is good to be. Insofar as human beings "demand" more than what "right now" ever could supply—*lasting* sense and completion—salvation has to stretch beyond this earth and its history. It has to import "heaven" and "eternity"—transcendent realities we can only symbolize dimly.

Traditional Christian soteriology (study of salvation) deals with both "right now" and "eternity." It has a sense and completion for both our existence in time and our existence beyond time. When it has lost its balance, its tension between now and then, it has failed the Incarnation and the full Catholic Christology. For instance, when certain communities of the apostolic period (while eyewitnesses of Jesus still lived) so concentrated on the end of the world that they neglected worldly institutions such as marriage and government, they failed the Incarnational truth that God really has joined divinity to our flesh and time. On the other hand, when present-day Christians so concentrate on reforming worldly institutions that they bracket or even deny the realities that traditional symbols such as eternity and heaven have sought to indicate, they fail the Incarnational truth that God has offered humanity a fulfillment history alone never could. In the first case, where Christians neglect the world, they open themselves to valid criticisms, such as those of Marxists, that religion is an opium—something the powerful offer the oppressed to keep their eyes off revolution. In the second case, where Christians neglect the profound experience and meaning in their tradition's transcendent symbols, they open themselves to valid criticisms that they have denatured the rich original vision.

The task for a contemporary Catholic soteriology, then, is to try to restore a balanced view, not simply by repeating old formulas but by creating fresh metaphors and applications. For instance, it might make Jesus' salvific function more impressive and credible if present-day theologians tried to show how appropriating Jesus' life and message can touch our very bodies. That would seem a powerful way of exhibiting the import faith has for our human experience "right now." Let us therefore attempt it, at least in sketch.

If God's own Word took flesh, as a Christology "from above" affirms, or if Jesus so made flesh a presence of divinity that one had to wonder whether he wasn't more than human, as a Christology from below affirms, then flesh—our embodied human being—is clearly valuable, good, divinizable. Catholic theology has often affirmed this proposition, but lately it has not affirmed it creatively enough to make it a powerful glad song. Two places where historically the tradition affirmed the goodness of bodily creation were in its opposition to Gnosticism, which called fleshly things ungodly (and so doubted the Logos' Incarnation), and in its opposition to Albigensianism, a heresy that denigrated the flesh and marriage. Further, in developing its sacramental system, the tradition made various material things "carriers" of divine grace. Thus, it gave bread, wine, water, and oil a solid vote of confidence. Impressing them on the bodily senses, and adding lovely music and words, the tradition echoed Psalm 150: "Let everything that breathes praise the Lord."

Nonetheless, Catholicism did relatively little to encourage physical regimes for the body of the average believer, and often it made marital use of the body a second-rate vocation (and so something suspect). Compared to some yogic regimes that developed in India and East Asia, Christianity was less than fully loving toward the body. It so stressed the soul that the body could become Saint Francis's "brother ass": just the beast of burden that carries us through the vale of tears earthly life is bound to be. In such documents as Pius XII's *Sacra Virginitas* (1954), the tradition was so interpreted that religious abstinence from sexual relationship seemed to appear a more perfect faith-way. Today we still lack a satisfactory Catholic theology of health, exercise, play, and sex, as we still lack a fully effective solidarity with the poor. The result is that our lives are less beautiful, graceful, joyous, and self-sacrificing than they could be. They are less than fully saved.

Other important zones of contemporary life and faith connect to these we are discussing. For instance, we need not journey far to find a Catholic neglect of the feminine. True enough, Catholic veneration of Mary introduced a feminine factor that was powerful in popular faith. But for women it produced a rather impossible role model (virgin and mother), and for men it did nothing to deter a repressive view of sex. In another direction, the relative inadequacy of our theology of the body, our concern for the body's salvation, surely has played in our slowness to embrace a radical commitment to social justice and ecology. There has been considerable championing of the rights of workers, but not enough to make the church a clear opponent of hazardous work, such as mining, laboring in mills, laboring in chemical factories. There has been virtually no popular or even scholarly attack on industrial pollution, the devastation of the oceans, or nuclear contamination. Catholic theologians have not clearly seen that because we have bodies nature is our home. They have not clearly seen that the Word's becoming flesh means that all natural and bodily things struggle to become whole and godly. For instance, in the four years (16 issues) 1976–1979, a leading American Catholic theological journal, *Theological Studies*, published nothing on ecology or the theology of nature.

An important part of renewing Jesus' salvific implications therefore lies ready in theological reflections that apply the incarnational principles of a high Christology to current issues of nature and the body. Two other dimensions also beg consideration. One is Jesus' salvation of our trans-worldly aspirations, and the other is his having saved us from sin. The first dimension takes us to the depths of human experience, whence cometh our best hopes. As historian Eric Voegelin has shown, profound human cultures everywhere have produced symbols of transcendence. Greek culture, for instance, rode the wings of its great tragedians and philosophers to a high, transcendent imagery of justice. Thus, Plato gave to his political analyses of justice the ballast of an artful myth of the judgment of the dead. Egyptian, Iranian, and Muslim cultures, to name just a few, have had equivalent symbolisms.

In such symbolisms, a people expresses its intuitions of how things "must" be, if fairness and decency are not to be chimeras. Unless we have lost all moral health, we "know," at the fine point of our spirits, that there ought to be some recompense for innocent suffering. The poor people of the slums know that life has dealt them a bad hand, and they struggle to hope that somehow things will change. The wealthy people who profit from the poor of the slums have to harden their consciences to avoid their own intuitions of what justice implies. So they tell themselves that the poor are shiftless, dirty, not worth loving "as themselves." When Jesus says that as we judge we shall be judged, he claims the center of this profound human sense of how things ought to be. Faith in Jesus therefore stretches beyond the realm of history, where full justice never obtains, to a realm of another order: the Kingdom of God. In the Kingdom, things *will* be as they ought to be, and even better.

We naturally think of justice in terms of persons' dealings with one another, but it has analogous applications to nature's dealings with us. The people who suffer from plague, famine, flood, or earthquake all receive less than what a "fair" human life implies. It is true that, insofar as creation is from nothingness, the Creator "owes" us nothing. But our full instinct is that to make persons, or other creatures, only for suffering or frustration is cruel and unworthy of "God." So we either abandon the very notion of God, which leaves us in a world without ultimate sense and hope, or we raise our eyes to further possibilities. "Eternal life" is precisely such a possibility. Believing in God, hoping for the fruition of the longings deep within us, we wonder whether there isn't true justice beyond the grave. For the Greeks, divinity was precisely deathlessness. For the Christians whom the Greeks influenced, the resurrection of Jesus symbolized the first fruits of a return to the Deathless One—a return to life as it ought to be. These are but symbols—arrows we shoot into mystery. But on occasions of deep suffering or joy, when we are especially human, they can seem more "true" than plain mortality. For us present authors, who have seen three of our parents die prematurely, they keep a salutary wonder alive. Would not a God as good as Jesus depicts recompense his beloved for all that they were shortchanged?

Jesus' having saved us from sin is the final motif we consider. It goes beyond the securing of our sense to the pardoning of our evil. For we human beings do miss the mark and fall short of the glory of God. We do abuse nature, hurt one another, injure our bodies and minds. We can be fools, saying in our hearts there is no God, no mystery honesty must honor. We can turn our backs on the stories of Israel and Jesus, where mystery becomes steadfast love. We have our excuses, our reasons, our exculpations, but ultimately they are hollow. Some responsible irresponsibility so infects us that we no longer say thanks for the light of our eyes, the air we breathe. Stupidly, we turn to pleasure and mammon. "Original" sin is the generality of this condition, the social construction of a "reality" truncated and poisoned. Personal sin is the affirmation of this condition, the "I" joining perversion somewhat awares. So deeply is this the underside of human history, so deeply does it stalk all our hearts, that sense and completeness seem shattered. On the stones of human hardness, human forgetfulness, the best of our instincts fly apart.

We all know sin, so there is no point rehearsing its countless variations. From petty slights that keep blood relatives shunning one another for decades, to massive desecrations such as germ warfare, sin is the good we would do and do not, the evil we would not do and do. It involves us in a terrible economy of retribution, a jungle law of eye for eye. The salvation that Jesus offers is the reversal of this jungle law. Instead of eye for eye it offers suffering love. Struck, abused, rejected, Jesus did not strike back, abuse back, reject back. By the goodness of his God, he stayed uncorrupted by what we humans do—by what the concrete evil humans who killed him did. The cross of Jesus is a shout that God endures our evil. The resurrection of Jesus is a quiet assurance that God's love is stronger than our evil. Place that shout and assurance at the constitutional center of a human assembly, and you have what the "church" ought to be. It ought to be the gathering that so opens to God's love that forgiveness is its middle name.

When forgiveness has been the church's middle name, human beings have felt wonderfully saved. They have heard a scriptural word that stressed mercy, not sacrifice. They have experienced sacraments of baptism, eucharist, penance and anointing that healed their festering self-hatred. Perhaps above all, they have become a community with a healed imagination. Most of what is possible to us human beings depends on what we can imagine. When we see the possibility of reconciliation, forgiveness, renewal—grasp the scenarios they might assume—we take charge of healing our future. All things are possible with God, Jesus the preacher assured. The Christ makes all things new, our canonical authors proclaimed. If we take a message like that to heart, embody it in our whole bearing, we will reconcile estranged spouses, motivate enslaved alcoholics, fiercely oppose the status quo. Basically, we all ask to be saved from lovelessness. The whole significance of the Word made flesh is that we have been saved from lovelessness—that even when our hearts condemn us, God is greater than our hearts.

THE CHRIST AND NON-CHRISTIANS

Through much of its history, the Catholic church has had only a fuzzy sense of its relations to non-Christians. The dictum of Cyprian (ca. 300) that "outside the church there is no salvation" crystallized a tendency toward exclusivism, while the biblical notion that Israel was to be a light to all nations (and so was not "elect" for itself) constrained the new Israel to try to serve the world. In its doctrine of baptism of desire, which said that persons who lead good lives implicitly want entry into Christ's Body, the church saw a tacit act of faith at work in the hearts of all persons of good will. In its doctrine of limbo, the place where the innocent unbaptized would enjoy a "natural" happiness after death, the church backed off from such generosity. Thus, for centuries missionaries such as Francis Xavier rushed through foreign lands, believing that unless they got holy water on pagans' foreheads heaven would be empty. The God who desired the salvation of all persons (1 Tim. 2:4) therefore seemed to have done rather poor work. The myriads who lived before Christ, and the myriads after Christ who never effectively heard his name, seemed bound to perish.

Non-Christians' actual reality broke this pessimistic theology. Just about all the foreign cultures that missionaries visited showed signs of impressive moral achievement. They surely begged salvation, from all sorts of ills, but equally surely God had not left herself without trace in their midst. Thus, the dignity of many American Indians, the wisdom of many Hindus, the deep peace of many Buddhists, the ardent piety of many Muslims forced honest observers to take their Christian pretensions down a peg. There were pagans more honest than many Christians. There were foreigners more refined. How could it be that God had not preceded the missionaries to their culture? How could it be that they had no portion in Christ?

Nonetheless, it was only among European intellectuals of the early eighteenth century that a universalist sense of concrete history started to emerge. As late as Bossuet's *Discours sur L'Histoire Universelle* (1681), the Augustinian pattern, where history centered in the church, continued. With Voltaire and the discovery of the sublimity of Chinese culture, things began to change, and with that change the Christian doctrine of salvation came into crisis. That crisis continued, indeed grew, in the Catholic church to the middle of the twentieth century, only abating in Vatican II's *Declaration on the Relationship of the Church to Non-Christian Religions.* The Holy Office did wither Leonard Feeney's "Boston Heresy" in 1949 (Feeney claimed that all modern persons had, through modern communications, sufficient knowledge to realize they had to join the Catholic church, and that therefore all who did not join would go to hell), but it did little positively to show how Christ lives in non-Christians.

The Vatican II declaration points out the special relation that Jews and Muslims have to Christians, in virtue of the biblical background and faith all three groups share. Jews and Muslims have themselves recognized this, for Jews have tended to look on Christians as a deviant Jewish sect that history treated kindly, while Muslims have considered Jews and Christians "people of the book" (and so distinct from other non-Muslims). It is with more distant peoples—Indians and East Asians, for instance—that the problem has seemed most acute. They apparently have had little historical contact with Christ, and so their virtue or wisdom seems not to derive from Christ's preaching or self-sacrifice. Have they then no salvation, or have they a salvation independent of Jesus? The divine desire to save all persons, which we mentioned above, made the first option repugnant, while Acts 4:12 ("And there is salvation in no one else, for there is no other name under heaven given among men by which we must be saved") made the second equally so.

Before turning to the most celebrated "solution" to this problem, Karl Rahner's theory of "anonymous Christians," let us try to specify it with cases even more acute than those of well-developed Hindus or Buddhists. Anthropologists furnish numerous such cases, and we can quickly take up three: Colin Turnbull's study of the Pygmies of the Congo Forest, his presentation of the mountain people (Ik) of the border area between Kenya and Uganda, and Napoleon Chagnon's study of the Yanomamo, who live along the border between Venezuela and Brazil. The Pygmies are a literary delight. They show all sorts of human foibles, but their love of their forest, their close-knit tribal life, and the way they sing to their God (who takes the physical form of the forest) all make one think that "primitive" humanity is in good shape. The mountain people called the Ik have become infamous in anthropological circles, either as an instance of an anthropologist's distortions or as an instance of what happens to a people when extraneous politics disrupts its traditional way of life. For the Ik come through as a horrible group: deceitful, loveless, avaricious, and cruel. Literally, they take food out of the mouths of children and the dying. Because they are no longer allowed to wander and hunt as they had for centuries, fighting starvation has made them give up most signs of humanity. Reading about them, one thinks of

Paul's harsh verdict in Romans (1:28,29): " . . . God gave them up to a base mind and to improper conduct. They were filled with all manner of wickedness, evil, covetousness, malice."

Nor are the Yanomamo much better. They spend their days preparing for war, engaging in war, or recovering from war. Other tribes are simply the enemy; fellow members of the tribes are competitors to subdue or outwit. The men abuse the women. The women abuse the children. Religiously, the principal function of the Yanomamo shamans seems to be to sniff hallucinogenic powders, in order to induce visions of fierce little demons who will aid the tribe in its battles. Socially, the only way Chagnon could keep the Yanomamo from taking his food was to stock up on peanut butter, which they thought was excrement.

Human culture apart from Christ is therefore a very mixed blessing. In the main it probably shows more need of salvation than "Christianized" cultures have, but that is a judgment neither indisputable nor sure. Many non-Christians are truly admirable (the old Pygmy Moke whom Turnbull describes comes to mind), and many aspects of Christian culture (its militarism, usury, and wastefulness toward nature) make it clear that Christ has not conquered the West. The ancient cultures of India, China, and Japan offered considerable sense and completion to their citizens. India offered the Hindu program of the *ashramas* (life stages), as a well-marked path toward salvation *(moksha)*. First in India and then farther East, Buddhism offered the eightfold path as a high way to union with ultimate reality *(nirvana)*. For millennial China, Confucian ethics and Taoist aesthetics provided high-minded spirituality. For Japan, Shinto love of nature and Buddhist philosophy of emptiness combined to form an exquisite taste. On the other hand, India burned widows, China bound women's feet, and Japan could be exquisitely cruel. The data on non-Christian cultures therefore invite several interpretations. Depending on what one is expecting, either God or Satan stands forth.

There is a parallel with Western peoples, including Western ex- or anti-Christians. A friend who worked organizing cooperatives among Jamaican field hands reports that the nominally Christian establishment there reacted with naked savagery, while the most dedicated reformers were ex-Christians now of Marxist bent. A similar pattern often occurs in the American professions. Some of the most dedicated scientists, doctors, lawyers, and social workers are repulsed by institutional religion, or even declare themselves atheists. Some of the most chauvinistic and bigoted politicians insist on prayer in the public schools. The blessings of religion on American soil are therefore also very mixed. When pilgrims went on their "errand in the wilderness," or pioneers headed West to establish "God's New Israel," they sometimes did not scruple to slaughter Indians like buffalo. When John D. Rockefeller and Andrew

Carnegie modeled the role of Christian businessmen, the Bible became businesslike.

The heart of the matter of any culture, any faith, any personal religion, then, is not determined easily or from without. Any culture, faith, or personal religion is worth precisely the authenticity—the honesty and love—it produces. Cheek by jowl, Christians are saints and sinners, as are Hottentots. From beholder to beholder, the presence or absence of grace is differently judged. Francis Xavier thought Japanese of the sixteenth century the most ethical people he had ever seen. Søren Kierkegaard thought Danes of the nineteenth century captives of an irreligious Christendom. Only by entering the theater of existential conscience can one come even close to the mystery of the real God's presence or absence. And in the theater of existential conscience, Christ's drama is persuasively the best interpretation of God's play for everyman.

Such is the point of Rahner's theory of anonymous Christianity. Convinced that the one God, in whom he believes because of Jesus Christ, has offered salvation in all persons' lives, Rahner distinguishes between salvation (revelation, grace) that is "transcendental" and salvation that is "categorical." Transcendental salvation is the offer of personal love that God, the one mystery into which all lives go, makes everywhere. Because of his reading of Jesus, Rahner thinks that God the creator, who must be present to all creation if it is to continue to be, is freely for all human beings also God the intimate lover. In technical terms, Rahner speaks of this state of affairs as "the supernatural existential." By that term he means that the de facto situation for all persons is a world of grace—a world where God offers love, sharing, communion with the very divine nature. Substantially, then, all human beings have an equal "chance" for salvation, in that all persons meet a reality whose mystery is God's own accepting and helping love.

The categorical side of salvation (revelation, grace) is the specific historical and cultural forms that mediate this supernatural existential. All human beings indwell a language, a set of traditions from the past, a common pool of values, and so forth. For Christians, the categories that derive from Jesus represent the most adequate express forms for transcendental grace. That is, what happened in Jesus is the definitive (once-for-all) declaration of this universal state of affairs. The way that Jesus related to God, related to his fellow human beings, went to his death, and was raised to divine life—all of this love persuades the Christian that Jesus is singular, nonpareil. Other religious geniuses may reflect other aspects of divinity. Individual Hindus, Muslims, or atheists may be holy indeed. But the mainline, most "privileged" categorical expression of God's universally salvific will and action are for the Christian Jesus and his authentic religion.

To put all this reasoning in a short formula, Rahner has spoken of anonymous Christians—persons who *do* the essentials of the authentic religion that Jesus inspires but don't use Christian forms or language. Anyone who really accepts the full challenge of human life, Rahner has said, takes on the lineaments of Jesus. In other words, Jesus, overall, is the "best" hermeneutic or interpretational key for what it means to be human. Wherever such humanity is achieved, Jesus applies. Of course, there are problems applying this notion, and it can seem offensive—seem to carry the old Christian superiority complex. But other theologians who have criticized Rahner for the "diplomatic" abuses to which his theory is liable seem to have missed his main point. Principally, Rahner's notion is an attempt to make sense, within the orbit of Catholic faith, of how Jesus functions in the salvation of the human non-Christian. The diplomatic communication of this sense is an important but secondary matter.

That Jesus "saves" all who come to full maturity, by being the most adequate personal symbol of the divine grace on which all full maturity depends, seems to us a great elucidation of Catholic doctrine. It holds together both the generosity that God's care for all persons implies and the stunning singularity that shone from the flesh of God's one Incarnate Word. For those who wish to maintain orthodox Christological and soteriological faith, that is a very precious accomplishment. For those who have a touch of humanity and common sense, it begets no undiplomatic chauvinism. All salvation is gratuitous—an excess from God's goodness. To receive salvation in specifically Christian categories is but a further excess. Those who appreciate generosity respond to it with a like largess: "Beloved, if God so loved us, we also ought to love one another" (1 John 4:11). In the case at hand, that means calling all persons of good will brothers and sisters in Christ's love.

CHRISTOLOGY AND SOCIAL LIBERATION

Rahner's reflections on Christ's functions in saving human beings from senselessness, incompleteness, and sin have led him to speak of Jesus as the "absolute savior." In the singular life and love of this man, God has disclosed his "eschatological" (definitive, once-for-all) bearing toward humankind. That bearing is one of steadfast love (the quality that the Hebrew Bible often associates with Yahweh). More precisely, it is the steadfast love of a parent. As God is fatherly toward Jesus, so God is fatherly toward us all. (We consider in the next chapter the development of God's "maternity" that current sensibilities postulate.) Insofar as this revelation goes to the depths of the human condition, furnishing the ultimate wherewithal to make life good, it does indeed bear us definitive glad tidings (gospel) of salvation. For it shouts that the great disclosure and deed for which our hearts have been set has occurred, to a measure we could never expect. Thus, absolutely, without any restrictions, Jesus bears us our exalted destiny. Without the substance of his message, of his love, we are a people sitting in darkness. With that substance, we are children of God, partakers of the divine nature (2 Pet. 1:4).

In a largely third-world context, the present generation of theologians, some of them students of Rahner, have given these theses about Christian salvation and eschatology a more social, practical, and often political focus. Two such Latin American theologians are José Miranda and Jon Sobrino, and it will pay us handsomely to attend to their interpretations of Christology and soteriology. Miranda is a philosopher and biblical scholar, quite influenced in both pursuits by Marxist theses. From his studies of the Hebrew Bible, he has concluded that the prime practical demand of the God of the prophets and Jesus is that we do justice. From his studies of existential philosophy and the Johannine literature of the New Testament, he has further concluded that genuine faith in Jesus empowers us to do justice. In both cases, Miranda opposes any notion of faith that divorces it from hope and love—from the concrete *praxis* or doing, where we put our bodies on the line. Biblical truth is not a matter of propositions. Rather, it is a matter of *doing* the truth (rendering others justice) and so coming to the light (see John 3:21).

Thus, Miranda's exegesis of the Johannine understanding of faith in Jesus ties directly to his social concerns. The Johannine understanding shows a longer period of development than that of most of the rest of the New Testament. It is therefore in some ways more mature. The Gospel and Epistles of John stress that salvation is not some distant, future event that will only arrive at the end of the world, when Jesus returns in full power (parousia). Rather, salvation is really present in our midst right now. The very coming of Jesus meant that God's glory shone from human flesh, sacramentalized human doings. What will occur at the world's consummation is powerfully operative in the present. Faith is the mode by which we open ourselves to such transforming, fulfilling salvation. Were we really to believe, we could embody heaven and eternity for present earth and time.

Linking this interpretation of Johannine faith with the conditions of depressed parts of the world such as Latin America, Miranda forges a powerful chain. To transform the hellish lives of his continent's poor would be an act of salvation that would marvelously display the incarnation of God's love, the power of God's grace. Sobrino and other Latin American Christians, among them a number of Brazilian bishops, agree with this inferential chain. Moreover, like Miranda they are quite willing to name the enemy, the powers of darkness that conspire against the salvation of the poor into a decent living. Phillip Berryman has recently translated part of the bishops' message in these ringing words:

> Capitalism must be overcome. It is the great wrong, the cumulative sin, the rotten root, the tree that bears us the fruit we know: poverty, hunger, sickness, and death to the great majority. For this reason the system of ownership of the means of production (of factories, of land, of commerce, of banks, of credit sources) must be overcome. . . . We want a world in which the fruits of labor are shared by everyone. We want a world in which one works not to get rich but to provide everyone with the necessities of life: food, health, a house, education, clothing, shoes, water, and light. We want a world in which money will be at the service of men, not man at the service of money. [Berryman, p. 61]

Those are not words of comfort for us who live in the prime capitalist country that exploits Latin America. But before we turn them aside, protecting our vulnerability, let us try to hear their connection with the biblical and traditional Christ. The salvation for which human beings truly hunger, the Bible and tradition say, is a sense, completion, and freedom from sin that love of God and love of neighbor "legalize." The "law" of Jesus' faithful is but his twofold command. Because God has loved us, we are to love one another, and the minimal sign of our love for one another is fair dealing. We know this from personal experience—from having been dealt with unfairly ourselves. Whether that occurred in the schoolyard or at home or at work, it told us that things incompatible with "God" (with the fullness of how things ought to be) were going on. And we were not only angered by such ungodliness, we were shamed. Read the literature of any exploited group and you will find that they are severely tempted to blame themselves. That of course compounds their suffering, by adding more interior division. When the Bible says that God favors the "poor," it goes to the heart of such suffering. God favors the poor because, in addition to their material wretchedness, they can easily think they are of no worth. But, as the prophet sensed, God can no more forget or account one of her creatures unworthwhile than a nursing mother can forget her child. Indeed, like a good mother, God's heart goes out above all to the most fragile of her children.

This sort of justice redresses the deep inequities of a world in which it is easy to prosper off the pain of fellow human beings. This sort of justice saves the lot of billions from cruel senselessness. For if "God" is not on the side of those who get a raw deal, they are of all born of woman the most to be pitied. In the beatitudes (e.g., Matt. 5:3–12), Jesus says that his fatherly God blesses those who get a raw deal. Their suffering wins a special pledge that one day things will be different. If we would but extend our own sense of how things ought to be different, but imagine our way into the lives of the world's most destitute peoples, we would start to entertain the changes that any Christian faith worth speaking about entails. For then we would verge on loving our neighbors as ourselves. The straitened imagination of the American 1970s, when the country retracted most of the new hope the 1960s had spawned, makes it imperative that we get this message clear. If the Bible and Christian tradition have any wisdom, we cannot serve mammon and prosper. The evangelical perfection of selling all that we have and giving it to the poor (Mark 10:21) may be utopian, but it symbolizes a powerful Christian truth. Utopias are the "no places," the ideal realms, where we imagine how things ought to be. It is easier for a camel to pass through the eye of a needle than for a rich person to enter God's utopia, because God's justice despises the disparities, the untruths, that make for "rich" and "poor."

Jon Sobrino, the Catholic theologian who has most fully mined the liberational implications of following Jesus, develops the original biblical truth existentially. Like Karl Rahner, who has written of the unreadiness of the church to embrace poverty, he soberly discloses our practical unbelief. For what counts in Christian profession, as we have already insisted, is not our sayings but our doings. The imitation of Christ most requisite in our time is following his law of love to justice, because in our time a great deal of human suffering is caused by humans. It is true that people have always been poor. It is true that there have always been inequity and unnecessary suffering. But today whole economies and cultures are warped because a relatively few people are extremely piggish. Properly, lovingly viewed, the world has enough resources to provide any sane population figure a decent standard of life. Properly, lovingly used, the human community has enough creativity and drive to feed, clothe, heal, and educate any sane population figure. The main reason we do not do these things is only partly a matter of imagination and energy. It is more a matter of will. Utopian as it may seem, therefore, Jesus' program is the only sort that cuts to the heart of the matter, because unless we have a new will, to power a new economy and polity, the best we will produce is band-aids.

So from the biblical Christ, through the theology of the Incarnation and of how Jesus' saves, we come to term at the contemporary passion for liberation. Many of our contemporaries want a world free of grinding poverty, of racism, of sexism, of war and profiteering. In Latin America, small cadres of liberationists have so upset governments that imprisonment, torture, and even murder have become the order of the day. In Nicaragua, they have even gained power, launching an experiment in Christian socialism. Latin America is perhaps the most Catholic locus of the fight for liberation, but its fight is more like than unlike similar struggles going on in other oppressed lands.

The regimes of recent Chile, Brazil, Uruguay, and other Latin American countries historically Catholic will finally be judged by the Spirit. So will the regimes of recent Western military-industrial complexes, recent Eastern totalitarianisms, and recent Vatican power-politicians. "For freedom Christ has set us free," Galatians 5:1 proclaims. The beginnings, deep tradition, and contemporary acuity of Christian faith add but polyphony. A central measure of Jesus' "worth" is the freedom, the health, the strength, and the joy he brings. A central measure is his absolute salvation. For Paul, such high pragmatism made Jesus God's power and wisdom. For Peter it left nowhere else to go. The Catholic experience of following Jesus, of living out the gamble that he is life's treasure, testifies that Jesus sends the Spirit. In the Catholic view, there is no better utopia: Jesus is the very Word of eternal life.

BIBLIOGRAPHY

Berryman, Phillip E. "Latin American Liberation Theology," in S. Torres and J. Eagleson, eds., *Theology in the Americas*. Maryknoll, N.Y.: Orbis, 1976, 20–83.
Caldicott, Helen. *Nuclear Madness*. Brookline, Mass.: Autumn Press, 1978.
Chagnon, Napoleon A. *Yanomamo: The Fierce People*. New York: Holt, Rinehart and Winston, 1968.
Dillard, Annie. *Pilgrim at Tinker Creek*. New York: Harper's Magazine Press, 1974.
Grollenberg, Lucas. *Jesus*. Philadelphia: Westminster, 1978.
Kasper, Walter. *Jesus the Christ*. New York: Paulist, 1977.
Lonergan, Bernard. *De Verbo Incarnato*. Rome: Gregorian University Press, 1964.
Lonergan, Bernard. *The Way to Nicea: The Dialectical Development of Trinitarian Theology*. Philadelphia: Westminster, 1976.
Mayr, Ernst. "Evolution," *Scientific American*, 239/3 (September 1978), 46–55.
Miranda, José. *Marx and the Bible*. Maryknoll, N.Y.: Orbis, 1974.
Miranda, José. *Being and the Messiah*. Maryknoll, N.Y.: Orbis, 1977.
O'Collins, Gerald. *What Are They Saying About Jesus?* New York: Paulist, 1977.
Pelikan, Jaroslav. *The Christian Tradition, 1: The Emergence of the Catholic Tradition (100–600)*. Chicago: University of Chicago Press, 1971.
Perkins, Pheme. *Reading the New Testament: An Introduction*. New York: Paulist, 1978.
Perrin, Norman. *Jesus and the Language of the Kingdom*. Philadelphia: Fortress, 1976.
Rahner, Karl. "Jesus Christ," in his *Foundations of Christian Faith*. New York: Seabury, 1978, 176–321.
Rahner, Karl. "Jesus Christ: History of Dogma and Theology," in Karl Rahner, et al., eds., *Sacramentum Mundi*, 3. New York: Herder and Herder, 1969, 193–209.
Rahner, Karl. "Observations on the Problem of the 'Anonymous Christian,'" *Theological Investigations*, 14. New York: Seabury, 1976, 280–294.

Rahner, Karl. "The Unreadiness of the Church's Members to Accept Poverty," *Theological Investigations*, 14. New York: Seabury, 1976, 270–279.

Schillebeeckx, Edward. *Jesus: An Experiment in Christology*. New York: Seabury, 1979.

Schilling, Harold K. *The New Consciousness in Science and Religion*. Philadelphia: United Church Press, 1973.

Sobrino, Jon. *Christology at the Crossroads*. Maryknoll, N.Y.: Orbis, 1978.

Teilhard de Chardin, Pierre. *The Phenomenon of Man*. New York: Harper & Row, 1959.

Thomas, Lewis. *The Medusa and the Snail*. New York: Viking, 1979.

Turnbull, Colin. *The Forest People*. New York: Simon and Schuster, 1962.

Turnbull, Colin. *The Mountain People*. New York: Simon and Schuster, 1972.

Vermes, Geza. *Jesus the Jew*. London: Collins/Fontana, 1973.

Voegelin, Eric. "Immortality: Experience and Symbol," *Harvard Theological Review*, LX (1967), 235–279.

Voegelin, Eric. *Plato*. Baton Rouge: Louisiana State University Press, 1966.

The Christian God **4**

OVERVIEW

The liberationists' concern with a God who makes us free springs from the biblical perception of deity. At the end of its conceptual chain, the biblical perception arrives at God our creator. The hidden God, who makes all human pretensions relative and demands that we live by faith, makes everything to be by his "I am." We glimpse something of such divine creativity in our own best works—enough to lift our gaze to a comprehensive work produced by artful love. The specifically Christian variations on the being of God the creator focus on the trinitarian processions. Developing scriptural hints, the early church fathers clarified descriptions of Father, Son, and Spirit. Probably the most powerful tool that the tradition developed, however, was the psychological analogy that first Augustine, and then Aquinas, elaborated. Both of these giants worked with their own consciousness, appropriating the biblical and patristic doctrine that human beings are "images" of divinity.

For the psychological analogy, the Father is the fathomless divine understanding, the Son is the Father's expressive word, and the Spirit is the substantial love that proceeds from their mutuality. These glimmers are valid still, though today we must strip them of rationalistic overtones. To do so, the indications that Rahner and others have given of how the Trinity enters our own experience are enormously helpful, for they spotlight God's love and work on our behalf. Finally, from the Trinity's communal existence, we can better see our own communal calling, while from our own creature-hood and suffering we can ponder God's pure perfection.

GOD THE CREATOR

In liberation theology, current reflection on Jesus' God finds a stimulus to discern how God labors for human beings' freedom. Doing that, it finds itself much at home with the God of the Hebrew Bible. For the God of Abraham, Isaac, and Jacob declared himself partner to the Hebrews' wanderings and time, and the prime moment of the Hebrews' time (whose memory was decisive in shaping the biblical form of the patriarchal legends) was the Exodus—the Hebrews' deliverance from Egypt under Moses. "Egypt" therefore became a prime symbol for slavery and bondage. It was the dismal "before" that preceded the "after" of entry into a land flowing with milk and honey. Settling in that land and establishing a monarchy came to have their own religious problems, for Israel did not fully resist the temptations to power politics and civil religion. As a result, the period of wandering in the "desert," when the Hebrews were free of Egypt and en route to their own land, became a religious paradigm. Despite the physical difficulties of unsettled life, there were spiritual compensations. Primarily, there were compensations of journeying with a living God in faith.

The distinctive quality of biblical religion, then, is its faith. In contrast to the nature-oriented religion of both its neighbors and other Bronze-Age peoples, Hebrew faith sought and found God in time— through history. There are qualifications to this thesis (nature orientations played their part in Israelite cult, and other peoples' religions contended with time), but they do not remove its core truth. The God that Jesus inherited from his people's beginnings was distinctively close and distinctively mysterious. That is the argument of Samuel Terrien, in his elegant volume on biblical theology, and it so organizes the data of the primal biblical texts that we find it persuasive. The elusive presence of the biblical deity was the objective correlative to distinctively biblical faith—the "outside" reality that summoned patriarchs and prophets to search for ultimacy in time.

Many indeed are the ramifications from this biblical center, but perhaps we should pause to develop a contemporary one. It has to do with forgiveness, which we found to be ingredient in the way that Jesus preached about his Father, and in the way that Jesus saves. How is it that so many situations develop in which justice and progress are lost because recrimination deadlocks the decisive parties? Internationally, the vacillation between cold war and detente that has marked Soviet-American relations since World War II is evidence that *homo internationalis* has far from come of age. Again and again, we have failed to muster the imagination and persuasion (the *peitho* that Plato made the catalyst of all successful politics) that would break vicious cycles, such as the arms race, and begin to make cycles of cooperation and building peace.

So too in such stunning examples of mutual recrimination as Northern Ireland and the Middle East. In Northern Ireland the world has an object lesson in how hatred is passed down from generation to generation. Before they even know what the words mean, little children use "Catholic" and "Protestant" as terms of abuse. And while it seems that a major cause of this situation is the economic exploitation that finally lies at England's door, there are no innocent parties. The biblical doctrine of forgiving one's enemies makes all the partners candidates for serious judgment.

So too in the Middle East. The breakthrough in relations between Egypt and Israel that occurred in the late 1970s was a welcome cessation from hatred unrelieved. However, it has hardly come to full flower, and the rise of militant pan-Islam threatens to make Arab-Jewish relations a new focus of an old notion of "holy war" (*jihad*). As in Northern Ireland, mutual accusation, well buttressed by facts, goes back almost to time immemorial. Palestinians surely have a solid case against those who despoiled them of their land. Jews surely have a solid case that being without a land of their own has given them their modern history of ghettos, pogroms, and holocaust. Neither Palestinian terrorists of the present generation nor Israelite terrorists of the past generation have much of a moral platform. Neither Arab nor Jewish "lawyers," haggling over minutiae of tortuous treaties, show the world a very magnanimous face. In the Middle East, as all around the world, we find "realism" often opposing forgiveness.

A principal reason this judgment can come to clarity is the alternative the Hebrew Bible holds out. There Yahweh, the sovereign King of all that breathes, is a God slow to anger and quick to forgive. And that is astounding, for a stiff-necked people who meet a God (an *elusive* presence) clearly out of their control might well have found things thoroughly otherwise. Because of their stubborn selfishness, they might well have found God principally a King of wrath. But no, it is not so. The depths of covenant theology, where the poets push the lawyers to the side, make God's fidelity to Israel a consequence not of Israel's good moral performance but of God's own self-consistency. Nothing so fragile as human "morality" determines relations with the living biblical God. Freely, that God who comes and goes as she wishes, who devastates all our idols of preconception—freely that God chooses to be slow to anger, quick to forgive.

Similarly, it was not because of any human comeliness that Yahweh chose ragtag Israelites to center a plan of universal salvation. It was because of Yahweh's own mysterious love. Were the people even to abandon the covenant, even to play the harlot and adulterate their faith, the God of Hosea would not give up loving them. Were individuals even to rise up in adolescent ingratitude, even to demand their putative "inheritance" and debase themselves to the care of pigs, the God of Jesus would rush out to meet them with forgiveness. From the free goodness of the biblical God, then, Christianity has glimpsed a rich potential for liberation. In our time, that could enable a theology of God the creator that would truly be creative.

For the gist of an imaginative theology of creation is the fecundity of love. It is true enough that God classically is the *ens a se* (self-sufficient being) who makes the world *ex nihilo* (from nothing). It is true enough that the world so made from nothingness manifests God's supreme power—the ultimate existential act Parmenides expressed in a simple declamatory "Is!" But neither God's being nor God's power "explains" creation satisfactorily. Neither fashions an analogue that makes us humans care passionately. Better are careful elucidations of human creative powers that illumine divine creativity by analogy. If so, there is little divorce between the God slow to anger and the God quick to create. Either way, the issue is the divine love. God is slow to anger—to want to "destroy" aberrant creation—because God is constancy-in-love. Equally, God is quick to forgive (re-create) and quick to communicate in the mysterious way that makes nothing something, because God is constancy-in-love. Classical Catholic theology of God as One *(de Deo Uno)* long saw that creation is not a once and for all affair. God has to conserve creatures in their being, and to concur in their actions. Continually, then, the divine love hurls "Is!" against nothingness. Continually God helps the universe participate in *ens a se*. And the best "motivation" we can conceive for this processive largess is nothing but God's own goodness. Creation comes from God's constancy-in-love.

A few homey parallels come to mind, to domesticate this biblical ontology (study of being). Consider, for instance, the vagaries of human work. Is it not the case that the labor we spontaneously call "creative" is largely labor of love? To make something, in the way that a creative artist or scientist does, is not a matter explained by nine-to-five. The artist or scientist may accommodate to "business" models, if only to appear less eccentric and odd, but models drawn from creative work itself make clocks and charts secondary. Primarily, creative work follows counsels and rhythms more internal. Thus, the sculptor has to "see" the form that begs to stand, the musician has to "hear" the melody that begs to be sung, the writer has to follow his or her characters, the theologian has to keep ascending to higher viewpoints. Even if these "creators" always take coffee at 10:15, always lock up at 5:30, the progress or stagnation of their work is nothing they can program. When there is no muse, the poet has to wait. When the muse appears, the poet has to work. "Sorry, banking hours are closed," is not poetic diction—nor is it scientific or theological. Archimedes obviously did not plan to grasp specific gravity while floating in the bath. Luther obviously did not choose to grasp justification in the toilet. Key insights almost always come unexpectedly, as the release of long months of ardent concentration. Almost always, they issue from a long gestation—from hiddenness, midnight kicks, false and then real pangs.

Remove the limitations, extrapolate the pure core, and you have a fragile tie to God's creativity. It is utterly interior, utterly self-controlled. For no external good does God create. Nothing outside the divine fullness lures God as a complement. Rather, God is intrinsically creative because, as the Johannine writers insist, God "is" love and love is intrinsically creative. We sense this in human love, whatever its kind. The heterosexual love that seeks marriage aims toward procreation. The love of friendship creates likemindedness and puts a glow on all the hours. The self-sacrificing love of *agape* makes the old order of Adam the new order of Christ.

So too in our work. Empirically, the farmer who deals with his or her fields personally, lovingly, gets a per acre yield no agribusiness can. The teacher who most loves the children brings out their best. Robert Pirsig, author of *Zen and the Art of Motorcycle Maintenance*, has described the mechanic to whom you should bring your machine. He is the one *not* distracted by hard rock, *not* jabbering about Sunday's game. For in good work there is absorption. One treats the fields, the children, the engines with respect—pays attention to them, listens for their needs. When the Taoist sage Chuang Tzu wanted to describe artful living, he told of a master butcher. A bad butcher wears out knives right and left—he hacks. A mediocre butcher can get by on a knife a year, but he still saws and chops. A master butcher keeps a knife a lifetime, so subtly does he carve. The sinews and ligaments seem to part of their own accord. At one with his materials' needs, in love with his materials' prospects, the master butcher creates works of art.

Love has a different "temperature" in the West, going among us less "coolly" than it does for Taoists, but its effects are similarly artful. Does that signify anything for the work-a-day world? It does indeed, E. F. Schumacher (author of *Small Is Beautiful*) says, for all good work needs tender loving care. To be creative—whether in human relations, scientific research, or the world of art—we have to nurture understanding with what finally can only be called love. For that reason, many of the most creative enterprises have long entailed apprenticeship. To know how technique and information turn creative, one must learn the care-ful atmosphere of front-line developments. Front-line developments move by solicitations of elegance, of harmony, of exactitude. They love the formula that just fits, the shape that just catches, the language perfectly apt. So too, we may think, with God's front-line developments. So too with God's creativity (God's DNA, quasars, particles, and frontal lobes). What a dazzling display of light and power. What a tribute to mysterious love. And the heart of it all, Christian faith holds, is the communication of divine love-life as it is in itself—the communication called "Incarnation" and "Grace."

GOD THE FATHER

The supreme instance of creativity, then, is divinity's presenting us with its own inner life. For Catholic theology, that inner life is trinitarian: a commonality of Father-Son-Spirit. Thus, in addition to its treatises *De Deo Uno* (On God as One), Catholic theology regularly spoke *De Deo Trino* (Of God as Three). In the popular mind, unfortunately, the Trinity seemed the most abstruse of the divine mysteries. Little children learned of St. Patrick's shamrock, or of the symbol of the triangle, but both children and adults found little help in structuring their faith towards a trinitarian God. Practically, as Rahner has noted, most modern Catholics have grown up as "monotheists," meaning in this case persons who so concentrate on the single ultimacy of God that they neglect God's intrinsic community. The alternative to "monotheism" is not "tritheism" (having three gods). It is an exegesis of the traditional symbol of God's plurality or communality that will keep unity and trinity in balancing polarity.

As a negative introduction to this exegesis, it may help to posit the reminder that *all* our discussion of God is halting and imperfect. For God really to be God, mystery must be to the fore. For "God" names the totality of beginning, foundation, and beyond that must ever recede from our sight. Thus, theo-logy in the strict sense (reflection on God herself), perches at the edge of our "world." The reality it would name always lies beyond, is always across the border. Indeed, it is "God" that gives us our borders, that defines our world. Thus, God and meaning run in tandem. At every turn where meaning heads into ultimacy, "God" appears. At every turn where "God" appears, meaning becomes mysterious (too full for our mastery).

A good illustration of this is the much bruited controversy about predestination and divine help *(De Auxiliis)* that preoccupied both Reformed and Catholic theology in the sixteenth and seventeenth centuries. In their rush to balance God's omniscience and human freedom, many of the controversialists forgot that divine action moves on a different plan than human action does. There is no "before" and "after" in divine knowledge, and so much of the problem of how we can be free if God knows "ahead of time" what we shall do is simply bad imagination.

So too with trinitarian reflection. None of it should aspire to blueprint the inner divine life. All of it is frail analogy, puny symbolization. For the Catholic tradition, we can get *some* dim sense of the divine nature, enough to clarify our way, but we can never remove the great mystery. After revelation as well as before, God remains hidden—the ultimacy eye has not seen, ear not heard, it has not entered the heart to conceive. Still, the "negative theology" that these religious truths sponsor has to leave a small part of the stage for a positive theology that marches human reason a few steps forward. Out of the Bible's theologies, Catholic tradition has speculated on the energies and relations of the Godhead, coming up with several privileged analogies. In presenting them here, our goal is mainly to suggest some of the enhancements of personal faith that trinitarian imagination may work.

For instance, building on the manifest speech of Jesus himself, Catholic faith has long begun its conception of God's inner life with the imagery of the "Father." Jesus called his God "Abba," and the first reflections of the Christian community that reached canonical status conceived Jesus as God's son. There originally was some ambiguity about this title "God's son," since its predominant meaning in the Old Testament had been something like "one favored by God," but in time Christian theology took it quite literally: Jesus was the strictly divine offspring of God. God the Father "generated" a divine Son; Jesus was the divine Son generated by God the Father. Thus, the bearing of God and Jesus to one another was relational: origin to originated.

The tradition tried to avoid any sense that this process took place in time or was a creation. The Father did not produce the Son as an artisan produces an artifact. The Father also did not produce the Son by something like sexual generation. There was no divine couple mating in eternity. Thus, by a negative (not this, not that) sort of process, the early church fathers groped after appropriate analogies. Continually, they agreed, the Father generates the Son: expresses himself in the Son substantially. It is the very active nature of divinity to have this outflowing character. Moreover, the outflow is not a giving that diminishes or parcels the source. All that the Father is flows over to or out into the Son. Generation communicates the Father's totality. So much is this the case that Father and Son differ only as two terms of an identifying relation. Father is origin and Son is originated. Apart from this difference, they are identical.

Now, what in our human experience comes closest to this sort of perfect relation and communication? Procreation and marital love come to mind, but for a complex of reasons, some good and some bad, the early fathers preferred not to use procreation and marital love. The bad reasons tie into the fears of sexuality and the body that warped patristic theology not a little. The good reasons tie into the realization that certain intellectual or spiritual processes are less finite than our bodily processes. Linking this realization with the biblical clue that God made men and women in the divine likeness, the early theologians located the image of God in our capacities to know and love. Influenced considerably by the Greek discovery of mind, they stressed what happens when we know. Influenced by the biblical forms of Hebrew anthropology (theory of human nature), they stressed what happens when we love. The most articulate result of these stresses was the Augustinian-Thomist "psychological analogy."

For Augustine of Hippo (354–430), the most influential of the Latin or Western fathers, our intellectual light is a participation in God's light. God's light, as it were, reaches down into our minds and hearts to provide our illumination, our spirituality. This is a prime way that Augustine concretizes his general dictum that "God is more intimate to me than I am to myself." Meditating on my own light, therefore, I can glimpse its source. Meditating on the structure of my light, I can glimpse the structure of its source. Through the *tour de force* meditation called the *De Trinitate*, Augustine probes the trinitarian God's structure. He takes guidance from the Johannine writings, which brim with references to God's light, life, and love. He also takes guidance from Neo-Platonic philosophy, which developed the theme of participation. But the powerhouse of the *De Trinitate* is Augustine's own introspective genius. That genius leads him to profound analyses of memory, understanding, and love, which become his counters for Father, Son, and Spirit.

To grasp the sense of Augustine's trinitarianism, one must make at least part of the journey with him. So, start to go back in your own mind, to remember. For instance, go through the past few hours, before you began reading these pages. Make a trail of bread crumbs from now to the time that you arose. Then try to jump farther back, to a week ago today. What was the most memorable thing that happened a week ago today? Dwell on that thing long enough to reproduce its rich circumstantiality. For instance, if your most memorable thing was buying a new coat, recall the way the coat first caught your eye, the way it felt when you first tried it on, the way you debated whether your budget would allow it. Then add some of the surrounding details: the other two coats you tried on, the perfume of the salesperson, the glaring neon light or the streaky triple mirror. Do you see how profuse are the circumstantial details that constitute even the most ordinary of our daily actions? Do you start to wonder at least a little about this extraordinary faculty called "memory," which can retrieve even how a past place smelled?

Were you to keep at your "anamnesis," your retrieving the past into the present, you might be able to reach things that happened when you were two years old. Indeed, psychologists might insist that you have memories back to the womb. Memory, then, is a rich thesaurus, a vast treasure trove. It holds a quasi-infinity of individual items; it recedes back to "time out of mind." Appreciating this, Augustine let memory symbolize God the Father. As the creative source of all that exists, God is somewhat like an inexhaustible treasure trove. Whatever has come to be participates in God—issues from the divine font. Thinking along this line, Buddhist philosophers spoke of the *Tathagatagarbha*—the "womb" of cosmic Buddhanature, from which all things are born. For Augustine, though, the special focus was memory's symbolization of precisely the Father. The Father was the unoriginated, primal partner in the Trinity. Outside of time, he was the "first." Where the Son derived from the Father, the Father did not derive. Were you to travel the divine fatherhood, you would never reach a beginning. Rather, the Father was the beginning, the origination, the dynamic ground zero. The memory of the divine mind is like an infinite universe. The most one can say about it is negative: It has no boundaries.

We have tried to take Augustine's drift and put it in more modern terms, but the general accent is his own. As the last books of the *Confessions* reveal, time (which of course correlates with memory) always fascinated Augustine. That is one reason he often sounds very modern, very existential. Trying to purify his insights into time, he associated the Father with the foundation of his own mentality. The Son he associated with his own act of understanding. Dependent on memory, understanding is in some ways its issue—its child and word. However rough the conception, it catches something of what the procession of the Son from the Father might be. The infinite regress of the divine paternity is so progressive as well that it generates a perfection expression. If one accents the whole life that the expression holds, then one tends to speak of the Father having generated a Son. If one accents the intelligibility of the process, its meaningfulness, then one tends to speak of the Father's having spoken forth a Word. Either way, the effort is to grasp how the Second Person is a perfect replication or image of the First. In language dear to Eastern Christianity, the Second Person is the First's eternal icon.

We shall keep at the psychological analogy through the next sections, spinning out Aquinas's variations on Augustine's beginnings and focusing on the Word and the Spirit. Let us pause here briefly, however, for a contemporary annotation. One of the more esoteric but potentially radical portions of current feminist theology is the effort to gain for women a full share in the notion that human beings are images of God. From forays into Eastern religions, feminists know that many cultures have symbolized divinity as male-female. They have done this by having both gods and goddesses, or by having bisexual, hermaphroditic deities. In some of the more developed theologies, the Goddess is as powerful as the God. That can be said, for instance, of much Hindu theology. It can be said of Mahayana Buddhist theology, insofar as the *Prajnaparamita* (the Perfection of Wisdom) is "The Mother of all Buddhas." It can also be said of Chinese theology, insofar as the Tao is a cosmic mother. Is it purer theology, or stronger patriarchy, that has removed the feminine from the theologies of the West?

Jews and Muslims (who in this simple division are "Western" religionists) can answer for themselves. Christian feminist theologians find the problem knotted. Patriarchy clearly has been very potent, but it is a patriarchy that goes back to Jesus himself. He may have treated women largely as men's equals, but he did not call his God "Mother." Whether we can change Jesus' diction, for instance by beginning his prayer, "Our Mother, who arc in heaven . . . ," is a more than interesting question. If we do change it, we have to take care not to crack the keystone of the whole Christian arch. If we do not change it, we have to explain how it is compatible with Christian freedom and love to insist on an archaism that contributes to many persons' inferior treatment. The problem would be less acute if the Catholic church did not abuse Jesus' diction and person by making them buttress male superiority. Even without such abuse, however, an important symbolico-conceptual issue would remain.

In our opinion, the Christian community ought to begin expanding its theology strictly so called to include God's motherhood. There are biblical hints of such a doctrine, for instance in Isaiah (46:3–4) and the Genesis account of creation. They might best be appropriated to the Spirit, but the First Personhood ought to be considered as well. It would *not* take much experience for feminine pronouns and references to God to become familiar (we know this from liturgical experiments). It *would* take much experience for all the implications of the reconceptualization behind those pronouns to emerge, but the growth and practical impact latent in such a reconceptualization seem worth the big investment. For though women surely have fathers, and can relate to Jesus' God, both women and men ought not to have their religion determined by a less than full symbolization of the parental relationship (which surely is one of the most formative for both the self and theology). Juliana of Norwich, a marvelous medieval English solitary, sensed this and spoke freely of God her Mother. Pope John Paul I sensed it and opined that we might with more justice call God Mother than Father. There is enough manysided tendency, then, to warrant a serious reconsideration. The historical limitations that follow Jesus' real humanity ought not to freeze our theology to the cultural sensibility of first-century Palestine.

THE LOGOS

Let us return to the psychological analogy. Before our discussion of the male-female aspects of God, we had begun to deal with the Second Person. Perhaps because he was more of an intellectualist than Augustine, Aquinas developed this part of the analogy more precisely. He had studied the doctrine of Aristotle that there are two prime acts of intellection, understanding, and judgment, and he had pondered carefully Aristotle's view that insight comes from grasping form in matter, intelligibility in phantasms or imagery. Appropriating his own profound intelligence, Aquinas realized that human acts of understanding issue an "inner word." The issue of Aristotle's first act was the concept. The issue of Aristotle's second act was the judgment. Concepts deal with *what* something is. Judgments deal with *whether* something is. (Today we see concepts in the form of scientific hypotheses, judgments in the form of scientific theories.) But both involve a process that Aquinas called "emanatio intelligibilis"—intelligible emanation. In that emanation he saw the most perfect analogy to the Word's procession from the Father.

For the sake of brevity, we shall illustrate only the emanation of concepts (the first act). In the interpretation of Bernard Lonergan, which we follow here, Aquinas resolutely made understanding ("insight") *pre*-conceptual. That is, we understand before we generate inner (and then outer, spoken) words; the subsequent word is the expression and result of the prior understanding. Consider, for instance, the following number sequence: 17–34–32–16–18–36–__–__. Assume that it has an intelligibility, study it, and fill in the last two blanks. The odds that you can fill in the last two blanks correctly simply by guessing are so remote that we can discount that possibility. If you have filled in the last two blanks correctly, you have understood the intelligibility of the sequence and so can give its "formula."

The two numbers that ought to go in the two blanks are 34 and 17. The formula is ×2, −2, ÷2, +2. What intercedes between your first acquaintance with the series, when it remains just a senseless string, and your confident expression of the last two numbers and the formula, is an act of understanding.

The issue of the Son from the Father is like the issue of the concept (whose outer expression is the formula) from the act of understanding. Thus, the Father is like a constant, endless, ongoing act of total understanding. The Son is like a constant, endless, ongoing conceptualization of that understanding. The "generation" is like a constant, endless, ongoing emanation of concept from act of understanding. That is a poor man's version of Aquinas's basic analogy for the Father-Son relation. He liked it because it was an instance of act from act. The act of conceptualization flows from the act of understanding. It involves no movement from potentiality or lack to actualization. If you regulate your thought about God as Aquinas did, using assumptions of Greek philosophy, you want to have no potentiality, no lack, in God. For your God is Pure Act, infinite perfection, being that lacks nothing. Your God does not change, suffer, or become. So utter is the divine "Is!" that there is no unfulfilled divine capacity or potentiality, no basis for change. There is no perfection for your God to acquire or to lose, for your God *is* all perfection. Therefore, intelligible emanation, act from act, appeals to you strongly.

Recently, this conception of God has come in for strong criticism, most pointedly in what is known as "process theology," and we shall take up such criticism below. For the moment, though, let us linger with Aquinas's view and achievement. Think again of that little insight you had in deriving the formula of the number sequence. It was a small flash of light, nothing monumental, but it is a precious clue. For in Aquinas's analogy, that light, magnified to the status that "divinity" implies, is what God is constantly being and doing. Thus, the divine "light" is not like a giant bank of bulbs over a football stadium. It is not a thing of physical wattage. It is more like the nearly instantaneous flash of meaning that comes only in highly developed brains. God's primal procession is an overflowing flash of meaning. The Word's expression of the Father is aboriginal intelligence.

Many indeed are the implications or extensions of this basic motif. For instance, the Logos (Greek "Word") was glimpsed by Pre-Socratic philosophers, who were unaware of Christianity, while they were pondering the relations between mind and nature. When they suspected an isomorphism, a parallelism, they took a momentous step. In theological clarification that step reads: All creation has a mental, logical aspect. All creation reflects the divine mind. If human beings, in virtue of their rationality, are "images" of divinity, subhuman beings are yet "vestiges" ("footprints"), for to be is to be mind-related. That is the truth in all idealistic philosophies, all philosophies that most prize mind, Western and Eastern alike. The Mind that founds this truth expresses itself in the Second Person. The Divine Logos is a cosmic Word. It would be overstepping the sure evidence to say that the authors of Colossians and John's gospel had a full ontology of the Logos, but they did move in the direction of the Logos as cosmic Word. For instance, they said, "All things were made through him, and without him nothing was made" (John 1:3). It would not be overstepping the sure evidence to say that church theologians, from the second century on, thought in terms of a cosmic Logos. From Justin Martyr to Origen, they were fascinated with this theme. Precisely how the confidence in the world's rationality that this theme sponsored contributed to the rise of Western science (which is a unique cultural phenomenon) would be a complicated historical question. Surely, however, it supported such confidence. When Einstein expressed his passionate conviction in the world's rationality ("God does not play dice"), he merely set a centuries-old faith in the modern context of quantum mechanics.

It would take us far afield to show that such a faith remains tenable despite such epistemological (concerning the theory of knowledge) developments as Heisenberg's principle of indeterminacy and such political developments as the Nazi holocaust of six million Jews. At its strongest, Heisenberg's principle concerns what we can know, not whether creation is isomorphic to divine mind. At its strongest, the holocaust concerns whether human beings may act absurdly, not whether God's logic is vitiated beyond rescue. There are enough workable theories about nature, enough hypotheses that have led to spaceships and nuclear explosions, to show that nature bears us intelligibility. There are enough political experiences that fit a persuasive story line to show that madness is not the biblical God's first name. So we prefer to stress that the whole thrust of our minds is for sense and meaning. The way we spontaneously think of nature and history postulates intelligibility. In such thrust and spontaneity, we validate the basic analogy behind theories of the Divine Logos.

Let us put this closer to home. Can a potter, whom we can take as an instance of human creativity, make pottery without intelligence? Does there not have to be some "sense," some "plan"? However intuitive, holistic, or aesthetic, an artistic work such as pottery demands understanding. There has to be some sort of picture or feel of the intended final product. There has to be some knowledge of one's materials, one's wheel, one's kiln. The temperature at which to fire, the temperature at which to glaze, the way to obtain the patterns, the way to obtain the colors—all these one has to understand. The Logos is the inclusive understanding of the global divine artifaction. In the divine artifaction, as Paul saw (Rom. 9:21), we are the pots, not the potter. That we have been made proves that we could be. Our "could be" depends on the divine mind, as our actual existence depends on the divine will.

Another instance of how we move within an ultimate "logic," how we image forth something of God's Son: human language. Tied inextricably to our "world," our sense and outline of reality, is our language. For that reason, Wittgenstein (the premier philosopher of language in recent times) laid down his much-quoted dictum: "The limits of my language are the limits of my world." For that reason, the decline in language skills among students is deeply threatening. If students cannot read, write, and speak precisely and clearly, they cannot *think* well. If they do not love their native language, they do not love their native *reality*. Manifestly, many students, as many citizens generally, do not read, write, speak, or think well. Manifestly, many do not live realistically. It is arguable, if not obvious, that those two propositions are intimately connected.

Not to live realistically, of course, is to condemn oneself to daily frustration. Ultimately, it is to drive oneself toward mental disease and sin. The jargon that rules government bureaucracies shows that their collective mind is largely dis-eased. The prose one finds in insurance policies, leases, or canon law suggests that their authors have a sinful mind to obscure. During the summer of 1977, the nation received a soap-opera-like lesson in a sinful mind to obscure. The parade of witnesses in the Watergate hearings "stonewalled": muttered and equivocated and "mis-spoke" themselves. Ultimately, they abused the Logos.

The "language" of God, of course is richer than human logic or syntax. The Word of God, become flesh, has a polymorphic (many-formed) significance. For the author of John, the Word's every gesture spoke eloquently. The first half of that gospel, in fact, is a book of "signs": changing water into wine, multiplying loaves and fishes, giving sight to a man born blind. Incarnate, the intelligence of God is subtle, powerful, much richer than syllogistic logic. It teaches by deed and silence as well as by word. Therefore, we must not make the divine Logos rationalistic. We must not divorce it from its heavenly context of love. Within the divine nature, the Word is an intelligence that breathes forth love. The "logic" of Christian religion therefore entails hearts as well as minds. The Word we join is Truth for freedom and life. All this brings us to the Spirit.

THE SPIRIT

The Spirit is the Third Person of the Trinity. As is true of both the Father and the Son, it is "Person" only analogously to the way that we humans are persons because, like the Father and the Son, it is unlimited. Further, the Spirit "proceeds" within the active life of the Trinity, as the Son "proceeds." Where the Son's procession is called "generation," the Spirit's procession is called "spiration." Father and Son spirate (breath forth) the Spirit. (This is the doctrine of the West; for the East, the Spirit proceeds from the Father.) The Spirit is the substantial fruit of the mutual knowledge of the Father and the Son, the love that their knowledge issues. No more than the Son is other than the Father is the Spirit other than the Father and the Son. It is other only relationally. Where the Father and Son spirate, the Spirit is spirated. Where they issue it is issued. Otherwise, Father, Son, and Spirit are completely one. They are three "persons" in one divine nature. Each is wholly God, wholly knowing, wholly loving. None is independent, a separate God. So there are not three gods. There is only one God who is a single community of three relationally distinct "persons."

Both Augustine and Aquinas agree that the Spirit parallels our inner psychology of love (as the Father and Son pattern with memory/understanding and conceptualization). Once again, however, Aquinas has the more exact analogy. For him, the best likeness to the Spirit's procession from the Father and the Son is the procession of our acts of love from our acts of judgment. Parallel to the way that concepts flow from acts of direct understanding ("insights"), acts of love flow from acts of reflective understanding or judgment. Acts of reflective understanding grasp a sufficiency of evidence. They occur when we realize that we have the grounds for saying that something is or is not so. A prime example of this process is scientific method. On the basis of intuition and experimentation, scientists form hypotheses—reasoned explanations of how things may be. It may be that certain kinds of viruses cause cancer. It may be that a bodily substance called interferon can fight some of them off. The critical work of science is to cross the gap from "maybe" to "is." That work goes on by testing one's hypotheses—verifying or disproving them.

When one achieves verification, a judgment follows spontaneously. Looked at as a final product, verification is the act of understanding that one does have grounds for saying something is so. Similarly, disproving is the act of understanding that one does have grounds for saying something is not so. That "saying" is a judgment, a committed assertion about reality. It is where truth or falsity occur. Perhaps putting this in more commonsense imagery will make it clearer.

Consider the proposition, "People in Somalia have pink hair." (It is hard to imagine where one would get that proposition, but suppose that someone saw an issue of *National Geographic* where the colors had run, so that natives of Somalia had pink afros.) On the face of it, there is nothing intrinsically contradictory in the proposition. People can dye their hair pink and live. Genes do strange things, as albinos demonstrate. So there "could be" people in Somalia with pink hair. But, would you bet your paycheck on it? Could we tempt you with 100 to 1 odds? Not likely. For you to take this proposition seriously, we would have to verify it, probably by showing you hundreds of pink-topped natives. Your skepticism shows that your mind has reflective postulates. When you are acting responsibly, you demand solid evidence for your committed judgments of reality. Rightly, you distrust untested or untestable propositions. You know that all sorts of people have lost their shirts in the stock market—because they took "maybe" for "is." If you read Shakespeare, you know that Othello ruined several lives because he took plausible evidence of his wife's infidelity for actual proof. Hang on to you skepticism, your distrust, your Shakespeare. Hand on to your demand for reasonable proof. It is a prime mark of God's image in you.

When we issue judgments, we intend, push forward towards, commit ourselves to "truth"—to how things are. And as we have a natural, spontaneous orientation toward truth, so we have a natural love for it—a natural respect, regard, benevolence. This is perhaps clearest in judgments we make about persons or important issues—in "value judgments." Here's an example of a value judgment.

Jack meets Jill. At first she seems a thin, pale, wishy washy type, unable to climb the smallest hill, let alone fetch a pail of water. But Jill has started a program of physical conditioning. Soon she runs five miles a day, fills herself out on Nautilus machines. When Jack meets her again she is climbing mountains, hauling huge vats of water. She has become lissome, lovely, graceful. Along with the improvement in her physical condition has come an improvement in her attitude toward life in general. She is no longer wishy-washy, will say a firm "yea, yea" or "nay, nay." To Jack she says mainly "yea, yea." Jack admires her taste. Before long, experience and reflection convince Jack that Jill is a terrific person. He has sufficient data, adequate grounds, for committing himself to the proposition, "This Jill is a good one." In that commitment, as act from act, Jack loves Jill. He goes out to her goodness as Pooh goes out to honey. A judgment of real being and goodness develops an inclusive flow of love. That is an analogy for the Spirit. (In concrete reality, of course, love is not so programmed. It comes as a suggestion early on, suffers anxieties in the middle, and by the end is a warm contentment. Jack may start to love Jill from the first, "yea, yea." But the main point seems valid: Judgments of goodness issue love spontaneously.)

On to the Holy Spirit. The experience Father and Son have of one another, their mutual acquaintance, involves something like a value judgment. Knowing one another, they "judge" that they are good. From this judgment flows an act of love. As was the case with the flow of the Word from the Father's self-understanding, the act of love passes directly from the act of value judgment. There is no potency involved, no lack of perfection. As fullness to fullness, divine knowledge passes into divine love. This passage is the procession of the Spirit. Like a breath of benevolence, joy, and delight, the Spirit proceeds from the relational unity of the Father and the Son. In the imagery of some of the early fathers, it is as the kiss of their love.

Further, there is a certain completion or roundness that the Spirit's procession brings. Images do not come easily at this point, but the Catholic tradition has talked of *perichoresis:* the mutual indwelling or coherence that the three persons have. The love that the Spirit personifies helps enable this mutual indwelling. It is like an atmosphere or suffusion, except that it is as real as the memorial Father and the logical Son. Memorial Father, logical Son, suffusive Spirit of love—each is wholly in, with, through, for the other. We can't imagine this sort of thing very well, for all our experiences are structured by limitation. But perhaps the suffusion of love that goes through a good family situation, or a good marriage, or an ardent friendship, or a warm parent-child relationship—perhaps it catches something of the Spirit. Such suffusive or atmospheric love is as real, and as important, as the partners it joins.

Without it, they not only are not joined, they also are not "themselves," not their full "I" and "you." The suffusive Spirit, then, is a sort of "We"—a sort of three that one and one make when they add in love.

The Spirit therefore saves the Christian Trinity from any appearance of being a merely intellectual affair. Where the Greek elements in traditional speculation led to a stress on mind and "logic," the Hebrew elements related presence and word to the "heart." Suffusively, the divine life that the three persons share is a blending of mind and heart. It is clarity and warmth conjoined. As such, we can appreciate its splendor, for our own best moments, our own peak experiences, are clarity and warmth conjoined. For instance, when we are in love (as we can be sure the three persons are), all is different. We perceive differently, associate differently, understand and judge differently. Thus, a land that appears rocky and barren to an outsider is for a native the prime site on earth. A child that to an outsider is wrinkled and red is for a parent cute as a button. The shyness that a stranger finds too great a burden a lover finds mysteriously attractive. The colleagues that a fledgling finds doddering and boring an old-timer finds comfortable and shrewd. Perhaps, then, the Spirit draws lovable particulars into the universal divine splendor. Perhaps divinity itself plays to join heart and mind.

Further, it would be fairly easy to write the Spirit a feminine persona. One could begin with biblical cues. There is the figure of the Spirit brooding over the waters of creation (Gen. 1:2). There is the Spirit's proximity to a creation in labor for fulfillment (Rom. 8:22–23). The work of our sanctification traditionally associates with the Spirit, as though she mothers divine life in our hearts. Whatever the original force of these tendencies, and whatever their utility today, they tell us that God can and does move subtly, indirectly, by persuasion as much as by force. Chinese thinkers saw this when they contemplated the Tao. The "Way" of nature is subtle, actively passive, gentle. As water wears the rock, as an infant rules its parents, as a woman persuades a man—so does Tao move. There is no reason not to credit these insights to the Spirit. There are many reasons for thinking the Spirit moves by *wu-wei*—passive action, light guidance of the flow.

Last, we probably do well to insist that the Spirit is more analogous to our *rational* loves, or that our love is at its best when it is rational. By this we do not mean cold or unfeeling. The reasons of the heart that Pascal praised unforgettably are both clear and warm. But so much current American culture debases love to sentimentalism that we have to warn that the Spirit's love fires mind even more than senses. This is clear both positively and negatively. Positively, the reports of those who consort most profoundly with God and instruct the tradition in God's deepest ways insist that mystical love chastens the senses. It is not a love that waxes sentimental. Rather, it burns away our illusions, in dark nights and clouds of unknowing. Eventually it goes beyond our imaginations, asking that we take God's existence as a simple invisible fact. Eventually, even, it goes beyond ordinary intellection, purifying the mind to a reason-fulfilling carte blanche. In these ways, deep love of God promotes the nicest, and sometimes the starkest, realism. It calls us to honor all evidence, to test all inspirations. It is sober and watchful, for its adversary (godless selfishness) is like a prowling lion, seeking whom it may devour.

Negatively, the shipwreck that regularly comes to those who base their religion on pure emotion testifies to the Spirit's rationality. In apostolic times, Paul had to remind ecstatic Corinthians that only a love which "edifies" (builds up) the community is a completely desirable gift. Through most ages of Christian history, overly emotional types have stirred crowds to frenzy, bizarre behavior, or certainty that the world would end in the next round year. One of the healthiest traits of the Catholic tradition is that its mainstream has tamed such emotionalism. At core, Catholic tradition respects reason. The Spirit promotes sweet reason. Sweet reason, peaceful intelligence, a joy that gives lucidity—these are marks of the Spirit. The best Catholic charismatics make them the crux of discernment.

RELIGIOUS EXPERIENCE OF THE CHRISTIAN GOD

The specifically Christian God is trinitarian and saving. In the next chapter, we shall consider the realistic world view that faith in this God promotes. We shall also consider the theological virtues (inner strengths) that a gracious share in this God's life has long been held to develop. Right now, however, we want to give a little phenomenology (description) of the religious (ultimate) experience that makes the Christian God credible. It is true, of course, that our approach to such experience is directed by our Christian convictions. Nonetheless, we think we can make a good case that the ultimate experience that all persons may receive, or that they have reported historically, suggest the portrait of divinity that Jesus and his followers have painted.

Concerning the "fatherhood" of God (which today we would prefer to render the "parenthood"), we suggest that many persons experience it when they move in spirit toward the depths of their selves or their world. In moments of quiet contemplation, for instance, one can travel recent memories or one's current spate of images down to the depths of the "I." There, perhaps under the questioning form, "Who really am I?," one can sense that personal identity passes out of our sight. The different parts of personal identity are like links on a submerged chain. What anchors them to the bottom we cannot fathom, for the base of who any of us is lies deep in mystery. It involves a beginning and a term we cannot clearly see. That beginning and term is the unoriginated originator. It is the self-sufficient first that alone keeps our regress from being *ad infinitum*—endless, without surcease. So does the Father appear in our midst. As Jesus drew all his identity from his relation to his source, his progenitor, so can we. Ultimately, we are children, offspring, of the fecund love that, as Dante saw, moves the stars. In our case, however, such love is personal. All that is uniquely human in us argues for that. Indeed, our best works image a fathomless capacity for creativity and effective self-expression. The artist and generator in us image God the Parent.

Concerning the Sonship of God, the Logos whom the Father speaks forth, we suggest that our experience of reason in nature, history, and the self moves in its train or pattern. When God speaks forth the divine primordiality, it flows as a light or intelligibility that may be participated in by finite forms. As we have tried to illustrate, that light flashes in each of our insights. Therefore, whenever we turn a "eureka" or a grasp of judgmental grounds toward ultimacy, we raise our minds toward the divine procession of God's Word. Playing variations on this elevation, early philosophers such as Pythagoras and Plato entertained the proposition that the world is formed by numbers. Physical scientists run in their tracks today, when they chalk on the board equations that they hope to verify as patterns that stars or particles follow. For, to think the world mathematically, and to find some of one's thought verified, is to experience profoundly the "logic" of creation. Warm that logic to a possible subservice of love and you have the universe participating in the first infra-trinitarian procession.

Third, concerning the procession of the Spirit, the religious experiences that weigh most heavily for us (as we take guidance from Karl Rahner) are those in which we are drawn to faith that God has given us divine love (the essence of our salvation) once and for all. That is, the Spirit pours forth in our hearts a love such that we can find our divine childhood—our being carried on the bosom of God—solid and unillusory. The tradition reports this experience, calling it an *arrabon* or down payment on the life we shall enjoy in heaven. The gift of the Spirit, then, is an earnest or marker that God will pay off the "debt" she has contracted in making us creatures who hope for a total fulfillment in interpersonal knowing and loving. The French Catholic existential philosopher Gabriel Marcel wrote in the grasp of such hope when he extrapolated from the experience of intense human love the spontaneous conviction, "You at least will never die." In his reading, when we fall profoundly in love we deal with something (a relation so good, or a soul so beautifully naked) that begs earnestly not to be eroded by time. The Song of Solomon was on the trail of this inference when it described love as "strong as death." Explicitly Christian conviction finds God's resurrecting love stronger than death. It is a work of the Spirit in human hearts to make the resurrection credible or strongly anticipated.

These three modalities to religious experience, which we argue suggest the trinitarian persons, may emerge most clearly when one probes with convictions formed by Catholic theological tradition, but they are by no means limited to Christians. We have advanced this proposition in another work, comparing Jesus' religious experiences with those of the Buddha. From that comparison, we have further proposed that future Catholic theology ought to do more with comparative religious studies than past Catholic theology has done. Thereby, it would remove much of the parochialism that makes it unattractive to a contemporary "global" consciousness—a consciousness that realizes we all share but one world-wide "village." Raymond Pannikar, whose own biography blends a Hindu with a Catholic background, is the prolific author in whose works you may find this thesis developed extensively.

When the three persons communicate *ad extra*, to persons not divine, they communicate "for us and our salvation." That is the nearly incredible conclusion to which the message of Jesus and the interior witness of the Spirit conduce. The backward reach of the "Father," the outward reach of the "Word," the circling return of the "Spirit"—they all, by God's free choice, enter space and time for our benefit. Aware and unaware, Christians have long actualized the substance of this grace in simple attitudes of affirmation. By "simple attitudes of affirmation" we mean saying yes—to the world, to other persons, to one's self and one's given life. The rather extraordinary spiritual journey that the famous United Nations diplomat Dag Hammarskjold recorded in his *Markings* pivoted on a day when there broke through his dark depression a deep and forceful "yes." From sources within him that played almost out of his control, he and the Spirit mustered a core word that overturned his whole outlook. Perhaps because he and Kierkegaard shared a common background, it is tempting to read his transforming act as a "leap" like that of Kierkegaard's knight of faith—a leap of nearly pure grace.

In less dramatic terms, the prime psychologist of the life cycle, Erik Erikson, has spoken of the human person's terminal virtue as the ability to love life in face of death. The view that Erikson develops of human time sees it as passing through age-specific crises. Thus, the adolescent years typically foist on us an "identity crisis" (this famous phrase comes from Erikson). Similarly, the years of middle adulthood tend to bring a crisis of generativity: Is our time, now fairly well along, showing us to be fruitful or barren? The terminal virtue or strength that human maturation postulates is "wisdom." By the time we come in sight of our approaching end, we face a critical task of mustering the wherewithal to call what we have done and become good—necessary, fitting, something with which we can die. It is not pure eisegesis (reading-in) to find the Spirit at work in all these crises, and at work especially in the terminal one. As she who "presides" over our experiences of God's love offered and effectively received, the Spirit groans the prayers of our depths, keeps the flames of our hopes flickering. For those who do make an effort to answer God's calls in conscience—who do, for all their failings, keep trying to be honest and to love—the Spirit works support and consolation. Where "the enemy of our human nature," as Loyola called Satan (and we may call whatever wills our destruction), tries to lure those who keep trying to depression and discouragement, the Spirit is encouraging, supportive, a bearer of possible ways through.

The God of Christian experience also is communitarian. That is, the three persons' own sociability and relatedness overflow into our human experiences of togetherness. We are most ourselves when we are in significant relationship to other persons (and to nature). The best societies or political groups are those that value the individual differences of their members. In the dialectic of these truths shines forth an expression of the Christian God. Rugged individualism is not the Catholic Christian way. Neither is a legalism that goes blind before individual circumstances. These are cardinal theses for the theology of the church, as we shall see below. We flag them here, however, because their ultimate warrant is the very nature of the God whom church life ought to bear. Father, Son, and Spirit say "We," not "I, I, I." Their identities are bound together. Would that our Christian identities were the same. Then the old patriarchal dictum would illumine present success: a brother helped by a brother is like a strong city.

The last observations we want to make about Christian religious experience of God deal with our creaturehood and God's suffering. Prompted by the whole story of salvation, Catholic theologians such as Rahner have read out of our experiences of contingency (non-necessity) and limitation, which force us to the truth that we have neither made nor controlled ourselves, a religious paradox. It is that we are *more* ourselves the *less* we stand apart from God in spurious independence. True self-realization, in other words, is finding one's destiny in the mystery of one's origin and term. Jesus puts this all concretely. Insofar as Jesus is signally human, signally a rich personality and free spirit, he argues powerfully that relation to God empowers rather than destroys individual selfhood. From humanistic psychology we get a complementary message. The most "realized" personalities have come to grips with the "nothingness," as Erikson calls it with reference to Gandhi, that bounds all human life. They have cast themselves upon the oceanic waters, made their peace with things out of their control. Doing so, they have been truthful to their creaturehood.

All creatures suffer—undergo, are done to as well as do. Most creatures also suffer in the sense that they endure pain. Does the image of

God in us argue that divinity too suffers? Does the way that suffering seems intertwined with our creativity or deep loves give us warrant to place "passion" in God? Traditional theology said no: God the Pure Act dwells outside the realm of suffering. True, God's Word assumed a passible flesh, but divinity itself did not suffer. In condemning patripassianism (a theory that the Father suffered with the Incarnate Son), the tradition concretized this view. Recently, "process theology," a loose school that owes much to the thought of Alfred North Whitehead and Charles Hartshorne, has contested the tradition on this point. It finds suffering so intrinsic to love, growth, caring, and other things we call positive that it wants to extrapolate it to God. As well, it points to the biblical portrait of God, for instance that of the prophet Hosea, where God grieves, is heartsore, makes himself vulnerable. Process theologians read the Bible as saying we do make a difference to the biblical God and so can "hurt" divinity.

Because of its conviction on this point, most process theology is willing to have a finite, limited God. That is the problem we see with admitting suffering in God: It runs to God's limitation. But the consensus of the overall tradition, we believe, goes against this point of view. It holds, rather, that a limited "God" is no real God. For that reason, we would prefer to take the indications of God's sufferings that either biblical texts or prime human experiences suggest with a quite careful and dexterous mind. Perhaps we can so analyze them that either vulnerability does not imply need or lack in God, or we can so correlate them with the mystery of the Incarnation that we can speak of God's having chosen to take a form in which divine personhood *can* suffer. However, developing either of these responses would take us away from the proper focus of this present work, so we leave you more notified than fully satisfied. You should know that some recent Catholic theologians, such as David Tracy, look favorably on the effort to place suffering in God, and that it remains to be seen whether they can dispose of the problems this view causes and win the general agreement of their peers.

BIBLIOGRAPHY

Bracken, Joseph. *What Are They Saying About the Trinity?* New York: Paulist, 1979.

Carmody, John. "A Next Step for Roman Catholic Theology," *Theology Today*, 32, (1976), 371–381.

Cobb, John B., Jr. and Griffin, David Ray. *Process Theology: An Introductory Exposition.* Philadelphia: Westminster, 1976.

Erikson, Erik, ed. *Adulthood.* New York: Norton, 1978.

Ford, Lewis S., *The Lure of God: A Biblical Background for Process Theism*. Philadephia: Fortress, 1978.

Gelpi, Donald. *Pentecostalism*. New York: Paulist, 1971.

Hammarskjold, Dag. *Markings*. New York: Viking, 1964.

Kierkegaard, Søren. *Fear and Trembling*. Princeton, N.J.: Princeton University Press, 1941.

Lonergan, Bernard. *De Deo Trino*. Rome: Gregorian University Press, 1964.

Lonergan, Bernard. *Verbum: Word and Idea in Aquinas*. Notre Dame, Ind.: University of Notre Dame Press, 1967.

Marcel, Gabriel. *The Mystery of Being*. Chicago: Regnery, 1960.

McDonnell, Kilian. *The Charismatic Renewal and Ecumenism*. New York: Paulist, 1978.

Merton, Thomas. *The Way of Chuang Tzu*. New York: New Directions, 1965.

Pannikar, R. *The Intra-Religious Dialogue*. New York: Paulist, 1978.

Pirsig, Robert. *Zen and the Art of Motorcycle Maintenance*. New York: Bantam, 1974.

Prestige, G. L. *God in Patristic Thought*. London: SPCK, 1959.

Rahner, Karl. "Remarks on the Dogmatic Treatise 'De Trinitate,' " *Theological Investigations*, 4. Baltimore: Helicon, 1966, 77–102.

Rahner, Karl. *The Trinity*. New York: Herder and Herder, 1970.

Scheffcyzk, Leo, et al. "God," in *Sacramentum Mundi*, 2, ed. Karl Rahner, et al. New York: Herder and Herder, 1968, 381–399.

Schumacher, E. F. *Good Work*. New York: Harper & Row, 1979.

Smulders, Pieter, et al. "Creation," in *Sacramentum Mundi*, 2, ed. Karl Rahner, et al. New York: Herder and Herder, 1968, 23–37.

Terrien, Samuel. *The Elusive Presence*. New York: Harper & Row, 1978.

Tracy, David. *Blessed Rage for Order*. New York: Seabury, 1975.

Trible, Phyllis. *God and the Rhetoric of Sexuality*. Philadelphia: Fortress, 1978.

Christian Realism 5

OVERVIEW

The Christian doctrine of God determines much in a "realistic" Christian outlook, but partner to this outlook is the Christian doctrine of human nature. How do "grace" and "sin" concretely shape this humanity we carry? What are the primary denotations and overtones these capital words ought to carry? Grace primarily denotes something ontological—the divine being that God desires to share. More substantial than any behavioral implications is the love-life, the *agape* grace imparts. By contrast, sin is the lovelessness by which we fail the exigencies of our humanity. It is our closure to God, our refusal to respond. All too concretely, we see this closure at work internationally, in our national injustices, and in more restricted personal zones. But the Catholic view of human nature, of grace and sin in the concrete, saves the core of the human person from depravity. It is not the way of the Catholic tradition first to suspect and distrust.

On the other hand, Catholics have their own share in the Lutheran doctrine of *simul justus et peccator*—simultaneously both just and a sinner. Whoever does not distort the facts of human performance knows many *peccatores*. A certain sobriety therefore hangs over Catholic estimates of the human condition. It is not the way of this tradition to be optimistic, but rather to hope. For hope, like faith and love, is a precisely theological virtue. It is strength to anticipate a good future from God. The Spirit alone gives this strength, at the deep level where sin would discourage us, as the Spirit alone makes us continue to believe and love. Ultimately, then, the humanity we seek is a more than human venture. Ultimately we owe our selves, as our hopes, to the goodness of God.

GRACE

"Grace" is the primary reason that Christianity is a gospel, a glad tidings. It puts into a single word the relationship God has chosen to have with us. Etymologically, grace means "favor." God grants us her favor—chooses to consider us children, friends, loved ones. Substantially, grace means divine life. It has not always meant this in Western Christian history, so let us begin our exposition with an Eastern Catholic theme. As developed by the Greek fathers, and modernized by Karl Rahner, it renders what we have said about the trinitarian God historical—"for us and our salvation."

Early Eastern Christianity took from Greek philosophy and culture what we can only call an ontological bent. Ontology is the study of being—the effort to understand how things are, what reality is. It is the core of philosophy. In classical Greek times, philosophy—the love of wisdom—could be a whole way of life. Socrates, Plato, and Aristotle effectively made it a religion: a way to encounter ultimate reality. Ontology, then, originally was a thing of passion and personal significance. It was not the arid "metaphysics" later periods knew.

For Christians influenced by classical Greek culture, what God is like, how God exists, whether we participate in God's being were exciting, pregnant issues. Chroniclers report that there were brawls in barber shops over the difference between saying the Logos is *like (homoiousios)* the Father and saying the Logos is the *same (homoousios)* as the Father. The difference was a single letter, a small Greek iota, but it had vast implications. Ultimately, it implied the difference between Nicene (orthodox) Christianity and Arianism (heresy). Since Arianism spread to the West and was powerful well into the sixth century, one iota marked a lot of history.

The temperament of the conciliar age was ontological (though also pastoral), because most of the early doctrinal debates took place in the East. As a result, patristic Christianity came to think of grace as divinization. Building on such clues as 2 Peter 1:4, which speaks of our becoming "partakers of the divine nature," and on Johannine writings, which speak of our "abiding" with God (as branches with a vine), the fathers conceived the life of faith as a participation in God's own life. Where the West, because of its Roman bent toward legalism, thought in terms of what we do, the East thought in terms of what we are. What we are in grace is participants in God's divine life. For the East the "new covenant" became an intrinsic tranformation. When God writes the new covenant of grace on the fleshy tablets of our hearts, he wonderfully transforms us. Principally, he makes us immortal *(athanatos)*, because immortality is divinity's prime attribute. God simply is, God simply lives. Thus, the radical new creation that Paul proclaimed became in

Greek minds a transformation of mortal human nature into divine deathlessness. As God resurrected Jesus into deathlessness, so God will resur-
rect the members of Jesus' "body." Grace—the faith-life we begin in
baptism—stretches out to heaven, but it begins deathlessness in time.
The *arrabon* or down payment of the Spirit was for Greeks exactly
that beginning.

This may seem rather abstract speculation, but it merely transposes
some concrete biblical motifs. For example, the relationship that the
God of Hebrew religious experience established through Moses led to
a pledge of sharing life through time. When Moses receives the divine
name (Exod. 3:14), it turns out to be indefinite and future-oriented: "I
am who I am—who I shall choose to be." In other words, the Hebrews
will learn Yahweh's "nature" by living with him through time. He is
not a god of natural seasons, not a god of sacred places; he is a God
humans learn through time. The covenant attempted to formalize this
relationship somewhat, but of course it largely failed. Yaweh is the creator of all order. No little treaty can bind or constrain him. If he chooses
to swear and not repent, to be faithful through all times, that is a form
of his sovereign freedom. It never removes the need for Israel, his partner
in the covenant, to find and follow him by faith. It never gives a contrac-
tual guarantee that removes the need for enduring his mystery. Only
a distorting, idolatrous god could be so guaranteed.

Through the prophetic period, Israel struggled to learn this prime
lesson. By the time of Isaiah (ca. 700 B.C.), it had become clear that for
the majority the lesson was too hard. Only a remnant could bear the
carte blanche a living God demands. Only a small remainder had the
heart and soul for deep faith. Christian experience has not been very
different. Numerically, the fraction of Christians who have not run to
laws, not hidden behind canons or indulgences or ritualistic prayers,
has been rather small. The carte blanche of deep faith so coincides with
profound humanity, with significant sanctity, that most of us do not
keep giving it. In terms of the famous battle line that Dostoveski drew,
we side against Christ, side with the Grand Inquisitor. The price of
Christ's freedom is stark (but joyous) faith. Not willing to pay this price,
we let Grand Inquisitors, priests, theologians, neighbors—any "rescuer"
we can find—give us tidy laws, tell us what to do. Thereby, we depreciate
grace to something medicinal—make it God's syrup for our little catarrh.

Not so was grace for the great Eastern fathers. Not so is it for Karl
Rahner. For them and him, grace is God's free love-life in us, the Trinity's processions taking up our mind and hearts. Technically, Rahner
calls this state of affairs the "supernatural existential." Everywhere, by
God's free choice, the Trinity offer human beings interpersonal communion. In place of the possibly impersonal relationship between a creator and a creature, the Trinity of persons have become for us as they

are in themselves. Using Rahner's terms, we can say that the "immanent" Trinity is the "economic" Trinity. The immanent Trinity is God actively interrelating through the processions—God the personal community. The economic Trinity is the God of the plan or dispensation we humans indwell (the Greeks called this an *economia* or "order"). Just as an individual human person need not disclose his or her inner self, so God need not. God could have been for us only a somewhat objective, detached creator, as we can be for other people only bosses, waiters, or token vendors. When we deal with other people that way, we show them but masks of our selves. On the other hand, when we open up, significant things can happen. God has "opened up" for us—made it possible for absolutely significant things to happen. If we but respond, we can participate in God's very own life.

How this actually occurs remains mysterious, as do all relations that open up and proceed heart to heart. But the biblical theme of sharing time prompts us to propose the analogy of a marriage. In a marriage people try to open up, to live heart to heart, to share time, resources, bodies, selves—life itself. They are bonded, for better or worse, for richer or poorer. Ideally, their bonding increases their individuality. Though older spouses may look alike, may slurp their tea the same way, in good marriages each partner grows as an independent personality. Analogously, the relation of grace does not collapse the self into God. It just further advances the faith-truth that we find our real selves in the divine mystery. Perhaps Paul thought of this when he set the relation between Christ and the church in marital imagery. Perhaps it was this the mystics had in mind when they discussed the nuptials of the soul with God.

At any rate, the sharing of life that marriage postulates is precisely what substantial grace entails. God and those whom she graces enjoy a common enterprise. More and more, their interests flow together. The Spirit so purifies the human self that it increasingly says, "I must decrease, God must increase." The Spirit so convinces the human self of God's care that the self can pray confidently about any of its hopes or fears. This is an important lesson, which any who want to pray deeply and regularly have to learn. There is nothing that can separate us from the love of God in Christ Jesus (Rom. 8:39), so there is nothing we cannot bring to God in prayer. If God really shares our life and time, then our worries about a job, our hopes for a child, our pain from a separation—all these are common property. Those who pray regularly learn how to share common property with God. They learn how to change distractions into renewals of the love-bond. Like Abraham, who haggled with God to try to save Sodom, they fight for causes they think right. Like Job, who accused God of injustice, they pour out their grievances. And like Jesus, who brought the Father his cup of sorrow, they finally say, "Thy will be done." For they want, in their best parts, to let God take care of their lives.

If the story of Christian salvation is credible, God's care of our lives is total. The Father numbers all the hairs of our heads. Therefore, like the lilies of the field, we shall prosper. Grace is the depths of this sort of confidence. It shows in a holy abandon. The end of our lives, our sort of "prosperity," like the bottom of our selves, passes out of sight. No worry of ours can change it a cubit. We all have finally to rely on God's goodness, whether we like it or not. We all have finally to trust we shall breathe tomorrow. Gracious Christian living makes this necessity an occasion of gratitude. It thanks God for the light of its eyes, for the air it breathes. The eucharist is precisely the primary Christian focus of such thanksgiving. Remembering Jesus, each eucharist expresses heartfelt thanks and praise.

In the next section, when we consider sin, we shall deal with the problematic patches that mar such a gracious scenario. Here, though, the accent is wholly positive. And the accent here is finally more important than any nuances reflection on sin may force. For the Catholic tradition takes deeply to heart Paul's conviction that where sin abounded grace has abounded more. There is no equality between the sin of the world and the grace of God. There is no question which is the victor. The light shone in the darkness and the darkness did not overcome it. The weakness tempted each heart but all hearts felt help for salvation. God, then, is a God on whom we can rely. However obscurely, the God of Jesus does only good work, operates only from love. Christian religion is as simple and as difficult as believing that. Its God is not too strange to be believed but too good. Again and again, our pusillanimity, our small-souledness, causes us to doubt God's goodness. So, we cannot believe God gives generously to those who come at the eleventh hour, as well as to those who work the full day, because we would not so give. We cannot believe God is a prodigal father, rushing out to forestall his churlish son, because we would not be. As Paul Ricoeur recently has shown, the logic of God is for us "excessive." God is more gracious by far than we.

The core meaning of grace, then, is sharing God's life. Western Christianity, however, has also discussed God's "operational" favor. That is, the West has underscored the fact that the Spirit helps us respond to opportunities and overcome temptations. Perhaps the simplest way to correlate this activity-oriented view of the West with the ontological view of the East is to emphasize the fairly obvious truth that an inert divine life would be both a contradiction in terms and a treasure little worth participating in. If divinity really does draw us into its life, the new sharing that that produces has to influence our behavior. When we are responsive, it soon produces a new horizon that configures everything differently. The "change of mind" that the New Testament calls *metanoia* is just such a new horizon. When we translate *metanoia* by "conversion," we ought to mean a restructuring of basic orientations. The dialectic that Paul works between sin and grace depends on this restructuring. Those who have entered the new, gracious life of Christ have a whole change of horizon. Whereas in the past their sinful minds could focus on little besides themselves, in the newness of Christ they open to a God of pure love. Whereas in the past they viewed their neighbors competitively, as opponents in a race to one small pie, in the present the Spirit lures them to love their neighbors as themselves. Paul's famous hymn to charity (1 Cor. 13) shows what this love looks like, as his juxtaposition of "flesh" and "spirit" (Gal. 5) dramatizes the differences between a sinful mind and a mind of grace.

We shall see more of the mind of grace below, when we consider the theological virtues (faith, hope, and charity). For this first description, however, we can conclude by stressing gratitude. Grace above all produces gratitude. In the summer of 1976, as most of you will recall, the United States put aside briefly its squabbles and greedy business-as-usual to celebrate its bicentennial. Against the backdrop of Watergate, which massively portrayed a sinful mind, July 4, 1976 was a day of grace. We watched this celebration from a far distance, in a hotel room in Hong Kong. When the regal clipper ships moved in stately order up the Hudson River, the tawdry junks of the past months withdrew to the mind's sidestreams. It was the one day of a six-months tour around the world when we were absolutely sure God blessed America.

SIN

Our description of grace has focused on the way that faith says things are between us and God. It has tried to report the traditional radicalness Catholic theology has seen in Jesus' eschatological (definitive) salvation. Were we human beings generously to open ourselves to God's gracious self-offer, the world would shine as a global sacrament. In this section we have to deal with the way things are in a different sense. Without subtracting anything of the radical transformation Jesus' salvation has accomplished, we have to deal with human frustration of God's tremendous offer—with the absurd self-frustration traditionally called "sin." So doing, we complicate somewhat the view of human nature developed thus far. Thus far, we have been stressing how human beings come from a good creator and are offered rich shares in the Trinity's inner life. Thus far, we have been opposing any doctrine of human depravity. Such opposition became rather dogmatic for the Catholic tradition at the Council of Trent (1545–1563), where the Roman church reacted to what it considered abuses of the Protestant reformers. From the mid-sixteenth to the mid-twentieth century, Trent dominated Roman Catholic religion. Through that period, Catholic theology tried to maintain a view of human nature that was moderate or median. It wanted to be to the left of pessimistic views, which saw human nature as corrupt to the core. It wanted to be to the right of certain humanisms, which thought the whole notion of sin ridiculous. Catholic theology often failed to hit its graceful mean, especially concerning sexuality, but on the whole the balanced goal it sought is something of which to be proud.

The doctrine of human depravity proves itself false *pragmatically*. Live by it and you will increase, not decrease, the fund of human woe. Stereotypically, the doctrine of human depravity associates with the Calvinist wing of the Reformation. Closer to the stereotypic Catholic view is Luther's *simul jusus et peccator*. In this phrase ("at once just and a sinner") Luther encapsuled his twofold sense that (a) human beings have been the recipients of a "justification" (being made right with God) that they can appropriate if they open their hearts wide in faith, and (b) this justification does not remove the need daily to recognize and confess one's distance from the all-holy God. Catholics can and should repeat most of this, for it is both an acute observation of human behavior and close to the biblical texts. But the ontological elaboration of grace that we stressed in the preceding section leaves the overall Catholic position with a different nuance.

The great influences on Luther were Paul and Augustine, both of whom had a somewhat moralistic or operational bent. The Johannine writings and the Greek fathers have been the fonts for a recent Catholic desire to go beyond moralism to the new being that grace imports. Since such an import is more substantial than moralistic changes could be, it gives a rather clear rationale for a Catholic desire to avoid the notion that grace is only "imputed" to us because of Christ's merits. Luther's writings encourage that notion. By contrast, a Catholic theology of grace that knows what it is doing makes the Holy Spirit a true renovator of human persons from the heart. Therefore, when Catholics repeat the formula "at once just and a sinner," they should make it clear that the formula does not mean schizophrenia. The "justice" that the Spirit gives is the good being God sees and loves in our cores. The sin that we all too evidently manifest is "merely" our unwillingness to let the Spirit invade us totally, "merely" our unwillingness to love.

This leads to the hypothesis that sin principally is lovelessness. Lovelessness can show itself as a prejudicial sourness and can abort colleagueship. A group might never become a circle of fellow workers, let alone of friends, because a majority might hold back the fair dealing and good will that collaboration or friendship demands. Tuck away in your mind's side corridor, then, the notion that sin often shows itself as a lack of *community.* Socially, it plays in the disorder, the fractiousness, the antagonism of people who refuse to cooperate. One advantage of this reading is that it links nicely with traditional reflections on evil. For a line of Catholic thought that goes back at least as far as Augustine sees evil as the privation of good—the lack of an order, being, or value that ought to be. Sin essentially is moral evil—evil that we choose. Contrasted with such natural evils as earthquakes or cancers, it lodges in human responsibility. Socially, then, much of our sin is a culpable privation of good. We refuse to go out to others in the love that would bring community, cooperation, justice, and mutual support.

It is hard to develop all this as systematically as we would wish, because an understanding of sin is more a ramification than a tidy deduction. Before we go very far, however, we want to make sure that the previous discussion of stereotypically Calvinist, Lutheran, and Catholic attitudes toward human nature does not leave a false impression. In actuality, individual members of those traditions are more than apt to "cross lines." For instance, one of the most loving, community-building couples we know have solid roots in the Calvinist tradition. Their home is just a powerhouse of good will. By contrast, we have sat in Catholic councils of education that effectively viewed students as weak and depraved. For example, we once heard a prominent Catholic scholar deliver himself of two educational observations. First, he had suffered considerably in his own education, so he saw no reason why his students should find learning a thing of joy. Second, in his mind's eye the degree process was like entering a large room through a small door, being soundly beaten as one crawled along, and then exiting through a larger door at the far end. This from a distinguished heir of the Catholic view of human nature.

Such attitudes develop neither education nor community nor joy. Rather, old cycles of lovelessness keep returning. That is sin's most depressing side. Our fathers ate sour grapes, so we daughters have our teeth on edge. Perhaps this is the most basic significance of "original" sin. It is not the tendency of current Catholic theologians to take the story of Adam and Eve literally. That story, in all the likelihood that literary and historical analyses can muster, is a subtle myth. As recent studies of human consciousness have amply shown, "myth" need not be pejorative. In this case, it simply says that a reflection on the human condition assumed the form of a story. The Genesis writers wanted to say that our human disorder is aboriginal. It goes back to any first "parent," any corporate personality, we can imagine. From the beginning, we have suffered an inability to keep sensual appetite under control of reason. From the beginning we have been "concupiscent." We have had to struggle to obey the light of God in our consciences, the promptings toward honesty and love. We have botched our relations with nature and with one another sexually. Like Adam, we all tend to foist responsibility off on Eve. Like Eve, we all tend to foist responsibility off on agents outside us. The result is suffering—a painful life outside the garden, outside intimacy with nature and God.

Original sin, thus, is something we all share. We all live, move, and have our being within it. Institutionalized, it erodes our money and banking. Given a code, it criminalizes our law. The Chinese sage Lao Tzu wanted to abolish all law, because he thought it made persons criminals. Lao Tzu had glimpsed something of original sin. The average person of good will who confronts a tax form, or an insurance policy, or a contract to write a book repeats Lao Tzu's intuition. He or she knows instinctively that a simple good order is missing sinfully. Those who praise our legal system, arguing that at least it gives some protection against pure might and greed, miss the cut of this theological argument. The very fact that pure might and greed are rampant possibilities shows we are a species disordered through and through. Our wars, our economies, our politics, our religions—they repeat one sorry story. None of them expresses a humanity pure, loving, honest, or good. None of them can stand confidently before Jesus or his God.

And, of course, we participate in these institutions, we benefit from some of their abuses, and often we promote their disorders. White-collar crime, for instance, goes with the drift of a nearly institutionalized tendency to gouge or cheat. Commonplace adultery goes with the drift of a nearly institutionalized tendency to seize a bit more gusto. Money is the root of a hundred political disorders. Power drives all sorts of people crazy. We know these nearly banal truths because they deface our own apartments. In our own neighborhood block, sin has cracked many a foundation. More precisely, most of us also know sin from personal malfeasance. Some way or other, *we* have cut corners: stolen, cheated, been unfaithful, ridden roughshod because of our ego. Even the apostle Paul moaned about the good that he would have done and did not, the evil that he would not have done and did. Sin therefore is the dreary business of the ever-grimey conscience. It is the heavy weight of being without the peace of God.

Even great saints have regularly denounced themselves as sinners, which shows that sin has layer upon layer. Those who find no gross evil on their conscience will learn, if they reflect more carefully, that their motivation regularly is impure. The pleasure taken in another's downfall, the joy taken in a cutting word—we collect such ugly little toads. The way we expand when someone flatters us, or the way we flatter others—they are similarly toady. Christian moralism of the past had little difficulty compiling lists of such deficiencies. As Diaz-Plaja has shown in the case of the Spanish, the capital sins can illumine a national character. But moralism bakes little bread for the massive hunger we suffer. The root of our sin is our failure to love. Socially, we need only love God with whole mind, heart, soul, and strength, and love our neighbors as ourselves, to have a holy community. Individually, we need only fulfill the Great Commandment to have the substance of human prosperity. The size of our income, the height of our station—they are unimportant. Were the Great Commandment our common directive, we would find all our times precious, all our gifts things to be shared.

"Sin," then, is a many-sided symbol for the fracture of humanity we suffer. It comes not from our finitude, not from our creatureliness, but from our failure to love. Insofar as it means fixating on idols rather than on the living God, sin is irreligion. Insofar as it means profiteering on the disadvantages, or even the sufferings of others, sin is deep injustice. But the constant in all instances of sin is closure to God or neighbor. Where love would keep us open, would insist that we try to attend, sin narrows us to the moment—the moment of pleasure, the moment of profit, the moment of disregard. The percentage of human suffering that comes from our closure is depressingly high. Sin therefore is the deep core of the slavery from which we beg liberation. Christ the Liberator is Christ the Savior from sin.

SOBRIETY

When we traveled the heights of the traditional understanding of Jesus, we glimpsed wonders and splendors. Jesus shows God to be better than ever we could conceive. But when we turned to the concrete human condition, the splendor gave way to deep darkness. From the gross sins of recent history (the massacres of Jews and Armenians, the torture chambers of a dozen dictatorships, the genocidal madness of Cambodia or Uganda) to the petty selfishness we all know, sin snatches away our joy. A mother who watches her child take its first steps on a ghetto street can rejoice only if she refuses to imagine the child's realistic future. An oriental mother who watches her Eurasian child has even less joy: simply for having a Western face, the child can have no place in Vietnam, Korea, or Japan. At home, black people remind us all of our deeply sinful national history. Red people do the same. American Orientals tell of detention during World War II. Chicanos tell of the sinful way we get our lettuce and grapes. Look carefully at any patch of American society, or of global society, then, and you will turn quite sober. It takes great faith to believe sin has not abounded more than grace.

As we mentioned in the beginning, sobriety is a hallmark of Karl Rahner's theology. Though he yields to no contemporary in his penetration of God's worldwide grace, Rahner is not your neighborhood consoler. He broods over the scene he surveys, and one often catches a groan.

De facto, judged on their performances, human beings are a trying lot. In the church, which is Rahner's most immediate society, human stupidity and lovelessness repulse millions from religion. In the recent history of his German nation, there is guilt for many lifetimes. The grace of God, come into our midst, meets terrible forces of resistance. Again and again, so many flee the light, because their deeds are evil, that the sun of justice seems beclouded. Reflecting on all this, Rahner's general outlook is very sober.

It is important for us to explain such sobriety rather carefully, because the practical attitude that one's view of grace and sin generates determines much of how one ventures into the world. We want "sobriety" to suggest neither a prejudice that human nature is vitiated by sin nor a grim-faced lack of joy. Rather, we want it to suggest that the Catholic Christian view of human nature urges us to be serious. There is a time to play, as well as a time to be serious, and it is a mark of maturity to discern which time has presently arrived. For the moment, let us concentrate on the time to be serious. It seems to suit the situation in our country and the church as they head into the 1980s. In our country, the beginning of the century's ninth decade found much talk about a new cold war, and a new registration of young men and women for military draft. In the church a conservative backlash was well under way. These were calls to be sober, judicious, a careful discerner of signs of the times.

Perhaps three "situational" descriptions can make such a reading clearer. Consider, for instance, the situation of a person who specializes in peace studies. If he or she is working from an explicitly Christian viewpoint, it is likely to be either that of one of the traditionally pacificist churches, such as the Mennonite, or of a fairly radical branch of a mainstream tradition, such as that of the Catholic Workers. Whatever the particular tradition, however, the Christian involved in peace studies finds the intransigence of most public policy very discouraging. The imbroglio in Iran, where fifty Americans were held hostage to students' demands for the return of the Shah, was a case in point. The entire thrust of the United States government's initial reaction was to lay down a hard line. One heard virtually nothing about the abuses of the Shah's regime, virtually nothing about America's role in supporting it. There was no creative effort to plan a scenario that would allow the aggrieved Iranians a platform, no empathetic realization that they most desired a forum in which to present to the world their evidences of the Shah's wrongdoings. As a result, the situation stalemated. Like kids in a schoolyard, each side sneered and jeered.

The person working in peace studies will be hard-put not to view such a reaction dolorously. It clearly seems just another instance of deploying bankrupt, basically dishonest policies. The fact is that the

United States did prop an inhumane regime in Iran, as it has propped inhumane regimes in many other countries. This fact did not, however, give sanction to the illegal and cruel way that the Iranian students held Americans hostage. It was not a wrong that justified another wrong. But it was such a basic ingredient in the snarled conflict that not to acknowledge it openly, not to provide for its obvious psychological force, was to choose a scenario destroyed from the outset. It was to choose illusion, dishonesty, and bad faith. Since this has happened again and again, writing a too solid portion of our country's recent diplomatic history, it reveals a systematic wrong-headedness. There is a light "out there" in the facts of international history that American leaders have been fleeing. If the Bible still bears us practical insight, they have been fleeing such a light because their deeds have been evil. One can, indeed must, hope to convert the doers of evil deeds, the avoiders of truth's light, from their sinful ways, but when the sinful scenario has become operative policy such hope must be rather modest. Trying to bring a country such as ours from chauvinistic self-serving to a foreign policy consonant with God's truth is not a work for those of short stamina. It is a missionary trek bound to be long-haul.

A second situation that tempers one's Christian judgment to sobriety is that of minority groups such as American blacks. They have enough history in hand at the present to be as unoptimistic as persons in peace studies. For close to twenty-five years, the American majority has had highly visible lessons in the breadth and depth of its racism. Even when one provides for the stridency of some of the teachers, and for the complexity of some of the economics involved, a very sober estimate of the will to change, the will to do justice, must emerge. If black youth presently are the nation's most underemployed, with statistics in some areas reaching to better than forty percent joblessness, there is no rosy future for a group who have had a dismal past. Black leaders therefore do well to keep their rage and despair from taking away all their peace or determination. Like persons in peace studies, they have to get set for a battle that will be a very long-haul. They may decide that white America collectively has an unreachable conscience, and so content themselves with very pragmatic, politico-economic strategies. They may realize that they have to work as hard on black pride as on black economics, if they are not to lose the present generations to despair. But whatever their strategies or realizations, they must realistically expect only to make haste slowly. Too much advantage accrues to the majority from the present arrangements for any but a deeply believing, saintly few to make sizeable changes readily. The American majority is neither deeply believing nor saintly.

We shall move into a third, smaller-scale situation momentarily, but before leaving these first two macroscopic situations we must note another pressure to sobriety. It is difficult in the present climate of American opinion even to offer such critical analyses as these. Harkening back to silly designations of the past, Americans have effectively claimed some mandate to be God's new chosen people, some manifest destiny to moralize to the world. We would do much better to moralize to ourselves. We would do better still to drop moralizing altogether and start dealing in sober theology. For sober theology, Americans are neither the best nor the brightest. We are rather just what our fruits show, and our fruits have been very mixed. The demagogic appeals to American pride in recent years have produced fruits thoroughly rotten, for they have been a shield against truth-seeing and truth-telling. It is not national pride, not falsely building the country up, that will set us free but truth-telling. It is not supposed tearing the country down that is our inner worm but lying and injustice.

Like large-scale situations, such as international conflicts or widespread racism, domestic difficulties regularly inculcate sobriety. Consider, for instance, the couple midway between happiness and divorce. In a representative script, they have been married eight years, have two children, and are in deep conflict. His great passion is his work, which more evenings than not keeps him out until eight or nine. Her energies are more dispersed, for she has the kids, the house, and a part-time job. She has the part-time job partly to keep her brain alive, partly because they think they need the money.

Unhappy with this state of affairs, the wife initiates a series of investigative hearings. Both researcher and prosecutor, she compiles briefs for a change. They ought to change their outlay of money, for they are getting deeper and deeper into debt. They ought to change their outlay of time, for they are growing farther and farther apart. Above all, they ought to change from the presently unjust distribution of housekeeping and child-rearing, for it is driving her crazy. Accused, the husband's first response is confusion. He knew that things had been rather hectic, but doesn't everyone in suburbia live that way?

The move beyond confusion, to action or nonaction, is where the couple come into crisis. As the husband decides to respond, so will their marriage go. Should he open himself to the light, accepting the validity of his wife's charges, their marriage can move to a new and deeper plane. Should he close himself to the light, refusing to discuss their problems, or to get counseling, or seriously to change his ways, their marriage is on the rocks. Look at the statistics in which marriages such as these now swim, and you will not be sanguine about the couple's prospects. Both parties, but especially the one who most offends justice, will have to be converted, if the marriage is to regain life or momentum, and conversion is a sobering affair.

Marital conversion usually goes hand in hand with mutual forgiveness. Trying to forget the shabby past, the partners pledge themselves to a new beginning. The effective solution to larger-scale situations, such as the racism and international standoff we described, equally entails conversion and forgiveness. That these terms are embarassingly unusual for those contexts is a first sign of how disordered the situations are. Soberingly, most countries of the world have gotten into the rut of doing business irreligiously. They may prate about "Christian" or "Muslim" values, if these adjectives seem good propaganda, but they make sure that the serious ethical programs implied in the Bible or the Koran stay far from the boardrooms of power. Both the Bible and the Koran paint a God who renders harsh judgment on human injustice. Both envision a social ideal of almsgiving and compassion. The Bible probably is clearer on conversion and forgiveness, but each Koranic *surah* begins, "In the name of Allah, the compassionate, the merciful." All this directly opposes the ordinary rules of the Middle Eastern game.

For Bernard Lonergan, the empirical inability of human beings to sustain social progress is a primary revelation of our need for salvation. The injustice we hand down, generation after generation, shows how sin has become our social contagion. To reverse this state of affairs, the Christian God introduced a new order of redemption. He would redeem those enslaved to injustice by a new law of the cross. On the cross, Jesus suffered expectable results for contesting an old regime of Satanic powers. He broke that regime, resurrecting to new possibilities, by suffering evil in love. The sober facts of the current human situation, as Christian theology comprehends them, lead to but one sure conclusion. We have not appropriated Jesus' modeling of God's new law, have not been willing to suffer the price of genuine prosperity. Our situation is just as stark as that. Until we do effectively suffer evil in love, things will change very little.

FAITH, HOPE, AND LOVE

But surely suffering evil in love, living by the law of the cross, is an unrealistic solution? Surely a sober appraisal of the way out of our basic human dilemma cannot demand a superhuman generosity? At the heart of these questions, one glimpses the depths of the Catholic theology of grace. The power to suffer evil in love is nothing less than God's own life. No one less than God's child possesses such power. The *agape* of God which overcomes sin and death, the *agape* of God from which nothing can separate us—this is thoroughly divine. History finally, and wryly, reveals that to be human we have to be more than human. To overturn the contagious ruination of humanity into which each generation is thrown, there must be incarnations of a divine love that recreates humanity at ruination's void.

In the previous sections, we spent sufficient time on the theme of grace as divinization to be able to say now that it is the ontological view that best meets the void of the problems of human sin. "Create in me a clean heart, O God, and put a new and right spirit within me," the Psalmist begged (51:10). Grace is God's ontological response to such petition. It is the new creation that the old ravaged order begs by its disorder. Here, however, we want to consider the "virtues" (powers) through which this new creation has traditionally been thought to work. Faith, hope, and love are the "theological" virtues because they most directly translate divine life into human strengths.

There is no completely adequate distinction of faith, hope, and love, for they interweave inextricably. Faith names the basic attitude of committing oneself to a mysterious God, hope names the attitude of living trustingly toward the future, and love names the warm creativity that is at core divine. Modern thought has tended to separate faith from knowledge, but that does violence to both biblical thought and to any shrewd observation. Our commitments color more than a little of our knowledge. The basic options we make dictate a great deal of what we "see." A good example of this is the usually rather bootless antagonism between doctrinaire atheism and doctrinaire theism. Where doctrinaire atheism sees in nature a terrible waste and disorder, doctrinaire theism argues that God is manifest in nature's overwhelming design. Where doctrinaire atheism assumes that "God" is a tool of exploitative upper classes, doctrinaire theism finds "God" to be the poor's one sure consolation. The "data" that the two sides use are supposedly the same. Each has equal access to evolutionary history, to economic history, to the sociology of Appalachia or Watts. Yet they conclude at diametrically opposite evaluations—because they are primed to see goodness or its lack.

Doctrinaire positions on just about anything tend to be unexperiential and uncritical. Where persons discourse on "God" from experience, and try to make all their assertions gravely, they find little surety. Nature, for instance, is both ordered (otherwise we could not understand it) and prodigally wasteful (most species run to extinction). Human beings are both so exploitative and so surprisingly good that they keep "God" an ever indecisive inference. To live sanely in the midst of such a situation, one has either to believe or to be atheistic rather carefully. The existential difference between careful belief and careful atheism can be very slight. Accepting the finality of mystery, both open the heart and wait.

For Catholic Christianity, faith has too often been an unmysterious matter of assenting to propositions. By and large, Protestant theology has done better at rendering the solid gravity of biblical faith. There one finds interpersonal commitment. There God is one's rock and salvation, one's defense against fear. Like a friend walking with a friend, the biblical person of faith trudges along with God. Thereby, mystery becomes an old familiar. If strange nights occur, when one has to wrestle with angels, or strange demands occur, like Abraham's need to sacrifice his son, they are exceptional testings. Ordinarily, life itself is faith's testing. Sufficient for most days is the evil thereof. God is so suprasensible, and fellow human beings can be so unattractive, that one only fulfills the twofold command of loving God and neighbor by leaping beyond "evidence." Suffering is so omnipresent, and the human heart is so deeply demanding, that assenting to propositions works little salvation.

Consider the situations we used above to establish a mood of sobriety. To believe that God cares for situations such as the Iranian standoff, or the racism that afflicts American blacks, or a shaky suburban marriage, one has to come to grips with human waywardness and divine mystery quite comprehensively. If we try to deal with such situations glibly, whether in supposed faith or supposed unbelief, they come back to slash us. God's "care" is sometimes as far from our expectations as the heavens are above the earth. God's "will" is sometimes as contrary to our desires as the will of the enemy would be. It is only at the bedrock, the level of fundamental options, that faith has any stability. It is only when we come in sight of a carte blanche, a blank check, that we are likely not to be swept away. "Though he slay me, yet will I trust him," Job was made to say. "Thy kingdom come, thy will be done," Jesus wrote on his check. Moving from the mystery of life and goodness, faith finds a commission of self, an abandon of self, that takes it across the mystery of death and evil. Accepting its postulates for sense and love as its defining vocations, the religious self finds the strength to call nonsense and hatred penultimate. Then, after living with such dispositions for a while, it finds them salutary. They conduce to ways of regarding the world, ways of regarding fellow humans, that bring out the image of God.

Implied in this description is a pragmatic test: Faith should make life good, make people happy. Employing this test, Catholic novelists have exposed many of faith's misuses. A line of literary critique runs from Ireland to the United States, carrying the judgments of authors such as James Joyce, Brian Moore, and Mary Gordon that Catholic faith easily can rob people of their joy. *Final Payments*, Mary Gordon's penetrating story of a young woman trying to break the grip of her father's fiercely conservative Catholicism, sets the robbery thesis smack in the middle of feminist liberation. The heroine, Isabel Moore, spent the flower of her young adulthood caring for her invalid father. She was cut off from the normal maturation that her friends underwent, buoyed up only by the "status" her sacrifices gave her in the myth-minded circle of her Irish-Catholic neighborhood. But she herself never believed the pieties and world-hatings that fed the religion of the parish biddies. Nor did she accept the harsh, self-righteous, intellectualist faith of her professorial father. When she was set free into the world of her secularist peers at the death of her father, she started a dizzy roller coaster ride from snatching greedily at sexual pleasure to suffering fits of self-laceration. Her dilemma became classic: Should she follow her hunger for pleasure, beauty, a happy life, or should she strive for the "real" satisfaction that comes from self-denial and good reputation?

Gordon's intelligence and skill are such that each horn of the dilemma shows itself hollow. The "simple" life of pleasure and refinement does not stand up for long, for it leads to injuring others—in this case, by adultery. The apparently more "simple" life of self-sacrifice collapses equally: Easily does it cover petty-mindedness, whining, pride, and stupidity. Before the reader's eyes, Isabel Moore acts out the profound battles involved in coming to a mature faith. For a mature faith is neither dehumanizing nor compatible with secular standards of "the good life." It says yes to the heart's longings for beauty and decent pleasure, no to the spirit's perverse ability both to canonize inferiority and to warp the heart's good longings. Ultimately, mature faith fights through to a God uncoopted by churchy religion, a love of neighbor uncoopted by "morality." It finds Christ's cross not where it chooses to declare the self a martyr but where daily life calls for integrity. It finds God's incarnation lovely—in sex, art, and friendship—without losing sight of the times when all mortal flesh must keep silent, all things passing are made relative. One can only achieve such a balance in the Spirit. Mature faith is a function of intense human effort that keeps giving itself over to grace.

In our opinion, then, mature Catholic faith says yes to the heart's spontaneous desires. It affirms that we have a vocation to develop, create, and take decent pleasure. The only caveat it puts on this affirmation is that we be willing honestly to see our vocation through. When it comes time to develop by refusing tawdry advancement or pleasure, will we take the next hard negative step? When it comes time to purify our creative talent by discipline, revision, greater honesty, will we make greater demands on ourselves? And when pleasure starts to get out of focus, to take us from more important things or to injure others, will we deny ourselves and let it go? These are test questions by which we can assay our faith's maturity. They concretize the Catholic view that human nature is not intrinsically depraved, while maintaining the sobriety about human waywardness that a hard look at human performance entails. With ourselves, as with other people, our first instinct should be cooperative. We should give our desires to enjoy the beach, or a good meal, or an attractive other person the benefit of the doubt. That way, we keep them from convoluting or festering inside. But we should also have the honesty and good humor to see how easily these desires try to take over the whole play. As we refuse to be foolish about others, to deny the facts when they abuse the benefit of the doubt, so we must refuse to be foolish about ourselves, to deny that we too easily lose balance.

Mingled with such a striving after mature, poised faith are strivings for a hope and a love that equally are gifts of the Spirit. We have to hope that some day we will grow mature, some day our desires will come to good fruition and balance. We have to love the selves we have been given, to compassionate their weaknesses and encourage their strengths. So too with the way we regard other people and nature. We have to hope that other people also will grow, have to love free their good desires. If, for example, we know a colleague who is overly concerned about money, always complaining that she gets less than her superiority to others ought to bring her, the prompting of the Spirit in us is not the one that makes her unattractiveness a case of petit-bourgeois envy. The woman *is* unattractively grasping, *does* burden you by her envy at others' success. But the Spirit inclines you to remember the signs of self-doubt she gives off, the evidences you have that something is difficult, her marital life, perhaps. What she does not need right now is another judgmental response that forces her to confront her demons ruthlessly. That is too much for her at the moment. She rather needs a sort of tolerance and indirect help that will get her ready for such a ruthless confrontation in the future. She needs a minor-league "suffering evil in love" that will briefly interrupt her vicious circles.

You can imagine the larger-scale elaborations of hope and love that might bring "antibodies" to the "diseased areas" of international war zones or scenes of national injustice. They regularly are the medicine most needed. What does little to cure any of the cancers at work in such places is a legalistic or punishing hard line. Soberly, one has to propose generous, self-sacrificing moves that both honor the truth of the situation and advance it toward a greater justice. One has to hope that forgiveness and new beginnings are possible, to love the smallest sign of good will that any party shows. This is terribly difficult work, complicated in most cases because one has to sell it to one's allies as much as to one's enemies. It is the sort of positive, simple effort to live out Christian precepts that easily brings derision.

Those who deride the bearer of hope and love often do so in the name of realism. It is unrealistic, they say, to speak of forgiveness, or of doing business in the light of full disclosure. People will take advantage of you. They will consider you weak and ram your good will down your throat. Both analytically and historically, the deriders have a weak case. Analytically, it is clear that all possibility of human community, and therefore of significant prosperity, goes out the door when (a) one has no mechanism for getting out of bitter antagonism, and (b) one cannot expect fair, honest dealing. Without forgiveness and honesty, interactions are from the outset off line. Historically, the wars and rumors of war that dominate the human story reveal a substructure of injuries unforgiven and trust continually destroyed. More positively, the few theoreticians of the human condition who have gained widespread respect—Plato, Confucius, Moses, Buddha, Aristotle, Jesus, Lao Tzu, and their like—have all been champions of humane treatment. From recent times, the signal figure who brought faith, hope, and love to programmatic political success was Mohandas Gandhi. His commitment was to *satyagraha*—the force of truth. Shrewdly, Gandhi developed tactics of arbitration that encouraged all adversaries to submit their positions to the light. Martin Luther King, Jr., and Cesar Chavez are the American "politicians" who have continued Gandhi's tradition. When the theological history of recent politics is written, they are likely to be the "statesmen" who prevail, the ones who leave some legacy worth emulating.

Realistically, then, Christian life commits one to considerable eccentricity and suffering. Realistically, human performance makes it imperative to *believe* that grace is stronger than sin. Soberly, one has to learn how to combine positive initiatives with frank post-mortems—how to be open and encouraging without getting destroyed. If one knows what true "prosperity" entails, the temptations to cheat for passing advantage will grow less and less luresome. If one knows what sort of politics usually brings popular prestige, less and less will one aspire to high status. Realistically, openness to God and intimacy with friends are treasures far less corruptible. Realistically, they give the lessons we most need. We need to know, solidly and unswervingly, that life is good enough to carry us through suffering. We need to know that God holds all time in her hand. We can only know these things if we experience the Spirit poured forth in our hearts. We can only know them if we venture forth to walk with a real, mysterious God in faith, hope, and love. When the mysterious God becomes not a figment but a daily assumption, a habit like eating and breathing, we shall begin to be realistic as the best products of the Catholic tradition have been.

BIBLIOGRAPHY

Berger, Klaus, et al. "Grace," in Karl Rahner, et al., eds., *Sacramentum Mundi*, 2. New York: Herder and Herder, 1968, 409–427.

Buckley, Michael J. "Transcendence, Truth, and Faith," *Theological Studies*, 39/4 (December 1978), 633–655.

Coleman, John A. "Situation for Modern Faith, *Theological Studies, 39/4 (December 1978), 601–632.*

Curran, Charles E. "Christian Conversion in the Writings of Bernard Lonergan," in Phillip McShane, ed., *Foundations of Theology*. Notre Dame, Ind.: University of Notre Dame Press, 1972, 41–59.

Davis, Charles. *A Question of Conscience*. New York: Harper & Row, 1967.

Diaz-Plaja, Fernando. *El Espanol y los Siete Pecados Capitales*. Madrid: Alianza Editorial, 1966.

Frost, William P. "A Decade of Hope Theology," *Theological Studies*, 39/1 (March 1978), 139–153.

Gordon, Mary. *Final Payments*. New York: Random House, Ballantine, 1978.

Guillet, Jacques, et al. *Discernment of Spirits*. Collegeville, MN.: Liturgical Press, 1970.

Lonergan, Bernard. *Grace and Freedom*. New York: Herder and Herder 1971.

Lynch, William F. *Images of Hope*. New York: Mentor-Omega, 1965.

McDermott, Brian O. "Original Sin: Recent Developments," *Theological Studies*, 38/3 (September 1977), 478–512.

Moore, Brian. *The Feast of Lupercal*. Boston: Little, Brown, 1957.

Powers, Joseph M. "The Art of Believing," *Theological Studies*, 39/4 (December 1978) 656–678.

Rahner, Karl. "Justified and Sinner at the Same Time," *Theological Investigations*, 6. Baltimore: Helicon, 1969, 218–230.

Rahner, Karl. *Nature and Grace*. New York: Sheed and Ward, 1964.

Rahner, Karl. "The Church of Sinners," *Theological Investigations*, 6. Baltimore: Helicon, 1969, 253–269.

Rahner, Karl. "The Sinful Church in the Decrees of Vatican II," *Theological Investigations*, 6. Baltimore: Helicon, 1969, 270–294.

Ricoeur, Paul. "The Logic of Jesus, The Logic of God," *Christianity and Crisis*, 39/20 (December 24, 1979), 324–327.

Schoonenberg, Piet, et al. "Sin," in Karl Rahner *et al.*, *Sacramentum Mundi*, 6. New York: Herder and Herder, 1970, 87–94.

Spicq, Ceslaus. *Agape in the New Testament*. St. Louis: B. Herder, 1966.

Vergote, Antoine. *Psychologie Religieuse*. Brussels: Charles Dessart, 1966.

Wilmore, Gayraud S. and Cone, James H., eds. *Black Theology: A Documentary History, 1966–1979*. Maryknoll, N.Y.: Orbis, 1979.

The Church 6

OVERVIEW

The community that sponsors Christian realism is the church, the assembly of Jesus' followers. Our first investigation is the church's original shape, the community Jesus likely had in mind. Jesus' mind, as New Testament analysis uncovers it, focused on the Kingdom of God. After Jesus' death and resurrection, his followers began to probe what he meant for the Kingdom. Slowly, they worked out a high Christology and an organization for service.

As it was developed, church faith and service pivoted on Word and Sacrament. Rooted in scripture, geared toward proclamation, the Christian assembly has attempted to body forth God's truth. By gathering to remember Jesus, and to celebrate their fellowship in his good news, Christians have fashioned graceful sacraments, above all the eucharist, which have provided saving help through the life cycle for millions.

Recent ecclesiology has spotlighted the different models by which the church has understood itself or could understand itself today. They show institutional, mystical, sacramental, servant, and heralding sides of what is ultimately a mysterious assembling by grace. By radical contemplation and radical politics, those models might gain greater acuity. By closer interpersonal relations, the local church might be more gracious.

The bugbear of current church order is ecumenical division, while that of current church moral authority is fear, especially of sexual love. A way around ecumenical division might be a greater stress on fundamentals, coupled with a stronger push toward scaramental intercommunion. A way through current moral crises might be greater faith that nothing can separate us from God's love.

THE COMMUNITY JESUS SPONSORED

As we noted in our first chapter, the Catholic church currently presents an ambiguous appearance. On the one hand, it remains an institution of immense size and significance. On the other hand, many of its faithful, especially in Europe and the United States, question its vitality and relevance. In order to get a contemporary theology of the church clearly in sight, therefore, we have to try to retrieve its original conception—to recall the community that Jesus himself likely had in mind.

Jesus preached the Kingdom of God. The focus of his teaching and healing was the new reign of divine power he saw dawning. Realizing this, recent New Testament scholarship has stressed the eschatological character of Jesus' ministry. Though we cannot be certain just what Jesus had in mind, the best guess is that he expected the Kingdom to consummate history. Whether or not Jesus linked this consummation to his own death is uncertain, but some interpreters read his depression in the Garden or cry of abandon on the cross as deep pain at the Kingdom's delay. At any rate, the proximity of the Kingdom accounts for Jesus' having made meager provision for the continuance of his work. The strata of the New Testament that go back to the historical Jesus contain little that deals with a "church." After Jesus' death, when communities of believers started to work out the problems of continuing his mission, ecclesiastical issues became more pressing. It is from such communities that many ecclesiastical interpretations of Jesus' teaching in the gospels derive. It is also such communities that furnish the context of Paul's epistles. Thus, even though it was not a paramount concern of Jesus himself, the theology of the church soon became an important New Testament concern.

Early Christians could derive the most important notions of what discipleship entailed from Jesus' own preaching and example. For example, following Jesus clearly entailed living a life of love structured by the twofold commandment. The love of God and the love of neighbor as oneself were the basic "law" Jesus had enjoined. He did not develop this to safeguard community order. Rather, he developed it as a brief statement on moral reality—on the core response that God's sovereignty and one's neighbor's value ought to evoke. To follow Jesus was to make his Father the prime treasure of one's life. It was to depend totally on this Father's goodness, to resolve totally to try to imitate this Father's love. Similarly, Jesus' example made it clear that he considered other men and women his brothers and sisters. They were members of God's family, objects of God's parental care. In the parable of the Good Samaritan, Jesus showed that all fellow human beings, but especially those in need, are our "neighbors." In the parable of the Prodigal Son, he showed that God is willing to forgive even the ungrateful. With notions such as these, Jesus' followers had the essentials of the "constitutional law" that their living together required.

In addition, they had other important directives. Jesus obviously had been a man of prayer. He had withdrawn from time to time into solitude; he had petitioned his Father for all his needs. Any group claiming to follow Jesus' way therefore would treasure prayer. Setting Jesus' example in the context of his Jewish faith, it would ponder the scriptures and try to bring the events of recent times—above all Jesus' death and resurrection—into the story of salvation those scriptures recorded. Clued by Jesus' example, then, the church organized much of its prayer, scripture reading, and effort to expand the story of salvation into "the breaking of the bread." That is, it developed the habit of congregating for a simple meal in celebration of Jesus' death and resurrection. As the services of the Jewish synagogue had included a sermon or exposition of scripture, so the early Christians, many of whom were Jews, began to preach at their congregational celebrations. They also began to associate their worship with provision for their poor, service of their needy. Thus, remembering Jesus, explaining their faith, and caring for the brothers and sisters dominated the early assemblies. Gathering together, Jesus' followers found in the breaking of the bread the nourishment they needed to sustain a hardy faith.

All this surely was quite informal. We know from Paul's letters that sometimes it was so informal it approached chaos. Various persons would claim the floor and run over one another in a babble of "inspired" utterances. Paul had to remind them that Christ's Spirit does not conduce to disorder. Speaking in tongues, to say nothing of swooning to unconsciousness, was not so important as a rational explanation of scripture or faith that edified fellow believers. Similarly, it was important that eucharistic groups maintain a genuine charity and a high moral tone. A genuine charity meant sharing goods openhandedly and refusing to split into cliques. A high moral tone meant remembering that this meal dealt with the body and blood of the Lord, not with things of "flesh." For the communities with whom Paul corresponded, many aspects of faith were still only poorly grasped. They had a passionate conviction that something marvelously new had occurred in Jesus' death and resurrection, but they were far from realizing its full implications.

More than a lack of experience lay behind this state of affairs. The early epistles suggest that Paul, as much as Jesus, expected an early consummation to history. In the lifetime of many still living, the Lord would return to finish his work. The second coming or return (*parousia*) of the risen Jesus so dominated Paul's thought that his early letters make little provision for secular affairs. Thus, he is more interested in what will happen to those who have died between the time of Christ's ascension and the second coming than he is in the long-range future of the church. This situation changed after some years, but it helps to explain Paul's counsel that people stay in the state (married or single) they presently were in, his unconcern about slavery, and so forth. The time was short, the Lord would soon return. Questions of marriage, or slavery, or relations with the secular authorities seemed beside the point.

By the end of the Pauline period it was clear that the parousia had been delayed. Thus, Romans took a longer, more historical view, and Ephesians seems almost cosmic. For these epistles, the followers of Jesus, like Israel, have a mission to all the world. They are to proclaim what happened in Jesus, so that all persons might know God's love. By the end of its first generation, then, the church had begun to realize that it did not exist for itself. It existed to keep Christ's message and love before the world. Indeed, for the author of Ephesians the church represented a great marital mystery. Those who believe in Christ share one life with him. If human beings have been made for God, the church is where they realize their vocation.

The last paragraphs have drawn on Pauline theology. As Catholic scripture scholar Raymond Brown's recent *The Community of the Beloved Disciple* shows in rich detail, there were early churches organized around other theologies. A number of them apparently traced their roots to an eyewitness of Jesus, called the "beloved disciple." The original members of such circles may well have been Palestinian Jews, including some followers of John the Baptist, who accepted Jesus as the Messiah. Others, including Samaritans, joined them, and before long they developed a high Christology, according to which Jesus had existed with God before his birth from Mary. This brought them into fierce conflict with Jews, who saw such a Christology as a blasphemous denial of traditional monotheism. It also made them open to Gentile converts.

A high Christology, conflict with the Jews, and "realized eschatology" (the final things already have happened in Jesus and the Spirit) are themes that distinguish the theology of the gospel of John and the Johannine epistles. By retrojection, then, we call the communities that held these beliefs "Johannine." At the stage of the epistles (ca. A.D. 100), the Johannine community had undergone schism, largely because some members had begun to downplay Jesus' humanity. Eventually, this latter group probably joined with Gnostics—heretics whose "secret knowledge" frequently included a denial of Jesus' full humanity. Whereas before this internal conflict the Johannine Christians seem to have had only the loosest governing structures, after it they apparently accepted the hierarchical structures other churches were developing and merged with them. They brought to the subsequent "Great Church" both their high Christology and their tradition of guidance by the Spirit.

The great doctrinal councils of the fourth and fifth centuries affirmed the high Christology of the Johannine tradition, and when the Johannine writings became part of the canonical New Testament their emphasis on the inner teaching of the Spirit became part of the great church's treasury. It lay in tension with more formal governments that had developed, and ever since there has been a tension in the Catholic view of church order. Because of its early controversies over doctrine, the church realized that it had to have authoritative teachers who could decide whether an interpretation was faithful to Jesus' original vision. The vagueness of the Johannine writings' criteria for orthodoxy suggests that their communities did not have such teachers, and that without them one was helpless against interpreters who claimed equally to represent tradition. By their problems, then, the Johannine churches showed the need for clearer authority structures.

On the other hand, the authorities mentioned in the rest of the New Testament are quite vague. Certainly they give no template for later structures, whether of teaching or liturgical leadership. Thus, when Catholics and Orthodox squabbled over questions of authority, neither side could settle the dispute by appealing to a clear New Testament picture. So too during the Reformation, when Catholics and Protestants squabbled over authority. Recent ecumenical discussion therefore has found the New Testament an opponent of later controversies. According to the scriptures, none of the "political" bases for later church division has sure standing. It may be that later developments had to come, and that some of them were better than others. None of the churches' forms of government, however, was clearly willed by God from the beginning.

John L. McKenzie is a respected Catholic biblical scholar who has been willing to read such New Testament evidence with an unblinking eye. In an article on ministerial structures in the New Testament, he shows that the situation of the early churches was neither uniform nor highly developed. Moreover, it seems that apostles—those who had seen the Lord—were not primarily church governors, that the churches described by Acts reached their decisions democratically, that we have no assurance a definite officer led the community in prayer, and that there was no *magisterium*—no ministry of authoritative teaching such as that which later Roman Catholicism developed. On the other hand, there was a permanent diaconate, a married clergy, and a corps of female ministers. With an eye to present ecumenical discussion, McKenzie infers that the problem for Roman Catholicism is to explain how it could develop traditions that curtailed the original New Testament diversity and freedom.

The general response that Roman Catholicism has made to observations such as McKenzie's is that with experience the church found it necessary to generate the offices and limitations it did. The rise of deviant teachings hastened the coming of the authoritative teacher. The milieu in which the ministry was to function made celibacy and excluding women advantageous. One can debate the wisdom of such historical decisions, and one can argue that conditions today require a change. But the general notion that doctrine and discipline have to develop, because later history raises new problems, is central to the Catholic understanding of the church. The church is not so chartered by the New Testament that it can never develop beyond the picture given there. The picture given there ought always to be a primary source of direction, and anything that seriously compromises that picture, especially anything that compromises the love and freedom it shows, ought nearly automatically to be vetoed. But under the Spirit the church must have the power to develop. Otherwise it can neither meet new challenges nor specify implications of its old faith.

Moreover, there is a significant sense in which the church precedes scripture. The New Testament, after all, was the product of two generations' worth of Christian experience. Most of it came from the collective memories of individual churches, and all of it had to meet the "sense of the faithful." In other words, all of it had to win approval as being consonant with the living, oral tradition by which the churches had long done business. The Johannine literature, for instance, won approval only after a considerable time. The Apocalypse was judged orthodox later still. Through all this "judging," the churches relied on the Spirit. What they remembered having received from their forebears in faith, and what they found solid through their daily practice, ultimately depended on the Spirit's illumination. When Catholic theology defends doctrinal development and the place of living tradition, it ought primarily to mean this vital experience of the Spirit. Below the utilities of such structural features as the episcopacy and the magisterium, the Spirit keeps the church indefectible.

That is not to deny that the Spirit uses scripture as the basic mirror in which the church discovers itself. The New Testament always retains a primary authority. Furthermore, the question of authority—of how power ought to be exercised in the church—receives in the New Testament a very instructive answer. When it looks in this mirror, the church discovers that all its power ought to be for service. Thus, Jesus says that he came not to be ministered unto but to minister. He says that those who wish to be great in his Kingdom must be the servants of all. Unforgettably, he girds himself with a servant's cloth and wipes the feet of his disciples. Station, power, office—according to the New Testament—are for service. It is by spending oneself for others in love that a Christian follows the Lord.

John L. McKenzie, again, has forced the Catholic community to confront this portion of its New Testament image. His recent *The New Testament Without Illusion* is an ironic study in the contrasts between the church of early times and the church of today. Without glorifying the archaic period, McKenzie shows that the church has regularly forgotten its original power-base. In place of service and spiritual reliance, it has taken to the ways of the world. Thus, where Jesus made it clear that money is a spiritual menace, the church has accumulated considerable wealth. Where Jesus made it clear that his followers ought not to lord it over others, as the "great men" of the world do, the church has built gilded thrones. The Mercedes that leave the Vatican are all too like the Mercedes that leave other government headquarters. The bureaucratic administration of church business is all too like the bureaucratic administration of other government business. By forgetting its early simplicity, poverty, and reason-to-be, the church has lost much of its distinction. Thereby, it has often failed to be the community Jesus sponsored.

CHRISTIAN MINISTRY TO WORD AND SACRAMENT

That is not to say the entire history of the church has been negative. Through high times of spiritual vitality and low times of spiritual defection, the Spirit has provided the faithful nourishment to survive. Principally, the Spirit has provided this through the ministry, the service, of Word and Sacraments. By preaching and reading scripture, the church has kept looking in the mirror, kept recalling whence its hope comes. By celebrating the sacraments, it has kept applying the good news to crucial moments of the life cycle. If we reflect on these modes of ecclesial self-actualization, we shall see how the "People of God" has managed to stay in existence. As well, we shall see more concretely how a creative understanding of service could make the church more effective today.

Bernard Cooke's magisterial treatment of Christian ministry provides a good summary of the history. He traces five guiding themes. There is first the ministry or service of forming Christian community. From New Testament times to the present, certain Christians have spent their lives keeping the church together, caring for its life. Second, there is the service of God's Word. Though this has overtones of following the Son, its principal motif has been preaching. Basing themselves on scripture, Christians have regularly tried to expose the meaning of their present times by reference to the paradigms of the past. Their "story" began with Old Testament events and pivoted on the event of Jesus. God would continue to treat them as he had treated their predecessors in faith, so every retelling of the biblical story, every remembering of Jesus' message and work, stirred up their faith.

It also stirred up their sense of distinctive identity. The story handed down in the scriptures was not a story "the world" found congenial.

Its standards of success and failure differed from those of most kings. From the Word of God, one learned that suffering was never very distant. Like forgiveness and love, it was almost a surety. However, the third focus of Christian ministry, service to the People of God, alleviated a great deal of suffering. Through both material alms and spiritual support, generations of Christians eased one another's burdens, of which the hospitals, schools, and soup kitchens that Christians established were absolute proof. The quiet, unpublicized support that friends gave the grieving, or clergy gave families who felt bereft, made this service strength to go on. It is hard to overestimate the importance of such strength. Life is always fragile, at least emotionally, and almost all of us owe our endurance to others who have supported us. Frequently, we have formed circles of mutual helping with them. In parishes, clubs, informal neighborhood friendships, we have been Christ to one another. That is the church at its unpretentious best.

In its ministry to judgment, the church has sought to increase individuals' sense of conscience, right doctrine, and healthy morality. Maturity in Christian faith entails growth in these things. Unfortunately, the church has also retarded individuals' growth on occasion, by treating them as lifelong children. Indeed, it has sometimes sought undue influence over consciences. But the general service of speaking up for the truth, clarifying the implications of faith, and demonstrating mature commitment has been vigorous in most ages. Today it seems clear that believers and unbelievers alike look to the church for moral guidance. In the main, they want to hear a clear trumpet, want to see a definite stand. The international problems we suffer today are so interwoven with basic moral issues that church leaders have a special obligation to judge well. When they show the world the compassion and insight the gospel can nurture, they make a better case than worldly power can.

The fifth theme that Cooke traces through church history is ministry to sacramentality. It is intrinsic to church life that we express faith through special signs. The most central of these have come to be known as the "sacraments," but lesser ones ("sacramentals") have also been useful. We shall discuss the sacraments momentarily. Sacramentals, such as holy water, candles, and incense, express the Catholic conviction that matter and religion are basically good. By opposing "religion" to Christian faith, as something man-made to something God-given, certain Protestant schools have contested this Catholic conviction. Religion, they have argued, is but a subtle form of idolatry. It is human beings trying to bootstrap their way to God. The God of Jesus Christ condemns all such bootstrapping. He saves us purely by grace and faith. The Catholic response ought to show some nuance. It is true that religion can overemphasize what human beings do. It is true that it can detract from God's utter priority. But it need not, and often it has not. Often it has simply extended the principles of the Incarnation.

If God chose to appear in our midst, to incarnate grace in a concrete human nature, then the things of our space, time, and senses have a certain divine sanction. Therefore, it is fitting that we use holy water, candles, and incense, as it is fitting that we use bread, wine, and oil. Protestants sometimes forget that human words are as liable to idolatry as human works. The Bible itself can be substituted for God. So while Paul Tillich and others are right in being proud of the "Protestant Principle," which says that no symbol can ever represent God adequately, it would be wrong to deduce from that principle an antisacramental conclusion. It would be wrong because it would be inhuman. God has not made us pure spirits but persons of flesh and blood. Christ has not spoken to us over telstar but through words, gestures, and deeds that engage our memories, imaginations, senses, and minds. The best sacramentalism knows that its things of sense become most pregnant when they are set in a reverential silence. It knows that the third dimension of grace demands a backdrop of divine mystery. None of this, however, obviates a ministry to the church's sacramentality. All of it argues that music, art, and dance can serve the Lord well.

Of Cooke's five themes, ministry to Word and ministry to Sacrament ring most familiar. In some ecclesiologies, they are the actions that actually form the church. The church exists where the Word is rightly preached and the sacraments are rightly celebrated. So intrinsic are these two functions that without them there would be no church. Preaching is not so visible on the average Catholic's horizon as it is on the average Protestant's, so we need to spend a little time explaining its theological significance. Basically, it ought to be a way for God's Word to take present form and be a two-edged sword here and now. "God's Word" is both the Logos, which symbolizes eternal truth, and scripture. Drawing upon scripture, the preacher ought to expose its message of judgment-and-grace so concretely that listeners can grasp its import for their own lives. That means a solid exegesis of the biblical text, and a keen awareness of current problems.

Essentially, the message of Christian scripture is that God's love both shines a light too bright for our consciences to bear and gives us the strength to accept that light. The great moment of the story that dramatizes this message is Jesus' passover from death to life. Jesus was slain for our sins and raised for our justification. His dying on the cross is the permanent judgment God makes on our human condition, while his ascension to glory is the permanent pledge God gives that all will be well. We live now between that judgment and that pledge. Every one of our days calls them both into play. Therefore, the message of Christian scripture, its core good news, is always relevant. Therefore, the discerning preacher always has a job. Whether that preacher chooses to concentrate on family life, business ethics, or neighborhood crime, the love of God that both judges us and holds out hope is a beacon of illumination. People ought to come to church precisely to gain such illumination. They ought to find in church a preaching that rivets time-honored biblical light to the problems and aspirations of this day.

The sacramental ministry of the church has much the same finality. It exists to bring the message of God's love where people live right now. The two sacraments which, by ecumenical consensus, are most important are baptism and the eucharist. They deal, respectively, with entrance into Christian life and Christian life's nurture. Baptism has a motif of cleansing. The water we pour is as a washing from sin, a preparing for grace. When churches celebrated baptism by immersion, a second motif was clearer. That was going down with Christ in death, rising with Christ to new life. It marked the basic rhythm into which the new Christian had been set. A third baptismal motif was entrance into the Christian community. Baptism was the Christian rite of initiation, the passage to fresh status as God's child. Whereas before baptism one stood outside the community of those who could fully celebrate God's grace, after baptism he or she was part of a chosen race, a royal priesthood.

The eucharist recalled Jesus' last supper with his disciples before his death. As the synoptic gospels portray it, that supper climaxed when Jesus identified himself with the bread and wine. Henceforth, those humble elements would carry his own intimate being. Symbolically, they would remind his followers that he was their true food and drink. Moreover, the eucharistic meal drew on biblical notions of the messianic banquet. Jewish thought contemporary with Jesus often imagined the coming of God's anointed leader, who would bring a time of prosperity, as a joyous feasting. Thus, the camaraderie of table companions seemed a good figure for the early Christians' fellowship. Their faith in Jesus enabled them to think they already had the first fruits of messianic times. Each eucharist therefore became an occasion for celebrating the fulfillment already come, and for stirring hope that heaven held still better things.

From early times, however, there also was the notion that the eucharist commemorated Jesus' sacrifice. So intimately was the last supper tied with Jesus' death on the cross that his followers could not celebrate it without recalling the climax to Jesus' self-gift. By medieval times theologians had so emphasized this aspect that the eucharist became a sort of allegory in which the separation of the elements stood for the sundering of Jesus' body. In the same way, they had grown overly precise about Jesus' presence in the elements, sponsoring concern about drops and crumbs. Reformation controversies hardened the Catholic position on "transubstantiation," so that the symbolic character of the bread and wine grew flat. Too easily, therefore, ordinary Catholics saw the consecration as something magical. Relatedly, they often participated in the Mass or eucharistic devotions with an overly literal mind. For too many, each Mass repeated the sacrifice of Calvary, while the red vigil light on the dark altar signaled a "prisoner" waiting to hear their petitions.

Those positions are not so much wrong as excessive. Placed at center stage, they caused many Catholics to miss the joy of banqueting together, celebrating Jesus' resurrection, and renewing their sense of mission. Each eucharist ought indeed to call to mind Jesus' passover from ordinary life through death to resurrection, but it ought to do this in such a way as to proclaim good news. There is a time to mourn and a time to rejoice. There can even be a time to mourn and a time to rejoice in each liturgy. But the total configuration should emerge as a good news. Otherwise, we have no gospel. Without a gospel, a compelling good news, we also have little incentive to be missionary. One only leaves the eucharist fired with a desire to communicate faith to others if that eucharist has refreshed wonderful vistas. Feeling part of God's family, remembering the story of God's love, seeing again the paradigm of Jesus' generosity—scripture and sacrament must effect these positive experiences. It is a great disservice so to perform them that they leave participants bored. Much talk about Sunday "obligation" and concern for rubrics has indeed been a great disservice. It has been means again tripping up ends. The ends of eucharistic celebration are joy and gratitude. Each remembrance of the Lord "until he comes" ought to help us find being a Christian our prime treasure.

The same holds for the other sacraments. When we confirm, marry, ordain, forgive, or anoint, the good news again should appear. In Karl Rahner's theology, these actions are "occasional" expressions of the church's basic sacramentality, ones that apply it suitably to crises or celebrations that have a quality of here-and-now. As the eschatological community of salvation, the definitive social "place" where God's victorious love abides, the church mainly serves the world a living symbolization of what God has done, what God has made possible. Mainly, it serves such concern and wisdom that "God" and "salvation" become credible. The sacraments ought simply to "apply" this basic sacramentality to significant moments in the life cycle. Confirmation, for instance, ought to color it for the important occasion of a young person's coming of age. Marriage ought to color it for the important occasion of two people formalizing their love, their desire to share life totally. At ordination the coloring is leadership and service in the community. At penance it is forgiveness for sin, repentance over wrong-doing, rededication to self-denial. At anointing, finally, the coloring is strengthening the body and spirit to bear sickness or impending death bravely, peacefully, in confidence that God provides.

Debates about the number of the sacraments, who may participate in them, their precise forms, and so forth, are secondary. It is understandable that the church should have concerned itself with them, as with the rights of the local pastor, the money offerings people make, or proper pre-sacramental instruction, but it is scandalous that those concerns sometimes have loomed larger than celebrating God's love. In good pastoral practice, the church rushes forth to *serve* God's love, minister God's joy and peace. Its instinct then is to be secondary, subservient, helpful. People seeking forgiveness, or marrying, or burying their loved ones know this in their bones. The needs and hopes that bring them are full of God's grace. The best pastoral practice moves by faith in God's prevenient grace. Sensitive to the occasion, it does its best to provide that grace, that love, the most beautiful forms.

Of course, there are times when such a service seems impossible. We ourselves recall coming from church and being introduced to a couple whose four-year-old had just drowned. He was playing by a brook, during a family picnic, and before anyone noticed he was under and gone. The people had come to church dumbly, mutely, by sheer instinct. It was their place of blind recourse. Nothing we could say could diminish their awful pain. No pious words were apt. We could only cry with them, and pray God would hold things together. Some days later, burial prayers and a Mass gave their pain and faith some outlet. The music, the words of hope, the reminder that Christ has conquered death all soothed their raw depths. The people survived their great deprivation. They found strength to go on. Never have we felt more inadequate, and never have we seen more clearly God's priority. Others plant, we water, but only God gives the increase. Good pastoral practice sets that over every door.

There also are times when the minister meets so tepid a faith that giving the sacraments risks becoming a charade. For instance, there are people who marry in the church just to satisfy social convention, or who come to confession with little repentance. In such cases, one has to try to develop the good will implied in their sheer coming. If that fails, the people should be discouraged from the sacrament. Their actual dispositions make some other form more honest. But usually a little deftness in translating the sacrament's intent to common language can fan the spark of faith that brought them. Just about all who marry want a ceremony that expresses their hopes. Just about everyone who comes to confession wants to leave feeling better. You can't leave feeling better unless you confront what makes you feel bad. Usually, sympathetic questioning can make that confrontation possible. Similarly, sympathetic explanation usually can make the Christian view of marriage apt and lovely. Marriage is a great act of faith, and Christ gives faith so human a face that marrying in his name easily becomes attractive.

MODELS OF THE CHURCH

Thus far, we have implicitly described the church as a community, constituted by Word and Sacrament, that bodies forth God's love. There are other models of the church, however, and Avery Dulles has done ecumenical theology the service of outlining them clearly. For instance, the traditional Catholic view of the church stressed its institutional structure. From Pope to laity, it was a "perfect society" pyramidal in shape. God had equipped the church with the juridical powers necessary to its task; the work of the church's "officers" was to exercise those powers so that Christians found sanctification. Balancing this rather cold model was a view of the church as a mystical communion. This view had sizeable support from scripture, especially from Paul's doctrine of the Mystical Body, and it stressed the church's mystery. Sharing God's life, extending the Incarnation, Christians' deepest meaning was hidden with God in Christ. The grace that flowed from vine to branches was Christians' great treasure, whose riches would only be fully revealed on the last day. Prior to that, holy living was the main task.

In recent times a third model has gained prominence. It presents the church as the basic sacrament that bodies forth God's grace. This is the Rahnerian view we developed above. It makes the communal being-there of Christians a sign of the world's inmost meaning. For instance, both evolution and history can gain direction from incarnate Christian love. Fourth, however, theologians who are more political have pushed the church in the direction of secular service. For them the church ought to be an avant-garde who minister to the poor, support causes that are just, pressure secular society to cleanse its conscience. Antiwar and antinuclear Christians often see the church in this light. They speak of a commitment to human liberation, and they ring true biblically. God wants justice, as well as pure worship. God wants effective love of our neighbors, as well as love of herself.

A fifth model that Dulles describes focuses the church on heralding the gospel. For it preaching, proclamation, and missionizing are the key ecclesial tasks. This model, too, has New Testament warrant. For instance, the early church clearly felt impelled to spread the story of Jesus to the ends of the earth. "Evangelization" is the word we hear for this today, and evangelical Christians often put "mainline" types to shame by their greater commitment to the church's mission.

Dulles is careful to show that none of his models is exclusive. Each has its measure of truth, and the mystery of the church is such that all are necessary if a full ecclesiology is to emerge. There is an institutional side to the church, inevitably, but it ought to serve the *personal* ends Jesus had in mind. There is a profound mystical side, but it should not make the church purely spiritual—so hidden that it ignores politics or economics. Sacramentality is intrinsic to the church's life, but so too are preaching and public service, especially to the poor. The models therefore counsel "both/and." The church ought to be both in the world and uncoopted by the world. It ought to be both a community of worship and a community of political impact.

Let us develop these last two "oughts." If we correlate them with the twofold commandment, they marshal a case for a church centered on radical contemplation and radical politics. In both cases, the word "radical" does not mean "violent" but "going to the root." By its obedience to the commandment to love God with whole mind, heart, soul, and strength, the church ought to become a community of radical contemplation. Its liturgy and solitary prayer ought to intend God precisely as God. God precisely as God is a living mystery of love more intimate than we are to ourselves. It is the "atmosphere" in which we live, move, and have our being. For the most part, good liturgical or private prayer simply directs faith in this "atmospheric" God so that it becomes personal and passionate.

Giving the mystery a personal face, letting Jesus body forth its humanity, we can share with God all our concerns and hopes. To do this commonly, Christians of times past have found the stylized prayers of the liturgy helpful. The only proviso is to make them occur gracefully, simply, as expressions fresh and apt. Too much liturgical prayer loses real worship among external forms. Too little liturgical prayer is slow, spare, and poetic. Those who lead it, as those who share it, need to retrieve its "mystagogic" character. That was the Greek term for celebrating God's atmospheric nearness.

In the next section we shall deal with current ecumenical problems, but this aside on liturgical prayer prompts a personal recollection. We have been impressed by the initiation in prayer that regular attendance at Mass inculcates, for we have found in ecumenical situations that many Christians are uneasy with contemplation. That may not be true of Orthodox, who have a splendidly mystagogic liturgy, nor of many Anglicans and Lutherans. It does seem true of other Protestants. So much was this the case in one ecumenical gathering that the proposal to pray deeply together, using various traditions' liturgical forms, became a divisive battleground. The problem was not the legalities of intercommunion. For this group they were quite minor. The problem was ease or unease in using any liturgical forms, including those of a eucharistic meal. Where common use of scripture was no problem, and retreat to private solitude left members free, common movement through traditional ceremonies caused difficulties. Our group did not have a good sense of how to let formulaic words focus attention on the mysterious God. It did not know how to share words and feelings ringed by silence. As a result, it experienced Word and Sacrament as antitheses. One sub-group had grown up on pure preaching and could not celebrate sacra-ments easily. The other, largely Catholic, sub-group had to work to understand their difficulty.

Without an education in radical contemplation, then, the church is not likely to worship its way toward unity. Without a sense of what it means, concretely, to be a group that constantly redefines itself by common lifting of minds and hearts, the church will continue to underval-ue God's Spirit.

There is a parallel on the side of action. Without a commitment to radical politics the church is not likely to fulfill the second great com-mandment, to love one's neighbor as oneself. It must have in the forefront of its self-modeling a sense that it stands in the polis, the city-state, as a champion of justice. Precisely what tactics this implies will always be a matter of prudence. We are not arguing for a specific set of programs. We are arguing that honesty and love are both the quintessence of good social life and the church's public business. It takes little imagination or experience to realize that honesty and love are precisely what a vast number of public situations critically lack. Be it the local school board, the state's welfare program, or the nation's intelligence gathering, a depressing amount of public business occurs dishonestly, covertly, and with little love. "Hard ball" is the name of the political game, "realisti-cally." "Realistically," politics is a jungle of power plays, a war of movers and shakers. Unless the church stand over against this crippling philoso-phy, a vicious pragmatism will face little opposition.

Radical politics, politics that goes to the roots, deals with the condi-tions of human beings' social flourishing. We shall take a more leisurely look at it in the chapter on social justice and liberation. Here the point is its ecclesiological implications. In our opinion, the church has an obligation to use its accumulated wisdom, its economic resources, and its political contacts in self-conscious pursuit of human beings' social flourishing. It must oppose the things that depress human beings, that deprive them of necessities and growth. Thus, rapacious land use, oppres-sive labor practices, wanton crime, bad housing, poor education, and inadequate medical care are all targets for church concern. To its great credit, the church frequently does champion those who suffer such abuses. We merely urge the transposition of this *diakonia,* this humane service, more deeply into the church's self-conception.

It ought to be clearer than it usually is that being a Christian, a church member, entails forthright standing for honesty and love, forth-right defense of justice. What "honesty," "love," and "justice" mean in particular cases has to be determined on the spot. Good Christians can differ in their evaluations. But the basic commitment to champion what is true, what is compassionate, what binds up wounds, is so central to following Jesus that Christian faith directly entails it. There can be no proper Christian faith where belief is merely private. There can be no proper Christian faith where belief simply props the status quo. All Christian faith has to be prophetic and political, if it wants to affirm with Irenaeus that "God's glory is human beings fully alive."

Radically contemplative and radically political, the church ought finally to be a community of forgiveness and personal concern. Insofar as the deepest social problem we human beings face is the cycles of antagonism that give us our wars and destructive competitions, the church's prime sacramentality is its ability to reverse such cycles. Nowhere is its otherworldliness, its divinity, more evident than in its ministry of reconciliation. By the law of the cross, which Jesus embodied perfectly, the church shows a way out of human antagonism. Refusing to return hurt for hurt, Christians break the vicious cycles that give us our broken homes, our jungle politics, our international confrontations. This is terribly difficult work, and terribly important. Suffering evil in love, refusing to fuel the destructive flames, is clearly superhuman. We simply do not have the goodness, of ourselves, to love that well. Whenever it happens that people endure evil without acting evilly in return, we can be sure God's Spirit is active. In the depths of such purity, she has convinced someone that because God has been loving he or she should be loving in return.

That is the social, very practical, import of the meditation on Jesus, the contemplation of Jesus' cross, which Christian faith has sponsored through the centuries. It has been one of humanity's last resorts against what Hobbes saw when he said "*homo homini lupus*"—human beings are to one another as wolves. To be sure, there are dangers in meditations on Jesus, contemplations of Jesus' cross. All good things have dangers; these have led to doormat-ism or the expectation life will be brutal. In our opinion, however, such dangers weigh less than the advantages that accrue when the church keeps Jesus' suffering central. Jesus' suffering is God's answer to our human evil, as Jesus' resurrection is God's pledge the victory is won. Walking the way of the cross, suffering for what is right, Christians keep both God's answer and God's pledge shining. Without them, the world sinks toward total darkness.

We are well aware that this sort of talk, this focus on suffering evil in love, goes down hard. Even when it is clearly a counterpoint to good news and resurrectional joy, it costs more than any of us pays gladly. The price of great humanity seems impossible. We are not saints, and we resent the fact that a good world, a just society, now demands sainthood. Nonetheless, it is well for us to have the issues set clearly. The sooner we realize Christ's demands, our utter need of the Spirit, the sooner genuine faith comes in sight. There is so much ersatz, phoney Christian faith that most of us are misled. As Kierkegaard saw in the case of nineteenth-century Denmark, "Christendom" has taken two-thirds of the gospel away. We grow up in a culture putatively "Christian"; we think we know what the gospel implies. In fact, our culture has watered the gospel to bourgeois morality or patriotism. Suffering, forgiveness, the price of justice—they always break such "culture Christianity." Bourgeois morality or patriotism are too thin for real skating. Therefore, paradoxically enough, our deeper crises serve God's mercy. God will not abandon us to the superficial humanity bourgeois morality or patriotism intend. He will force us, through either creativity or suffering, to glimpse true human stature sometime.

The lesson for the church might be to focus more directly on the ministry of reconciliation. As Bernard Cooke has shown in reflecting on the sacrament of penance, the church's ministry in this sacrament equates judgment with reconciliation. That would seem to argue for its broader and more creative use. In ecumenical gatherings, for instance, penance could be coupled with eucharistic celebration, so that both Christians' common responsibility for their division and their substantial unity were acted out ritually. With but a little imagination, the sacrament of penance could serve other situations that cry out for healing, for reconciliation with both God and neighbor. In that case, "radical politics" would assume the humble form of tearing up rotten, misdirected roots and planting new beginnings. As well, it would properly involve Christians in one another's social welfare.

For example, what does a couple on the verge of divorce-by-superficiality most need? What do their relatives and friends most have to risk? Could it not be Christianizing "I never promised you a rose garden," warmly being willing to share the pain? If we stand by alienated spouses, or alienated children, or alienated friends, stubbornly refusing to let Christian love flee their courts, we do work like Jesus.' We often do it at cost, and we usually do it badly. But even to try to do it is to be the church at its best. Even to try to absorb human pain is to conform to the mind of Christ.

If this is so, models that encourage the church to legalism or impersonalism are simply noxious. The work of reconciliation, as the work of radical contemplation and radical politics, has to proceed in freedom and love. Studies we have seen of the current revision of Canon Law suggest church leaders are still far from realizing this. The code now likely to emerge remains impersonal, legalistic, a series of letters choking Christ's Spirit. It contrasts starkly with Jesus' way of dealing with people, and no reference to human waywardness can defend it. With such misunderstanding near its top, the church needs no enemies outside.

Once and for all, we have to realize there is no Christian authority functioning impersonally. Any body or officer claiming to represent God has to deal with individuals concretely. Be it divorces, dispensations from religious vows, sins petty or sins great, the minister of Christ's love must know the heart with which he or she deals. (So too with local political conditions, local business practices, national policies of defense.) Where one cannot deal with actual persons, one has recourse only to general principles, and general principles never brought anyone to penance or joy.

The most promising ecclesial development we've seen recently is the rise of what Latin Americans call *comunidades de base*. These are groups of small scale, where members can know one another well. Often they gather at peril, persecuted by unjust civil regimes. Their focus is a study of scripture and a eucharistic sharing that rivet faith on present circumstances. Regularly this spotlights Christ's cross. All try to listen to the Spirit from the heart. All try to muster the courage to walk Jesus' hard way, forgiving their enemies and persevering after justice. They are primed to bear one another's burdens. The joy of one is the joy of all. So, at least, do we idealize a community such as Ernesto Cardenal's Solentiname, for such communities are the best model of current church life we've seen.

Last, a word for those who do not enjoy a model local church. Many parishes are neither vital grass-roots communities nor places of impressive reconciliation. Having being bored by many sermons without insight, we know that many parishoners hear little of God's word. Having been depressed by lifeless eucharists, we know that many parishoners experience little sacramental joy. Usually, such failures are not the result of ill will or hypocrisy. In their bones, most priests and parishoners want something better. Gradually, however, busyness and distraction have taken their toll. The result is tepidity, perfunctoriness.

In such a case, we can only encourage individuals to take initiative and seek out a better community. If a better community cannot be found, it is probably time to start one. Even a handful of Christians who meet regularly to ruminate on scripture, share their religious experiences, and celebrate the Lord's Supper realizes the essence of the church. The essence of the church is sharing Jesus' faith, hope, and love. Is that not worth fighting for?

CATHOLIC ECUMENICAL PROBLEMS

Early in the twentieth century Protestants began a movement toward the reunion of their disparate churches. Subsequently, Orthodox and Roman Catholics joined in. Since Vatican II Catholics have had regular contacts with Protestants and Orthodox. In bilateral theological commissions, especially, they have made good progress in removing age-old differences. Presently, Catholic-Orthodox dialogue is promising. Other aspects of the ecumenical "movement" seem to have slumped. Nonetheless, any serious ecclesiology has to try to relate the splintered churches to the main church. The bibliography offers several historical treatments. Our focus here will be positive suggestions.

First, we assume that all Christians deeply desire reunion. There are signs this is not the case, but we read the general ecclesiology of the Catholic tradition as a judgment it should be. Scripturally, the classical text is John 17, where Jesus prays for his followers' unity. Traditionally, the first "mark" of the true church has been unity. The psychology of sectarian identity explains much of the initial opposition to reunion. Many groups define themselves by contradistinction to others. Separatist practices develop lives of their own, and power-bearers oppose change. It is understandable, then, that churches are reluctant to make the sacrifices full reunion demands. It is also sinful, if one takes division to be the church's prime failure—the prime excuse for the world not to believe.

Second, we leave the specifics of other churches' sins to themselves and concentrate on our own. How do we Catholics manifest a sinful will to remain divided from other members of Christ? In part we do this by suffering the psychodynamics just mentioned. Most American Catholics define themselves by distinction from Protestants. "We" have the Mass, the Pope, an unmarried clergy, nuns, an international orientation, a strict sexual morality, and other such emblems. "They" do not. More sophisticated Catholics make qualifications (Anglicans, Lutherans, and Orthodox have the Mass, essentially; Baptists can have a strict sexual morality), but in the main a "we" and "they" mentality prevails. Indeed, much of the confusion among ordinary Catholics since Vatican II stems from the diminishment of the clear-cut differences that feed such a mentality. With the Mass no longer in Latin, Friday no longer a day of abstinence, agitation for a married clergy, nuns in lay garb, the widespread practice of contraception, increased study of the Bible—with these developments one needs a program to discern the Catholics from the other guys.

We sympathize with the loss traditional Catholics feel today, but too much sympathy risks a desire to see the church remain divided. Brian Moore's slim novel *Catholics* shows too much sympathy, but it is splendid on the human costs change involves. In it traditional monks, called to obey radical changes of an imaginary Vatican IV, suffer a severe crisis of faith. The old ways have proven solid as a rock. The new ways (pivoted on an invitation to Buddhists!) are dubious indeed. In Moore's portrayal, unity is less valuable than the intensity possible when lines are rigid and doctrines stark.

Catholics puts part of the stand-off well. So do Walker Percy's *Love in the Ruins*, which mocks the spiritual wasteland we owe to the modern loss of faith, and the signers of the recent Hartford Appeal. Across denominational lines, the signers call on the church to repudiate American secularism (denial of a transcendent, other-worldly God). They have a good point, but also a severe problem. The good point is that secularism denatures human beings and denatures Christian faith. The severe problem is that they seem to think in doctrinal or propositional terms, and so to miss the real, existential battles.

If one believes God desires all persons' salvation, and has become available to all persons as the gracious mystery holding their lives, then determinations of "faith" or "unfaith" must be more than propositional. However desirable it is to have clear enunciations of what Christians believe, it is more imperative to have keen intuitions of God's free presence. Many persons who deny propositional presentations of God, Christ, considerable portions of traditional morality, and "transcendence" give rich evidence of being faithful to God's Spirit. If they are honest and loving, they "know" God. God is always more preconceptual than clearly grasped, always better evidenced by how one lives than by what one says. Those who do the truth come to God's light. Those who act lovingly manifest God's Spirit. Doctrines and names and uniforms are secondary. Primary is loving the divine mystery of life passionately and loving one's neighbor as oneself.

Let us take this back to ecumenism. Vatican II's *Decree On Ecumenism* (#11) speaks of a "hierarchy of truths." Some portions of Christian faith are more basic than others. Were we to concentrate on the basics and translate them into experiential terms, we might remove most obstacles to reunion. (We might also open Christianity to all persons of good will.) Rahner has argued that Christianity has three cardinal mysteries: Trinity, Grace, and Incarnation. We have followed him in trying to render these three mysteries contemporary and experiential. Were theologians to concentrate on such fundamentals, and church leaders to make them the touchstone of communion, they could cut through a dozen ecumenical roadblocks. For instance, Roman Catholics share the essence of life's meaning with anyone who, explicitly or implicitly, makes Jesus the decisive interpretation of how to live. Explicitly, all who confess Jesus to be Lord and Savior seem oriented to this interpretation. Implicitly, all who follow the twofold commandment, or suffer for justice, or accept death trustingly probably make an equivalent confession. At the least, a God as good as Jesus' Father interprets such generosity savingly.

Though Jesus surely is the center of Christianity, we might develop analogous approaches to the two other cardinal mysteries. The effort in all three cases would be to cut to the bone of what really is necessary for intercommunion. (By "intercommunion" we mean both a general sharing of church life and a specific sharing of the eucharist.) Behind it is the assumption that persons finally summarize themselves in what recent moral theologians have called a "fundamental option"—a basic yes or no to God. Such an option or core act is never fully clear, but the effort to get to it greatly clarifies the nub of the ecumenical matter: Does one live as Jesus did?

We suspect many Christian theologians lose a properly ruthless clarity because (a) they have not appropriated the notion of a hierarchy of Christian truths, (b) they do not hear the call to unity as a divine imperative, and (c) they live in a sort of ghetto and so do not realize how trivial the outside world finds Christians' differences. In the horizon of the world religions, for instance, all Christians hold far more in common than they hold apart. Simply by bowing to Jesus, their orientations toward nature, society, self, and God are all distinctive. This commonality appears all the stronger against a horizon of nonbelief. It is true that outsiders' observations on matters such as these have limited value, but many ordinary Christians share outsiders' impressions. People in many churches' pews feel theologians and church leaders diddle with nonessentials.

At the time of the separation of Eastern and Western Christianity (1054), a few doctrinal issues were important, but the major causes were differences of temperament, historical pressures, and disciplinary disagreements. At the time of the separation of Western Christianity into Protestant and Catholic camps, doctrinal matters bulked larger. The doctrinal differences between Orthodox and Catholics on the Trinity (does the Spirit proceed just from the Father or from the Son as well?) have diminished, but those on church government remain. The Reformation disputes about salvation by faith alone, scripture alone being Christianity's norm, the primacy of private conscience, the status of laypeople, and the like have withered away. In all these cases, theologians of both traditions have reached a solid reconciliation. Even more prickly issues, such as the place of Peter and the place of Mary, have largely been smoothed. Papal infallibility remains a sore point, but there too progress is possible, for recent historical studies have shown how this dogma received legitimately diverse interpretations. Globally speaking, then, the times are ripe for a new thrust toward unity. How might it come?

First, there would have to be great sensitivity to the questions of conscience that remain, and a way found to honor them. A powerful development of two convictions might succeed. One is God's will that Christians be one. The other is that there is a great difference between essentials and accidentals. Were essentials bare and profound enough, they could make almost all points of division accidental. For instance, among those who agree that Jesus is the decisive interpretation of human life, differences in understanding the eucharist seem accidental. Between transubstantiation and consubstantiation, or transubstantiation and symbolic interpretations, there need not be cause for division. All celebrate Jesus' decisiveness, which could suffice for communion. So too with papal primacy. It could be an accidental matter, requiring only an agreement that, historically and doctrinally, the Petrine ministry has been important.

The point to such analysis is not to skip over hard questions. It is to find a way to keep hard (but relatively secondary) questions from keeping Christians apart. We ought by now to be sophisticated enough to make the church a pluralistic community. Rahner sees the church of the future as pluralistic, and we see pluralism as an ecumenical gateway. Let the various traditions continue their distinctive ways, but let those distinctive ways not bulk larger than common faith in Jesus' decisiveness. Concretely, let them not keep Christians from sharing the same table, the same supper. The eucharist is the great sign of the church's communion. Including scripture, it bodies forth God's Word. Were the churches to sacrifice their self-identities sufficiently to allow (better, to encourage) intercommunion, they would virtually destroy their division. That single agreement could suffice.

A venerable Christian maxim says, "In necessary things, unity; in doubtful things, liberty; in all things, charity." Would that this maxim ruled Catholic practice. We shall see its application to the current crisis in the church's moral authority momentarily. Here its application to the ecumenical impasse need only be brief. First, only a few things in Christian faith are necessary. Though we would hold the twofold commandment and the three cardinal mysteries, all views reduce to the love necessary for salvation. Second, the doubtful things are correspondingly many. Only a little of "faith" or "order," to use the Protestant distinction, is at the top of the hierarchy of truths. Whether a church has an episcopal, presbyterial, or congregational authority, for instance, could be a matter of free choice, since it was such at the beginning. Third, exercising charity in all things means considering all other Christians friends, brothers and sisters, one's betters in parts of Christ's teaching or practice. If a Pope treats non-Catholics lovingly, as John XXIII did, he removes two-thirds of their problems. If Baptists and Anglicans treat one another lovingly, they need not worship apart. As many of our economic problems lodge in the will, so do many of our ecumenical problems. The mind and imagination open a way, but the will holds back. Ecumenical prayer for reunion therefore ought to be mainly a begging for conversion: Create in us, O God, a new will, that we may be one, as You and Jesus are.

CATHOLIC MORAL CRISES

There is a broader notion of ecumenism, where the focus is not simply Christians' reunion but improved relations with either all religionists or all persons of good will. For the dialogues implied there,

Christians have to translate their faith into "humanistic" terms. For instance, they have to show how the radical contemplation and radical politics that Jesus stimulates comprise a human program broad and deep. Catholics, for further instance, have to show how the papacy is a form of government that can work well—can be efficient, loving, and servant. For many persons of good will, the recent Popes' social encyclicals have been admirable exercises of religious governing and teaching authority. By their concern for the poor, for peace, for all that would reverse injustice, the Popes have won great respect. Outside the church, such teaching has been spadework preparing ecumenical (worldwide) good will. Unfortunately, the same is not true for much Catholic teaching about private morality. Critics both outside the church and in have judged that teaching lacking. This is the main point of our title "Catholic Moral Crises."

Sigmund Freud was a sort of Antichrist to church leaders early in this century, but when he described human health as the ability to love and to work, his psychoanalytic insight was keen. We shall consider the theology of work in the next chapter, when we deal with personal Christian living. Love pervades all Christian theology, since it is our best clue to God and grace, but here its connotation is erotic, as it was for Freud. Eros—love that pursues beauty and self-fulfillment—is central to the church's current moral crises. While we do not find Freud's diagnosis of human health complete (we would add politics and prayer), we do prefer his stress on eros to the church's avoidance of it. That is this section's theme.

Within the Catholic community, the pressing issues that now polarize the faithful radiate from eros. For intellectuals, tensions remain over what Lonergan calls "the pure desire to know." Do scientists, scholars, and artists have the right freely to pursue the beauty of truth? In the most acute case, do theologians have the right freely to pursue the beauty of revealed truth? This is a complex issue, for theologians who want to represent the church's tradition, or to serve its teaching office, have to be docile to the past and the magisterium. Nonetheless, unless Catholic faith encourages intellectual eros, it cannot be the humane "way" the best contemporary talent seeks. The God of Catholic faith must be a coruscant Truth, a luminous Beauty, a total sponsor of human creativity. Unless the church serves such a God, the most fully alive will have in conscience to spurn official membership. Without descending to invidious details, let us say that the magisterium needs to improve its image here.

However, the more popular issues that radiate from eros directly concern sex. It is abortion, divorce, contraception, celibacy, homosexuality, women's rights and ordination that stake off the area most controverted. In conservatives' eyes, recent theological trends have been a wholesale capitulation to secular hedonism. In liberals' eyes, the church must be hauled, kicking and screaming, into contemporary reality. There are points on each side, but a fair tally shows many good persons, sound in judgment and healthy in psyche, finding official Catholic sexual morality repressive. We do not have the space for all the ins and outs, so let us home to the heart of the matter: Is this finding valid? Does it explain much of the current malaise?

Earlier we quoted Andrew Greeley's opinion that the current crisis in the church, the brackets so many Catholics now place around portions of the hierarchy's teaching, flashed forth when Paul VI's *Humanae Vitae* reiterated the traditional ban on "artificial" contraception. Interpreters may disagree with Greeley's making *Humanae Vitae* the cause, considering it more a symptom, but few of them disagree with his using it as a benchmark. By all statistical indices, American Catholics have rejected *Humanae Vitae*. They simply do not find its teaching compelling. Some agree, others blindly obey, but the majority do not. For the majority, the encyclical is out of touch with both the realities of current family life and a mature view of human sexuality.

The current realities of family life—economic, psychological, feminist, and more—make birth control an imperative for most couples. A mature view of sexuality does not agree that every conjugal act has to be open to procreation, for it conceives morality in terms of basic options and overall goals, not individual acts. If a couple try to make their shared life fruitful in love, the number of children they have, or whether they have children at all, is optional. Having decided the best scenario for their particular marriage, they should take the best means to pursue it. Chemical or mechanical contraceptives are no more "artificial" than chemical or mechanical technology in farming or medicine. Nonchemical contraceptives are better, insofar as they avoid undesirable side effects, and new advances in rhythm may make it attractive. But few are drawn to rhythm by the argument that each act of intercourse has a right to pursue fertilization. That smacks of biologism—of separating organs and functions from the person they should subserve. One does not argue that the ear has a right to pursue hearing, and so veto earmuffs. Why should one argue that way for genital organs?

Though a majority of American Catholics say one shouldn't argue that way, it is instructive to probe the church's official position. On the positive side, there is a commendable concern for human life. Analogies between technological intervention in conception and technological intervention in farming or medicine limp, because neither farming nor most medicine directly involves the rise of a new human person. Insofar as reverence for the human person has been the hallmark of the church's social morality, *Humanae Vitae* is consistent with *Pacem in Terris* or *Populorum Progressio*.

Extrinsic to the contraceptive issue, but in fact crucially important, is the question of past teaching. When Paul VI received a majority report from his panel of experts that favored changing traditional prohibitions, he came into doctrinal crisis. Not seeing how he could depart from his predecessors' teaching without tearing magisterial authority apart, he chose to repeat the past prohibitions. Though neither they nor *Humanae Vitae* itself fulfilled the stringent conditions of infallibility (*ex cathedra*, formal pronouncement), the influence of the monarchical model of the church, where the Supreme Pontiff is the pyramid top directly connected to God, hedged Paul's freedom to change. Coupled with his positive concern to protect human life, this dubious ecclesiology proved more powerful than the advice of his experts.

A darker influence still was the traditional view that marriage has a twofold purpose, procreation and the spouses' mutual support. In that view, which has only fallen away in the last decade, procreation clearly was the primary end, and the secondary end of the spouses' mutual support often justified sexual relations as "a remedy for concupiscence." The apostle Paul had said it is better to marry than burn (1 Cor. 7:9), and many Catholic theologians, themselves unmarried, knew little about the profounder "support" conjugal sex can bring. They therefore relegated personal considerations to subordinate status, and saw contraception as the frustration of marriage's main reason to be. Leon Uris's novel of Northern Ireland, *Trinity*, suggests how this can destroy a marriage. In it an Irish-Catholic wife grows cold toward her husband because she is advised by her parish priest that sexual love and pleasure are sinful apart from a procreative intent. That opinion has a hefty forebear in Augustine, who also taught that original sin is passed along through intercourse. Thus, eros has had good grounds for thinking Catholic faith its enemy.

If contraception has been central in the recent moral crisis, divorce and abortion have also played a part. Each is at least as complex as contraception. A majority of church members do not support the official Catholic intransigence about divorce. Surveys show that a majority feel a person whose marriage has gone on the rocks often should be able to remarry. The official teaching has on its side Jesus' repudiation of divorce, but there is a counter-argument that Jesus did not mean to prop destructive situations, nor to forbid a second love that could help genuine faith. We commend church leaders for defending the ideal of lifelong fidelity, but perhaps they have been unecumenical in not countenancing Protestant and Orthodox experience, which has found some divorces charitable.

The majority of the Catholic populace do support the official condemnation of abortion. Though the statistics require some qualification, few Catholics would promote abortion. Whether they believe conception is the beginning of a true human person or not, the majority think the fetus a potential person having the right to life. We agree with this and find abortion tragic. However, we do not agree with many of the political tactics that zealous anti-abortionists adopt. The rights of the unborn, however pressing, are not the only consideration. There are persons of good will who believe abortion moral, and the argument that the poor suffer disproportionately from restrictive abortion legislation is persuasive. Thus, the vision that makes opposition to abortion a political candidate's rise or fall seems to us shortsighted.

We distinguish, then, between a religious claim on conscience and the politics proper to a pluralistic society. Having voiced their opinions, and lobbied decently, anti-abortionists ought to let the chips fall where they will. Had God been monomaniacal about evil, we would have no freedom. The best Catholic responses have been positive—for instance, offering reluctant mothers-to-be adoptive homes for their babies. Expanding this, perhaps Catholics could hasten the day when it would be acceptable for married couples to put up for adoption infants they did not plan to have or cannot raise happily.

With divorce and abortion, good Catholic instincts have somewhat foundered on eros, as they have with contraception. For if one finds erotic love an energy that can make human beings creative, happy, and generous, then one will not deny it to those whose first marriages go awry. We once knew a woman of thirty, mother of boys eight and five, whose husband divorced her for a sleeker model. She was close to a breakdown from unhappiness, so it was a significant "salvation" when she found a good man to love her and the children. For all four, the second marriage has been beneficial. Only legalism, powered by ignorance or fear of erotic love, could call it sinful. Similarly, ignorance or fear of erotic love plays in much failure to understand how two people can produce an unwanted child. Erotic love can include a desire to be fruitful in children, but it need not. The good it brings just the two lovers can suffice. It does not justify abortion, but it partly explains some abortions. Had the church been less fixated on procreation, more appreciative of personal eros, its response to abortion could have been more effective.

Celibacy, homosexuality, and women's rights in the church complete the roster we can handle here. By celibacy we mean the Catholic church law that requires priests to remain unmarried and sexually inactive. The Eastern church has never accepted this law. In the West it dates from the Council of Elvira (about 306), and the Protestant Reformers, with their scriptural orientation, subsequently rejected it. How much the celibacy of its clergy, who have been the bulk of its theologians, has shaped the Catholic church's views of sex, marriage, and women is hard to determine. Without being offensive, one may say it has some-times made them unexperiential or less than fully balanced. The canons on marriage in the Code of 1917 are one evidence for this judgment. The general impression of outsiders is another. For example, an eminent Jewish scholar sometimes begins classes with the observation that as Jews' preoccupations with food offer entry to their religious system, so do Catholics' preoccupations with sex. We suspect an unmarried clergy has benefited the Catholic church, allowing many ministers to travel or serve freely, but also has deprived it of experiences that could have made its theology and pastoral practice more realistic. Combining the late rise of celibacy with such deprivation, we believe a church that loves freedom would make it optional.

Parallel to the experiential deprivations the church has suffered from the compulsory celibacy of its clergy are the deprivations it has suffered from their all being male. Lately those sufferings have lessened, as more women have become theologians, and women's past ministries to the church, whether as single, religious, or married, have been crucial. But the fact that women have not been Catholic priests, or bearers of official power, has meant little feminine insight at the top. If God created us male and female, two sexes diversely equal, Catholic tradition has wob-bled one-sidedly. Lately that has caught up with us. Probably the greatest threat to the American church's credibility now is its structural sexism. Until women receive equal opportunity in things Catholic, those who consider sexism a sin will regard things Catholic warily. It does little good to bolster sexism by appeals to scripture or tradition, for that just makes them enemies of current standards of justice. Plato said we should call things godly because they are good, not call things good because they are "godly." Unless the Catholic church follows Plato's injunction, rejecting injustice wherever it occurs, it will oppose the good of God's having created us male and female.

The anti-eroticism one sees here is misogynism—fear of the feminine. Largely through male projection, the dangers in erotic energy are laid on women. Both Buddhist and Christian "fathers" made woman a temp-tress, the daughter of Mara (Satan) or the daughter of Eve. Augustine, Jerome, and Chrysostom were fonts of Christian misogynism, but the theologians who followed them were legion. The parallel reaction to homosexuals is sometimes called "homophobia." It is a convoluted phe-nomenon. We have little competence to bare its psychoanalytic roots, so our observations will be spare. Recently our city, Wichita, hosted a highly emotional debate over a city ordinance that had guaranteed cer-tain civil rights (protection from discrimination in housing, employment, restaurant service, etc.) to gays. Led by local Evangelicals and Catholics, a repeal movement brought the ordinance to a referendum, where it was rejected overwhelmingly. We calculated that if Wichita had the average percentage of gays (10 percent), and three-quarters of them voted to keep the ordinance, about 5 percent of the straight population voted to defend gays' civil rights. That is ominous. Even more ominous is its religious base. The Catholic bishop, who ordinarily keeps the lowest of profiles, was so agitated he made the front page. Legally or not, he would fire any professed homosexual, sexually active or not, from the Catholic school system.

As the recent book of John McNeill, one of our teachers, has shown, it is not certain that homosexuality is Christians' enemy. As local observation has shown, the churches' homophobia helps police harass gay people and sometimes ruin their lives. What allows human beings of purportedly Christian faith not only to injure other persons grievously but to cloak those injuries in the garb of religious virtue? What deep fear or perversion takes our kind so far from the twofold commandment, Jesus' kindness, or mere mental health? By its ugly fruits, homophobia shows itself Christ's antithesis.

By its ugly fruits, fear of eros or women shows itself biblical "flesh" (human nature closed to God). The Pauline exultation that *nothing* can separate us from God's love opposes all such fear. Without that exultation, faith in our founder has gone dead. In various permutations, the crux of the church's current moral crises is its unfaith, its fear. Freezing humanity and love, unfaith freezes church authority. The real authority of the Body of Christ is its experiential wisdom, its manifest power to save. The church Jesus sponsored is as far and as near as that, as far and as near as Jesus' love.

In visionary moments, Karl Rahner has ruminated about the shape of the Christian church in the future. The guiding thread in his ruminations has been the notion of "diaspora" (scatteredness). As the Jews were scattered after the destruction of Jerusalem in A.D. 70, so Christians increasingly seem scattered throughout a secular world. The hospitable basin of Western civilization called "Christendom" is no more. Though the passing of Christendom is by no means all loss (often Christendom confused faith with ethnicity), it does require a sober estimate of the Christian future. For Rahner the way of "life" passes through a bold, imaginative freedom. If common culture no longer supports Catholic faith, that faith must be chosen willingly. One happy result could be the development of a church without fear. Having little "position" or "influence" to lose, Catholics could choose church leaders for their lovableness and wisdom. They could be open to all species of truth (see Phil. 4:8), and so truly ecumenical, democratic, and constructively critical of society. They could make a church solid at the grass-roots and pluralistic. That is a church reminiscent of Paul's great vision—a community of Christ's freedom and love.

BIBLIOGRAPHY

Bassett, William W. "Canon Law and Reform: An Agenda for a New Beginning," in D. Tracy, H. Küng, and J. Metz, eds., *Toward Vatican III.* New York: Seabury, 1978, 196–213.

Berger, Peter L. and Neuhaus, Richard John, eds. *Against the World for the World: The Hartford Appeal and the Future of American Religion.* New York: Seabury, 1976.

Brown, Raymond E. *The Community of the Beloved Disciple.* New York: Paulist, 1979.

Brown, Raymond E., et al. eds. *Mary in the New Testament.* Philadelphia: Fortress, 1978.

Brown, Raymond E., et al. eds. *Peter in the New Testament.* Minneapolis/New York: Augsburg/Paulist, 1973.

Brown, Robert McAfee. *The Ecumenical Revolution.* Garden City, N.Y.: Doubleday, 1969.

Callahan, Daniel. *Abortion: Law, Choice & Morality.* New York: Macmillan, 1970.

Cardenal, Ernesto. *The Gospel in Solentiname.* Maryknoll, N.Y.: Orbis, 1978.

Cooke, Bernard. *Ministry to Word and Sacrament.* Philadelphia: Fortress, 1976.

Doherty, Dennis, ed. *Dimensions of Human Sexuality.* Garden City, N.Y.: Doubleday, 1979.

Dulles, Avery. *Models of the Church.* Garden City, N.Y.: Doubleday, 1974.

Dulles, Avery. *The Resilient Church.* Garden City, N.Y.: Doubleday, 1977.

Ford, John T. "Infallibility: Recent Studies," *Theological Studies,* 40/2, (June 1979), 273–305.

Granfield, Patrick. *The Papacy in Transition.* Garden City, N.Y.: Doubleday, 1980.

Green, Thomas J. "Revision of Canon Law: Theological Implications," *Theological Studies,* 40/4, (December 1979), 593–679.

Grollenberg, Lucas. *Paul.* Philadelphia: Westminister, 1978.

Kilmartin, Edward. *Toward Reunion: The Orthodox and Roman Catholic Churches.* New York: Paulist, 1979.

Kosnick, Anthony, et al. *Human Sexuality: New Directions in American Catholic Thought.* Garden City, N.Y.: Doubleday, 1979.

Küng, Hans. *Infallible? An Inquiry.* Garden City, N.Y.: Doubleday, Image, 1972.

Küng, Hans. *On Being a Christian.* New York: Pocket Books, 1978.

McKenzie, John. "Ministerial Structures in the New Testament," in H. Küng and W. Kasper, eds., *The Plurality of Ministries.* New York: Herder and Herder, 1972, 13–22.

McKenzie, John L. *The New Testament Without Illusion.* Chicago: Thomas More, 1980.

McNeill, John J. *The Church and the Homosexual.* New York: Pocket Books, 1978.

Moore, Brian. *Catholics.* New York: Holt, Rinehart and Winston, 1972.

Noonan, John T. Jr. *A Private Choice: Abortion in America in the Seventies.* New York: The Free Press, 1979.

Percy, Walker. *Love in the Ruins.* New York: Avon, 1978.

Rahner, Karl. *The Church and the Sacraments.* New York: Herder and Herder, 1963.

Rahner, Karl. *The Shape of the Church to Come.* New York: Seabury, 1974.

Personal Christian Living 7

OVERVIEW

Where the previous chapter dealt with ecclesial aspects of Christianity, this chapter deals with the Christian self. It begins with the current theological interest in story. We all have a tale to tell, and its substance is our self. History, biography, and autobiography converge on such telling, as does biblical narrative. For the individual, religious traditions have staged the life cycle with both ceremonies and received wisdom. The Hindu schema of four *ashramas* was a powerful influence on India. In the West, Christians spoke of three successive "ways." A major index of those ways' development was the sort of prayer each urged. The shift from purgative to illuminative living, for instance, often correlated with a move from meditation to contemplation. "Contemplation" has had various connotations in Christian history, and it is useful to explain them. The profoundest has been the mystics' effort to know God as God.

Some would argue that contemplation in the mystics' sense is bound to be elitist. Others, stressing the common foundation all Christian vocations have in baptism and grace, would not withhold it from any who find it attractive. For all persons—married or single, religious or lay—God does the contemplative calling. So prayer is a way the vocations share, but there are other ways they differ. For instance, by their vows religious oppose the "world," and by their service they confound it. Single persons' service can do the same, though singles now need a clearer theology of vocation. Married couples try to grow to one flesh, and to raise the next generation. For the latter task they need imaginative help, which could return us to the theology of story. Finally, all Christians contend with eros and agape, work, play, and nature. We reflect on these contentions briefly, trying to set them in the horizon of adventure.

A CATHOLIC THEOLOGY OF STORY

The self is an irreducible pole of reality, so any adequate theology pays the self careful attention. This runs the danger of egocentricity, but most religions are quick to put up safeguards. For example, Buddhism teaches that the ego is an illusion, and Christianity teaches that the ego must die. Moreover, the dangers of irrelevance are not less than the dangers of egocentricity, and without careful attention to the self theology would seem quite irrelevant. For the self is the concrete subject that revelation addresses, the concrete object of Jesus' saving concern. We begin, therefore, with a recent theological interest that takes the self's history seriously.

Fusing recent literary criticism with developmental psychology, Catholics have lately joined the movement of American theologians toward "story." Biblical theology, we have come to realize, often assumes a narrative mode. History, biography, and autobiography unfold as narratives. For this chapter on personal Christian living, autobiography seems most apposite. Communities tell tales of their past, of where they came from and how they grew, but so do individual selves. We have always known this instinctively; the modern move "inside," towards subjectivity, has only made it clearer. For instance, modern literature has studied the self's dramas, through stunning probes of memory, imagination, and the subconscious. Marcel Proust and James Joyce show the wealth such probes can retrieve. Psychoanalysis, whether Freudian or Jungian, has developed disciplined recall (anamnesis) and the analysis of dreams. Recent philosophy, both existentialist and phenomenological, has emphasized our temporality, which makes us "projects" or ineluctable dramas. Even history has come to fuse the social and the individual. William Clebsch's recent book, *Christianity in European History*, periodizes almost two thousand years according to representative Christian "types": a philosopher like Boethius, a prelate like Gregory.

Catholic theologians such as John Dunne and John Shea have made this story bear concretely on Christian faith. Searching God through personal space and time, they have brought "salvation history" to the individual life trajectory. They depend on schemas of the life cycle, such as Erik Erikson's, which theorize about the "typical" crises and strengths that childhood, adolescence, adulthood, and old age entail. Future theology of story likely will employ developmental studies directly focused on faith, such as James Fowler's. However, whatever the theoretical scaffolding, the prime matter of a Catholic theology of story should be a three-way interaction among personal temporal experience, Jesus' paradigmatic tale, and divine mystery. Let us elucidate this triad.

Placed in space and time, having a psychosomatic constitution that gives us a "world" and a march toward death, we human beings all indwell unique narratives. We all are both tellers and tales. What we become, the "I" we each bespeak, is a mixture of things done to us and things we do. In the beginning, our parents did the procreative thing—gave us our genetic material. We grew in a protective womb, symbiotic with our mothers, and then suffered the traumas of gasping for breath, fighting off light, being separate. It took many months for this separateness to take hold, many months for us to realize our independence. In the terrible twos we pushed off negatively. Each "no" and "I won't" flexed our little egos. And so it went, through schooling, the first job, the first love affair. Each day brought its quantum of experience, its packet of pressures and responses. If the guiding angels were good, we grew in an atmosphere of support. Our parents were loving, our neighborhood was safe. If mystery marked us for harder things, our home waters were brackish, our neighborhood was vicious. Either way, most of us kept struggling to develop, for that was our nature, our epigenetic fate. We postulated growth as we postulated food. Piaget and other observers of children make such postulates almost ironclad.

Typically, our scenarios have changed since "maturity." Under all the illusion, some autonomy has been real. We have made choices about what we would study, where we would work, whom we would date. However conditioned, they were in part our own creations. For example, though a person could have studied medicine, she considered literature more fulfilling. Though she could have studied literature academically, she chose creative writing. For her it made literature more compelling. Though she entertained Bob, mesomorphic and gabby, she responded to Jim, witty and quiet. So now she lives with Jim, shares parenthood with Jim, and wonders occasionally what "Mrs. Bob" is doing. In the morning, after the kids have exploded to the school bus, she sets aside her coffee and turns to the next chapter. What happens to green frog and pink pig, now that they have escaped wicked weasel? An hour later, when it is clear she should not have listened to pig and put them in the mudpuddle, she gazes at the blossoming cherry tree and daydreams. Would it have been better to go to grad school, to be lecturing now on the brothers Grimm? Would it have been better to have skipped words and fancies altogether, to be dissecting green frogs rather than imagining them? "Two roads diverged in a yellow wood"—and she sits by a cherry tree. "Time, time, time, what have you done to me? What have I done with you?"

The Christian introvert muses into Jesus. What did time do to Jesus? What did Jesus do with time? We know so little of Jesus' story, in terms of hard fact, that imagination leaps too willingly. From the earliest apocrypha, Christians have embellished the child Jesus. Under Gnostic influence, they made him a tiny Hercules, scattering giants and bringing

Satan low. For medievals, the child Jesus clung to Christopher, who carried him across the stream. But the core of Jesus' story, the firm reality reining fancy in, is his passion and death. Whatever his personal history, Jesus died on Calvary in witness to his God. Unto that end, he loved his Abba with whole mind, heart, soul, and strength. Unto that end, he loved his neighbors—his disciples, enemies, and us—as fellow children of God. The death that comes to all of us surely came to him early. He capped his thirty years with its conscious embrace. Feeling his Father's hands, he commended his spirit. His death has become our principal lesson. We are to use time to end as Jesus did, to pass into God.

Paul spoke of our lives being hidden with Christ in God. We are bound to find mysterious the Abba who seized Jesus. If God looms more imperatively at death, she has been with us from the beginning. No more than a nursing mother could the Spirit forget her charges. Various religious traditions have devised ideal stagings, as so to grow more intimate with divine mystery. Hindus, for example, have spoken of four *ashramas* or life stations. In youth, one should study with a guru, be apprenticed to a master. Obedient, poor, chaste, one should study the tradition, the Vedas, and learn from the master's model what the tradition concretely intends. When the tradition has become second nature, one should return to the world. Marrying, engaging in business, taking civic roles, one should let early virtue encloister. Sex and money, power and production—they will develop early virtue. So will responsibility for a child, or an elderly parent, or a family business.

By the time one's hair is grey and there are grandchildren, one has enough of family and business life. After mid-life, the spirit grows reflective. It wants time to sort things out, retreat from business. So the third classical stage was "forest dwelling." Leaving the world, one goes back to meditation. But whereas traditional truths first were long and wide, now they are very deep. Experience revealed the pervasiveness of desire. Long years made *karma* persuasive. If forest dwelling achieved the breakthrough it sought, there came enlightenment. At one with the universal Atman, the Spirit that is the world's soul, the realized Hindu ended as a wandering *sannyasin*, a sage stripped and free. The whole world was his oyster; he taught with a begging bowl. The message was: All life is instinct with God. Atman abides in every person and corner. Wisdom is union with Atman. The story has that happy ending.

Christian notions of the life cycle, the ideal faith-story, took a somewhat different direction. Because Jesus' life was a battleground of sin and love, Christian biography began with purgation from sin and ended with union through love. The purgative "way" was a path for beginners. Those who became serious about faith, who wanted to work at sanctity, set to asceticism. They disciplined the body through fasting, work, and stripes. They disciplined the mind, through meditation, study, and obedi-ence. The goal was to throw off old, selfish habits, to put on the "mind" of Christ. The goal was immersion in the tradition, filling up on biblical scenes.

In a few years, the generous could expect a transition. Habituated to external discipline and virtue, their next tasks were more interior. In prayer, they usually grew tired of meditation. Reflecting on traditional "truths," probing biblical scenes, making firm resolutions—it all seemed more and more arid. From the depths, the Spirit asked something sim-pler. "Abide, gaze, attend," she said. In a word, "contemplate." Where meditation was ratiocinative and discursive, contemplation was affective and collected. Where meditation stressed the mind, contemplation stressed the heart. For the transition sought "illumination." One wanted to "know" in a deep, interpersonal way. With Jesus, one wanted not head to head but heart to heart. Thus, the illuminative way tended to move down into darkness. Paradoxically, it overshadowed the mind, put thought in the shade. For slowly one was "understanding" that God is no thing. Slowly the mystery, the living too-fullness, was coming home.

Illumination had an energy to pervade one's whole life. Spouse, chil-dren, friends—they all became more complex, and so only graspable by great simplicity. The spouse unanalyzable one learned by embracing. The kids flying everywhere stayed apples of one's eye. Where an old friend had first been likeminded, now he or she was a fellow pilgrim. Moving together, friends communicated by silence as much as speech. They relied on one another unquestioningly, felt fully broken in. Now and then, light broke the cloud, to show how marvelous these simplicities were.

The denouement of the Christian story was the unitive way. More and more, mystery was the traveling companion. The God of Moses, with us as he would, became a present reality. If he chose, this was strictly mystical, strictly a thing undergone. Grasping the soul, God espoused it experientially. Delighted, the soul wanted more and more to decrease, that God be all in all. Delighted, the body felt tears of joy, overflowing gratitude for brother sun and sister moon. Ignatius's tears, Francis's joy, Teresa's nuptials blaze the unitive message. John Berchmans, one of the Jesuit "boy" saints, put unitive living humbly. He was playing billiards, the hagiographers say, when someone asked what he would do if he knew he were to die the next hour. "Keep playing billiards," he said. Whatever was honest, decent, permitted could carry God's presence. Whatever the purified spirit felt could be God's inspiration. All things were clean to the clean. Only evil minds would find them evil. The grace of union largely burned away concupiscence, making nature supple and transparent.

When we excavate from such Christian piety nuggets still relevent today, we find the centrality of God's mystery. Time unfolds from a Beginning to a Beyond. Our stories, with all their circumstantial specificity, are tales with a single moral. We have to learn to love life in face of death. On the way, we have to learn how living and dying are paradoxical. The seed that falls in the ground burgeons in the spring. By dying Jesus became Lord. The "good life," full of foam and gusto, may be a species of dying. The penthouse pad can imprison the spirit. So, illumination reflects from union toward purgation. All the Christian ways cross the cross. Yet Christian storytellers delight in resurrecting myth and symbol. They make us all hope to grow round and full. Then, we would be light as little children. Then, time could take us outside.

CONTEMPLATION

The Catholic notion of the three "ways" could have fit all church members, but few nonprofessionals appropriated it. For common folk, prayer and moral fidelity staked out an apparently more pedestrian way. Prayer was usually vocal: Our Father, Hail Mary, the Rosary. The moral fidelity was to the commandments, as the Catechism detailed them. But under such apparent simplicity, many grew spiritually wise. Tutored by the Spirit, they turned their prayers to loving converse, their morality to self-sacrifice. By the simplest of sapiential regimes—bare pondering of their experience—they achieved a balance between this-worldliness and other-worldliness, the now of grace and glory's not-yet.

Unpretentiously, such folk sometimes realized the pith of the Catholic matter. No matter how their experiences went, where their lives took them, it could turn to religious profit. Were they to achieve financial success, they could praise God for his bounties. Were they to suffer hard times, they could learn deeper detachment. Even their sins could work thanksgiving, as the Easter vigil sang: O happy fault, which merited so great and such a Redeemer. What anthropologist Robert Redfield called "the little tradition" also wrote "divine comedies." Many simple people, uneducated in express theology, let God purge them, enlighten them, fill more and more of their days. Living with a traditional Catholic family in Madrid, we saw this centuries-old pattern continuing. The widowed grandmother, wrinkled and all in black, spent her time in two occupations. She cooked the family's meals, and she prayed. If cooking took six hours each day, praying took more.

We do not say cooking and praying exhaust sanctity. Blaise Pascal, the brilliant seventeenth-century scientist, shows how traditional faith's journey can be many-sided. But we do find personal Catholicism implying serious prayer, on both historical and theological grounds. Historically, all professional religionists have been obligated to regular prayer, and all pious laity have been commended it. Theologically, prayer is probably the most distinctively religious act. That was comparativist Friedrich Heiler's opinion, and theological analysis confirms it. Lifting heart and mind to God, one directly limits the "world." Whether at public liturgy or private prie-dieu, the person who tries to pray enters the spiritual lists (combats). From Antony in the desert to the abbot of Moore's *Catholics*, serious prayer has meant trying one's convictions. Persevering prayer puts both God and self to the test. If nothing "happens" at prayer, no light or help appears, what can "God" mean? If nothing happens at prayer, how can the self claim faith? Expressly or not, many Catholics know these questions. That may be why many avoid serious prayer.

It is true that work can be prayerful. "To work is to pray" is a venerable monastic dictum. It is also true that contemplative prayer builds on natural dispositions. It comes more easily to old people than to young, to introverts than to extroverts. But there is solid testimony from humanistic psychology than maturity entails both interiority and exteriority, as there is solid testimony it entails both "masculine" and "feminine" traits. More compellingly, there is solid testimony from Christian experience that contemplation can enhance almost all personalities. If they find a proper form, almost all who believe can profit from quiet, imagination, centering, and peace. For that reason, contemplation is more than faith's testing. Through the centuries, it has also been faith's nurture.

But what is contemplation? How do we take it here? First, it is not meditation. Meditation, in Christian parlance, is the discursive mental work we mentioned above. (Eastern "meditation," as in Hinduism or Buddhism, is usually not discursive, so there is a Western-Eastern terminological difference.) As we mentioned above, contemplation often succeeds meditation, when the spirit grows weary with discursion. Second, contemplation may work in vocal prayer, or it may avoid express words. The simple faithful we tried to sketch above often prayed the Rosary throughout their lives. For many, however, the words were not the prime focus. Through the words, they sent affections to God. The words held their imaginations, kept them from daydreams or distractions. Or the words served slow pondering: Our *Father*—that God should be parental! Full of *grace*— that a teenage girl should bear God! Smoothed by long usage, the words slipped by while the heart held loving converse. Repeated vocal prayers did not grow wearisome, were not just empty clatter, because communion flowed beneath them. They could be empty clatter, as Rosaries at wakes or sing-song litanies show, but they did not have be. In the deeply religious, they were slow, loving, contemplative.

Third, contemplation could employ the senses and imagination. Loyola's *Spiritual Exercises* offer a clear method. Take a scene from the gospel—Jesus being baptized by John. Contemplate this scene, by applying each of your senses. See the water of the river Jordan. Note the steep hill behind. Watch Jesus go down before the Baptist. Mark his humility, his grace. Then hear what he and John tell one another. Listen to the changing of the guard. Was either of them shouting? Did the heavenly voice startle both? Then sniff the air, smell the water, catch the organic rushes. Feel the dirt of the shore, the texture of John's girdle, the tangle of Jesus' hair. Savor with Jesus the baptismal water. Taste his wet flowing robe. In every way, imagine yourself a contemporary, a witness to that happening. With little thought, few ideas, let your senses do the praying. Let them help you *be* there—poised, receptive, watchful, admiring. You are doing what thousands before you have done. You are gazing on the Lord—as illiterate peasants did in Chartres, following the stained glass stories; as street sweepers did in St. Peter's, before the "Pietà."

However, the heart of contemplative prayer has been its dark nights or clouds of unknowing. Dark nights recall John of the Cross. His classical writings on mysticism describe a cleansing of the senses that mediates between the purgative and illuminative ways, and a cleansing of the spirit that mediates between the illuminative and unitative ways. In both cases, the Spirit labors to teach us how God is God. During the dark night of the senses, she weans us from imagination, thought, and feelings. Though the stress contemplation places on love assumes that warmth and peace often come, the Spirit qualifies our enjoyment. In early spiritual experience, we need the support of consolation—bright ideas, good feelings, peak experiences. God gives these helps, but not so that we confuse them with divinity. Against our tendency to wrap snugly in consolation, the Spirit teaches us that consolation is God's *gift*. Against our tendency to be upset during "desolation" (the absence of consolation), she teaches us that patient fidelity purifies.

Thus, a primary "illumination" is the relativity of emotion. Emotion is a sensorium of God, an instrument of the Spirit, but it is not divinity. God's love is totally fulfilling, but to experience God's love totally, we have to put human selfishness aside. The depths of self-abnegation come in the dark night of the spirit. There the Spirit works our detachment not just from good feelings but from much "faith," "hope," and "love." Insofar as these theological virtues have not penetrated to our core, and so shone as utterly God's doing, we tend to lean on them, rather than purely on God. As good feelings can screen the self from God, so can imperfect virtue. Those whom God purifies profoundly, in the antechamber to the nuptial suite, are burned of all self-reliance. In John of the Cross' experience, they often feel abandoned. But the Spirit keeps a flame of love living, so that one day their embers reblaze. Then union is regular and amazing. Then they are free as a bird. The slightest attachment to things ungodly can keep the soul fettered, so the night of the spirit would raze all attachment.

There is profound wisdom in John's contemplative program, as in his complementary program of asceticism. The terminology of both programs, though, is rather forbidding. "Dark nights," "the ascent of Mount Carmel" may seem only for heroes. That is not so, but it shows the church's wisdom in encouraging other terminologies. One that recently has returned to favor stems from an anonymous fourteenth-century English classic, *The Cloud of Unknowing*. William Johnston and Basil Pennington are two current writers who have used the *Cloud* to good effect. Essentially, the *Cloud* describes the overshadowing of the mind that occurs when prayer becomes serious. Those drawn to an interior simplicity find that thoughts no longer satisfy. Their tendency is to become discouraged, and so to give up on prayer. A wise spiritual director will show them how their unease may be progress.

God wants a being-to-being relationship. Only that is deep enough to satisfy. To achieve that, God makes us dissatisfied with superficial relationships. Coming into our consciousness, the divine mystery wraps us in opaqueness. We cannot think God as such, because God as such is infinite, immense, too "thick." But we can entertain God as such, can attend and love. The *Cloud* advises just such attention. If it helps, we may take a simple word, such as "love" or "God," and use it to beat against the cloud. That way, we have an arrow to direct our attention. But whether we use an arrow or not, our whole effort ought to be to quiet down, to rest in the center. There God encourages a simple being-with. The *Cloud* is so convinced of the surpassing value of this being-with that it fights off all competitors. There is nothing we can do for our own salvation, or for the good of others, that compares with this direct communion. For the *Cloud*, it justifies contemplative living experientially.

If we set traditional teaching such as that of John of the Cross and the *Cloud* in a contemporary framework such as Rahner's, it becomes more testimony about divine mystery and grace. Rahner works from the slightly different Ignatian tradition, but his analyses of its times of "consolation," his going behind *The Spiritual Exercises*, takes other schools into account. We are so made that transparent communion with God is the core of our desire. Only God as God can meet the thrust of our minds and hearts, but God as God is too pure for our sin. So the Spirit loves us to a certain "adequacy." Contemplation is nothing more than that. Working, praying, making love, witnessing politically, we are called by the Spirit to open. When we open, God as God can both invade us and use us. When we open, our work, prayer, making love, and witnessing politically can be sacramental. "Opening," of course, is more than a bit of sleepy attention. At term, it is total generosity. But even those who don't reach total generosity, who are not nominees for canonization, can let time and the Spirit erode their spurious defenses. Even such as we can learn wisdom by suffering the Spirit.

The overwhelming value of contemplative prayer, then, is its foundation in bedrock essentials. If God is, and is *God*, then everything is theological. God is so encompassing that nothing is real apart from him. In other words, we can only see any entity or relation truthfully by estimating its Godwardness. For personal living, this means a happy condemnation to mystery. In the horizon of Christian grace, all stories would unfold a wonderful climax. If we would, we could hear invitations to a marriage. If we would, we could commune with the All. Were that to happen, every spot would be lovely. Were that to happen, the Father would be meat and drink. Jesus lived out from the Father. Contemplation can help us do the same.

MARRIAGE AND FAMILY LIFE

In dialectical method, the juxtaposition or conflict of a thesis and its antithesis is supposed to bring synthetic light. That comes to mind here, because following contemplation with family life will seem to many antithetical. Traditionally, vowed religious were the church's contemplatives. They had the leisure for instruction, asceticism, and lengthy prayer. Married people did well to make a morning offering, a noon Angelus, and an evening examination of conscience. "Now I lay me down to sleep, exhausted and distracted," the parent of six usually said. Thus, a first question for a contemporary Catholic theology of marriage and family life might be: Is contemplation possible? Testimony from many quarters shows it is. For instance, *The Wind Is Rising*, produced by the Quixote Center, has several essays by married people that deal with serious prayer. When they are convinced of its value, even harried parents can make time for quiet converse with God. Seizing some free time, when the kids are away or asleep, they focus all the whirl toward the cloud.

We begin with this conviction because marriage cannot be a solidly Christian vocation unless it has access to faith's deepest roots. Faith's deepest roots are God's love. God's love can come in many ways, but contemplation is prominent among them. Therefore, our theology of marriage will make it emerge compatible with contemplation. The "one flesh" two spouses intend will be as exciting an adventure, as rich a potentiality, as the other Christian vocations. As much as they, it will translate commending one's Spirit into God's care. We suspect few marriage counselors urge couples to share contemplation, but that just judges most counselors. Anyone who knows contemplation's power to reknit raveled sleeves of care will urge it enthusiastically. For the constant reclarification marriage needs, and the constant forgiveness, it is a marvelous resource.

Below we consider marital eros, and its link with *agape* (God's love). At that point, we connect this section with the moral crises discussed above. For the moment, though, let us stress family life. In the traditional finality of marriage, it was primary. Two persons came together that their love might issue children. Begetting children and raising them was marriage's prime reason-to-be. Bracketing the possible biologism, let us appropriate that view's wisdom. Children do externalize spouses' love. Their begetting and raising does weave cords of common concern. Anne Morrow Lindbergh's *Gift from the Sea* gave the past generation poetic lessons in such themes. Sensitive to time, she saw it fashioning marriage like

> an oyster, with small shells clinging to its humped back. Sprawling and uneven, it has the irregularity of something growing. It looks rather like the house of a big family, pushing out one addition after another to hold its teeming life—here a sleeping porch for children, and there is a veranda for the play-pen; here a garage for the extra car and there is a shed for the bicycles. [Lindbergh, p. 8o].

No matter that Lindbergh's images came from the upper class. Her basic insight obtained for all: Time shared is bonds woven. The great weavers of bonds are children.

Stereotypically, women have championed this wisdom. Like the old wicca (wise woman), they have kept close ties with nature. Nature is growing, including, organic. So would most traditional women have marriage be. Counter to men's absorption with work has been women's traditional absorption with children. Obviously, these assignments are up for grabs today. So, Christian theology of marriage has to make more of parenting for men, and of work for women, than it did in the past. We shall take up women's work at the end of this chapter. Men's parenting is apt right here.

In our view, parenting ideally involves both spouses, with their definite quotients of reason and emotion. If a father actually is more sober, let the tasks of sobriety be his. But if he actually is more tender-minded, then let the tasks of tender-mindedness be his. William James divided persons into tender- and tough-minded. We think a child needs, or at least profits from, a man who is rational and emotional and a woman who is the same. Apart from tasks biologically determined, such as nursing or giving birth, fatherhood and motherhood are mainly parenthood. Parenthood supervises sex-specific initiations, for we continue to have men's and women's groups, but its main task is giving physical and emotional support, inculcating tradition, and guiding offspring to freedom.

Most theologians attend little to children, and that is a loss. Were they to attend seriously, they might realize how much imagination good catechesis demands. The traditional catechisms, with their definitions and memory drills, were the work of underachievers. There is far more we might accomplish, had we the playfulness. For instance, there are wide extensions for the theology of story. Children all love stories, all respond to "once upon a time." Elie Wiesel has preserved for contemporary Jews the Hasidic genius with stories. Would that some disciple of Rahner had grown up in a Hasidic-like tradition. Then fairy tales that exorcise children's fears, rhymes that help them love language, might radiate from a Christian center. Then we might plunge to the psyche to baptize Oedipus and Electra. Theology can only gain by involving itself with creative imagination, and who better to keep it interesting than children? "Once upon a time," children know, is both now and never. It bears upon here and now, but it comes from Narnia, utopia, a place of free play. If little ones make up the Kingdom, it is a place of free play. The implication parents hear is that free play in the family assimilates it to the Kingdom.

All our duties are lighter when we recess regularly for free play. To be sure, there is a time for fact, and strict history. All time is not for free play. However, in an age of executive parents, fact needs little protection. It is creative intuition, healthy imagination, that the national endowments must guard. It is shared play, and the joy it nurtures, that many kids most need. Entering their play and education, we can do a great deal for their faith. We can show it is a happy sharing, with a church of good times.

The extensions to conjugal love are important. Previously, we sketched the dolors of Catholic anti-eroticism. Sexual play is something few Christians have handled well. For instance, few have known how to let love be randy. Few have applauded the male-female duel. The hint's of God's passion, the places in Hosea and the song of Solomon, most theologians have allegorized. Therefore, most bedrooms have turned out the lights.

Eros goes out to the beautiful and the fulfilling. That is obvious in sex, but true also in study and art. Are disorders in sexual eros more profound than those in study and art? Is that why we have fixated there? If we compared evils, our fixation has been a serious mistake. Indeed, our fixation has meant not letting people realize, from their own experience, how demanding erotic love becomes. To stand on its edge, and see more than one's own fulfillment, takes one toward agape. Many couples attain this, but few without much labor. The sadness Aristotle found after coition shows that sexual eros is no full religion. No finite good long satisfies, not even our intensest union. Only when intense union moves in a horizon of unrestricted love, open to God's more, can it finally not be frustrating. To ask it to be the whole, or even the prime, is to taste ashes of idolatry.

We put the matter of sexual union elliptically, that fine matters stay fine. The base line, though, is urging marital eros on. As Montessori kids explore and explore, so should married couples. Kindling their imaginations, tuning their wits, let them try all decent options. If God is a consuming fire, Plato was right to call eros a god. We have shown how a god can be an idol. Let us now show it a sacrament. In other words, let us bring conjugal eros to the sanctuary, as we have brought eating and drinking. Plunging the paschal candle into the baptismal water, let us celebrate Christ's union with the church.

RELIGIOUS AND SINGLE LIFE

In this section "religious life" means consecration to God through public vows of poverty, chastity, and obedience. Thus, it means monks, nuns, brothers, and many priests. Through church history, they have been an inestimable resource.

Their beginnings go back to the desert, where zealous Christians early sought relief from the world. More positively, they sought total absorption with God. From the Edict of Milan (313), which set Christians free from Roman persecution, religious life prospered. Community living became the rule, in both the East and the West, for experience showed that total absorption with God was not for the untutored.

It was for the poor. Taking Jesus' beatitudes and counsel seriously, early monks and nuns lived with few material things. They wanted to be free for prayer, service, or pilgrimage. Similarly, they wanted to be free of family burdens, and to fix all their eros on God. So they made Jesus' counsel of chastity matter of a second vow. Obedience capped their dedication, for it reached deep into the will. To follow the will of another, who stood for God and the common good, was deep asceticism.

Insofar as these vows go against worldly instincts, they spotlight the witness of religious' *being*. By what they are, or what they try to become, religious symbolize the eschaton. The eschaton is God's free consummation. It takes us outside the world. By their existential style, religious ought to witness that God surpasses the world, that the eschaton is heavenly. They ought ontologically to be a sort of scandal. Other, different, possessed of Jesus' peculiar values, religious confound a horizon limited to money, pleasure, and individual freedom. If the beholder's eye sees only those, they are offensive.

That is something of the tradition of religious' being. Complementing it, as action complements essence, have been religious' works. Their services, in schools, hospitals, missionary outposts and more, have been a second witness. Mother Teresa of Calcutta, now recognized worldwide through the Nobel Prize, is scion of a centuries-old line. Vincent de Paul, Louise de Marillac, and countless others embraced the poor wholeheartedly. It is Mother Teresa's charism to have embraced the most abject poor in an age of rampant luxury. The nations of the North, who can afford noble prizes, find her utterly unearthly. The nations of the South, who scarcely share earth with the North, find her one of their own. One need not embrace Mother Teresa's conservative theology to applaud her saintliness. She continues religious' venerable tradition of showing the average person biographic possibilities he or she probably never glimpsed.

In the contemporary context, religious face a cluster of serious problems. Since Vatican II, almost all groups have been preoccupied with "renewal." They have lost a significant fraction of their membership, and have felt somewhat adrift. That may be changing now, as though they have turned a corner. The authors of one sociologically based study, *Shaping the Coming Age of Religious Life*, think recent times represent a shift in the conception of religious life as drastic as that of great changes in the past. We suspect they are right. If the Vatican II ecclesiology of "the People of God" takes hold, so that lay Christians no longer consider themselves second-class, religious life will have to be chosen for intrinsic merits. That will probably diminish the number of religious, but deepen and clarify their vocation. The gift of religious vocation, especially that of virginity, may be rarer than past ages assumed. Nonetheless, when it brings persons to maturity and freedom for service, it is a most powerful index of God. Out of deep contemplation and supportive community lives, religious can put the heavenly Jerusalem on Main Street. All but the pure contemplatives among them want this; we pray church authorities grant them the freedom to attempt it.

Historically, single Catholics have received worse than short shrift. Neither "special" like religious, nor "normal" like married folk, they have easily seemed eccentric. "Bachelor" and "old maid," for instance, have not been positive terms. There are signs this is changing. Single Christians still grope for a theology of their vocation, but perhaps with less sense of inferiority. They draw ambiguous support from the common culture, where singles' economic clout and recreational needs have won considerable attention, and from the liberation of both women and gays. However, sexuality remains a pressing issue, for our moral theology doesn't quite know what to advise. From the past it receives the stern verdict that all intercourse outside marriage is grievously sinful. From the present it receives joshings that continence went out with the ark. The individual person has always had to make the final decision, but he or she does so today midst swirls of cultural confusion.

As the needle returns to the well-worn groove, so does this return us to eros. The close ties between sex and love, body and spirit, argue that traditional morality had much wisdom. The generous evidences of repression that traditional morality caused argue that things need to be more flexible now. In the absence of sufficient precisely contemporary experience, singles' sexual activity demands especially prudent discernment. When an attraction arises, honest prayer will be a giant help. Things *are* different because of cultural changes. Our travel, variety of work roles, awareness of psychological forces, and controls on fertility make us somewhat untraditional. Until the full implications of this change clarify, we have to go case by case.

A great advantage of being single is the freedom it can offer. Those who want to serve in a variety of situations, or who feel drawn to works especially absorbing, may find singleness God's provision. Dag Hammarskjöld working at the United Nations comes to mind. Slowly, he found that his work fit his (hard-won) faith and was a preoccupying vocation. Less dramatically, there comes to mind an aunt who spent forty years at the same hospital. She trained there as a student nurse and died there near retirement. For decades she lived in a single room, breakfasting for 7¢ a day. She was Santa Claus to several families, a good friend to dozens outside. If opportunity offered, she would travel on the shortest notice. If opportunity did not offer, she was content with the usual rounds. In time she took over the outpatient department, serving the poor from teeth to toes. With little incongruity, she would go from Lenten devotions to a clinic on V.D. Her main resource, though, was early morning Mass. Having nursed and buried her own mother, she moved into the nurses' home. From there it was but a skip to the chapel, and before long she was hearing Mass daily before dawn. Though she died rather young, there was a sense of fulfillment. Her solitude had not been loneliness, for she had a wealth of good deeds.

Passing from one vocation to another, especially through divorce or widowhood, throws many into a state they had not expected. Whatever the duration, it is something come from God. Christian providence justifies that conviction, but something more recent could enhance it. That is the understanding, again implicit in Vatican II's ecclesiology, that all the Christian vocations are more like than different. Whether one is married, a religious, or single, one is first a member of Christ. Catholics are a long ways from fully realizing this, as those who have left one state for another too often learn. One who leaves home for religious life can still suffer incomprehension. One who leaves religious life to marry can still find bitterness. The person, especially the woman, newly singled is a social irregularity. If divorced, she is almost a triple threat. This is a sad commentary on our faith. To find, for instance, that friends from religious life consider a common habit more important than a common faith is saddening, even angering. However right it is that religious shore one another up, a blindness to deeper things suggests idolatry. Analogues from other vocations suggest the same. Below our legitimate vocational differences, we ought to be neither Jew nor Gentile, slave nor free, male nor female, married, religious, nor single. We ought to be brothers and sisters.

WORK, PLAY, AND ECOLOGY

Work cuts across all the Christian vocations. Married persons work, inside and outside the home, to keep the family going. Religious work in fields and classrooms. Single persons staff offices, factories, schools, and hospitals. If Freud's dictum about human health is true concerning love, it is equally true concerning work. Unless they find their work satisfying, most persons do not write happy stories. Thus, the Genesis association of work with the fall does not mean we should help labor be painful. Rather, we often most clearly image God by interacting with materials, natural or human, creatively. By making, doing, serving, we redeem most of our time. Contemplation is a doing, as well as an undergoing, but here "work" will mean action. What light do Christian convictions shed on active work? What do they counsel for this great portion?

Though he is no friend of Marx, Eric Voegelin has given the author of *Das Kapital* his due regarding work. Marx was the first significant labor theoretician, the first to show work's economic and philosophical depths. As is common knowledge, his view was rather grim. The average laborer in industrial England was little better than chattel. It took that most advanced country decades to pass laws limiting laborers' hours. In the late eighteenth and early nineteenth centuries, 14- to 15-hour days were common. So, from simple observation, Marx saw that most persons experienced work as alienation. It stood between them and nature, them and society, them and their selves. Whereas the preindustrial artisan often had a satisfying craft, the factory worker did mindless tasks mid absolutely wretched working conditions. Mindlessness and damaging conditions continue in the United States today. The assembly line is a straight recipe for boredom; the conditions in the mills, steel or textile, remain hazardous. What keeps us from changing such obvious inhumaneness? Why does so much work continue alienation?

Much of the answer is greed. As a society, we place greater value on profit than on work-fulfillment. Therefore Christians, as well as Marxists, have summonses to lay on the unbridled capitalist's door. For, when he forced his hearers to choose between God and mammon, Jesus strongly bridled capitalism. Despite certain Christian bodies' close identification with capitalist drive and prosperity, bridling it remains the first Christian instinct. Fortunately, the brunt of recent Catholic social doctrine has played this trick in spades. From Leo XIII to John Paul II, Popes have qualified the rights of capitalism. In other creative theology, the verdict is even starker. Latin American theologians, for instance, see North American and European capitalism at the root of their people's poverty. Looking at Chile, they even see it alongside their people's politics: ITT and the CIA were instrumental in Allende's downfall.

More personally and positively, economists such as the Catholic E. F. Schumacher have proposed an excellent alternative. Schumacher's posthumous *Good Work* repeats themes from his early *Small Is Beautiful*, including those of its essay "Buddhist Economics." In that essay, a main point is simplicity. Too much Western work goes for complicated nonessentials. By contrast, the Buddhist ethic Schumacher learned about in Burma emphasized spareness and the worker's welfare. For example, clothing was to be functional and simple. True Buddhists would rather produce uncut cloth that can be draped elegantly than a peacock variety of high fashionables. The uncut cloth cost little, in time as well as money, and it did not feed vanity. More generally, what happened to the worker, and to the recipient of the work, was more important than what happened to the bank account. If either worker or recipient suffered diminishment (alienation), work had gone wrong somehow. For work ought to occasion spiritual growth. It ought to supply fundamental needs, advance the worker's self-expression, and encourage cooperation. Any other, negative, result would make work irrational, inhuman.

Studs Terkel's interviews with working people show that much Western work is indeed inhuman. From waitress to mechanic, his interlocutors are frustrated. Women suffer special frustrations, as do minorities. Sexism, rampant in our work culture, lays vicious hands on the clerical pool. Indeed, women suffer discrimination by every objective index. In pay, power, or promotion, they come up short. Things are changing slowly, but with great resistance. When it colludes with profit and power, sexism makes a diabolical trinity.

Thus a full equalization of women is potent theologically. If they stay free of male aberration, women managers might redeem business. For humane administration, as humane work overall, focuses first on persons. Women's current biologico-cultural inheritance tends to make a personal focus instinctive. It is the rare woman who is not sensitive interpersonally. It is the rare woman who, if not manipulated by male pressures, would not rather cooperate than compete. Were we to join feminist labor theory and Christian instinct like Schumacher's, we could be as critical as Marxists and far more constructive.

The Scott Bader Commonwealth, with which Schumacher was associated, tried to make work a fair sharing. It insisted on units of small scale, so that workers could know one another, and on an equitable distribution of profits. Schumacher lamented that a seven to one salary ratio, top to bottom, was the best Scott Bader could accomplish, but if you compare salaries of the head of ITT and a lowly clerk, you might call Scott Bader a paradise. At ITT the ratio would be about seventy to one.

Of course, salary ratios, and even working conditions, are not the whole story. Christian labor reform means doing all we can to make work a form of self-expression and service. Refusing to produce junk, insisting on quality, focusing on basic needs, we ought to work in the image of our parental God, who labors always for our growth and healing.

A hinge between work and play is poetry, the old fashioned *poesis*. Yesterday *poesis* meant "making"—crafting, fashioning, creating. Today it is little different: Good poets craft words to diamond hardness by disciplined imagination. Imagination has to well up from the unconscious, and then fit itself to forms or patterns. The free, finally uncontrollable welling-up is a species of play. The fitting to forms and patterns is more onerous, a species of work. So the poet is both player and worker, both *homo ludens* and *homo faber*. When you find your own *poesis*, you find half your imaging of God. Wisdom played before God, and then entered the form of creation.

It is hard to balance play and discipline in the study, even harder when the poet runs into business. In the study one must trick free fancy to make new suggestions—to reach back to childhood, wonder what if the farmer's daughter. . . . The tricks of discipline are less subtle, but equally important. Whoever said genius is ninety percent hard work knew wherof she spoke. Having set fancy free, one has to corral it and then set it to plowing. There is no substitute for regular plowing, if one wants either productivity or an uncramped style. Where method acting would discuss a scene two hours, Laurence Olivier would walk through it ten times. It is by doing that a creation plays out its potentials, by baking that dough becomes bread. So creative art, however humble, means lessons in freedom and discipline. Play stands on the side of freedom, work on the side of discipline, but they serve a common coinage. The happy worker loves labor for its creativity, plays onerously to advance the self.

There is little play when creativity runs into business. Too often those who bankroll innovation devour the revenues. As a rule, those who create receive ten percent, those who produce ninety. Even when lucre keeps its hands off creativity itself (which is far from always), its "reality" sours the play. To be sure, poetry is not simon-purity. Many artists have a walleye on the ledger. But those who give our culture its fresh vision have a childlike vulnerability. The play portion of their creativity, the fancy they mine, makes them confused by money and profits. What have they to do with making something beautiful? What do they know of the spirit or the muse?

Exercise is an area where the body can share in play. True, the body can share in play through sport or song or dance. But exercise is more democratic, demands fewer special skills. Also, it has venerable connections with religion, especially in the East.

If you run, swim, do aerobic dance, you can discipline your body to play. Once you're in shape, so your muscles don't protest, you can begin to go beyond the physical. Of course, the physical always remains, but there is also rhythm-unto-freedom, unto Zen no-mind or Chinese Tao. You can feel a groove, a circuit, a "way." When it comes, you start to run integrally. Your body does not fight your mind. Your spirit trains all your senses, recording the impact at your feet, the wind at your cheek, the purr of your pulminary engines. And it plays these recordings to the God of creation, who made matter for such communion.

By making play somatic, of the body, we have stumbled into nature, which summons ecology. "Ecology" can name something scientific, but also a cast of mind. Scientifically, it denotes the interdependencies of living systems: the marshlands and the tidewaters, the beavers and the trees. As a cast of mind, it conjures process theology: creation as a living web, an endless reticulation. The systems of nature move and interrelate, and we are systems of nature. In the wilderness this is beyond dispute, which argues for wilderness preservation. It is still persuasive in the Kansas Flint Hills, but by Kansas City you can start to lose it. Most of Chicago has lost it, and New York can barely remember. The urban way has a lot of amnesia, and that explains a great deal of pollution. However, the urban way also promotes higher culture, so there are solid questions of trade-off. Still, the judicious know that some trade-offs are crazy, some choices badly set. When we are asked to choose between nature and culture, ecology and art, we ought to suspect the askers. Too often they have an axe to grind, a business that will prosper. So let the listener beware: a smoggy ballet is no bargain.

Catholic theology has not been strong on ecological insight, as Christian theology in general has not. Lynn White's seminal article on the historical roots of the ecological crisis indicted Christians for an abusive attitude toward nature, and though respondents have lessened many of White's claims, they retain a kernel of explanation. The authors of Genesis had a pastoral past, but their successors went after culture. Zionism finally restored land to Jewish consciousness, but exile, diaspora, and prejudice long made it an alienation. The various stocks in the Christian pool brewed a European industriousness. Finding it profitable, they read Genesis as a writ to subdue the land, if need be by brutal plowing. The counter-paradigms, such as Benedictine stewardship and Franciscan naturalism, lost out in both farming and business. In the main, Western Christians grew up feeling superior to nature, which allowed them frequently to despoil it. The forests could fall, the buffalo thin, in the name of Westward-hoing. One wonders, even, whether Amerindians weren't decimated because their closeness to nature made them appear somehow subhuman to whites.

Amerindians, or course, were more "ecological" than their white antagonists. Though some of our lore about them is unhelpfully romantic, it is true that they honored nature. The plant to be cut, the deer to be shot merited an explanation. In the hard cycle of lives, where one survived off the other, hunting kept a poignant sadness. Similarly, farming kept a touching gentleness, for it dealt with a pregnant mother. To tread heavily on the Earth in the days of Spring was to injure a living matron. When we consider the American earth today, we do well to remember that history. The strip-miner's myth has ousted the myth of the matron, and what has taken her place? Along Love Canal, beside Niagara Falls, people grow leaden from chemical pollution. There is no life where their children play, no water still untoxic. Farther west the story changes its scene, but sings of acid rain.

Though its own practice cautions against great expectations, Eastern religion might be an ecological ally. The Logos and Wisdom emerged as the Tao made nature China's prime divinity. Return to nature, Lao Tzu said, if you wish to find your own essence. The uncarved block is the better self, the Tao moves patiently like water. Chuang Tzu had the same naturalism but he put it more pungently. It is better to drag your tail in the mud, to be contented like the turtle. If you drag your tail to court, you are more than likely to lose it. As a Zen Buddhist finds nature one, so does a Chuangtzuian Taoist. In any logic worth its salt, that would make for an ecological religion. Contemporary Japan shows that scarcity of logic is not peculiarly Western—smog may soon erode its rock gardens.

For Catholic theologians ecological reform will be hard, if our population continues to be urban. Without a firm footing in the land, we shall have to work through pollution's human tolls. Still, those are manifest enough for the bells to ring, the wise to get to typing. Jesus cannot be pantocrator, Lord of all, if the all is rotten and polluted. The air we breathe, the food we eat, the water we swim must be purer. If that means an economy of steady-state, an advance toward Ernest Callenbach's "Ecotopia," so be it. By its fruits, the economics of "bigger is better" shows itself doubtful. So does the theology of "nature is a slave, a pawn of our good pleasure."

BIBLIOGRAPHY

Bettelheim, Bruno. *The Uses of Enchantment: The Meaning and Importance of Fairy Tales.* New York: Vintage, 1977.
Cada, Lawrence, et al. *Shaping the Coming Age of Religious Life.* New York: Seabury, 1979.

Callahan, William and Cardman, Francine, eds. *The Wind Is Rising*. Hyattsville, Md.: Quixote Center, 1978.

Callenbach, Ernest. *Ecotopia*. New York: Bantam, 1977.

Carmody, John. *The Progressive Pilgrim*. Notre Dame, Ind.: Fides/Claretian, 1980.

Clebsch, William A. *Christianity in European History*. New York: Oxford, 1979.

Dunne, John S. *A Search for God in Time and Memory*. New York: Macmillan, 1969.

Erikson, Erik H. ed. *Adulthood*. New York: Norton, 1978.

Fowler, James and Lovin, Robin. *Trajectories in Faith*. Nashville, Tenn.: Abingdon, 1980.

John of the Cross. *Collected Works*. Washington, D.C.: Institute of Carmelite Studies, 1973.

Johnston, William, ed. *The Cloud of Unknowing*. Garden City, N.Y.: Doubleday, 1973.

Johnston, William. *The Inner Eye of Love*. New York: Harper & Row, 1978.

Lindbergh, Anne Morrow. *Gift from the Sea*. New York: Vintage, 1955.

McDonagh, Enda. "New Horizons in Christian Marriage," in his *Doing the Truth* (Notre Dame, Ind.: University of Notre Dame Press, 1979), 168–178.

Milhaven, John Giles. "Conjugal Sexual Love and Contemporary Moral Theology," *Theological Studies*, 35 (1974), 692–710.

Pennington, M. Basil. *Daily We Touch Him*. Garden City, N.Y.: Doubleday, 1977.

Rahner, Hugo. *Man at Play*. New York: Herder and Herder, 1972.

Rahner, Karl. *Spiritual Exercises*. New York: Herder and Herder, 1965.

Rahner, Karl. *The Dynamic Element in the Church*. New York: Herder and Herder, 1964.

Rahner, Karl. *Theological Investigations, XVI: Experience of the Spirit*. New York: Seabury, 1979.

Schumacher, E. F. *Good Work*. New York: Harper & Row, 1979.

Schumacher, E. F. *Small is Beautiful*. New York: Harper & Row, 1973.

Shea, John. *Stories of God*. Chicago: Thomas More, 1978.

Sheehan, George. *Dr. Sheehan on Running*. New York: Bantam, 1978.

Spring, David and Spring, Eileen, eds. *Ecology and Religion in History*. New York: Harper & Row, 1974.

Stevens, Edward. *Business Ethics*. New York: Paulist, 1979.

Terkel, Studs. *Working*. New York: Pantheon Books, 1974.

Voegelin, Eric. *From Enlightenment to Revolution*. Durham, N.C.: Duke University Press, 1975.

Weaver, Mary Jo. "Singleness," *Commonweal*, CVI/19 (October 26, 1979), 588–591.

White, Lynn. "The Historical Roots of Our Ecological Crisis," in D. Spring and E. Spring, eds., *Ecology and Religion in History* (New York: Harper & Row, 1974).

Whitehead, Evelyn and Whitehead, James. *Christian Life Patterns*. Garden City, N.Y.: Doubleday, 1979.

Social Justice and Liberation 8

OVERVIEW

Although Catholic ethics has always had a social dimension, that dimension has come to the fore in the last ninety years. Perhaps its best known form is the stream of papal encyclicals begun by Leo XIII in 1891. We use a recent study of their central focus, the dignity of the human person, to present traditional Catholic teaching on social justice.

Through more individualistic ventures, theologians on the Continent and in the Americas have pointedly turned "social" into "political." The European stimulus in this direction has been dialogue with Marxist theory. North American political theology also has had a theoretical interest, but the liberation movements of blacks and women probably have been more influential. Racism and sexism are pervasive social flaws that show injustice's deep biases. From their experiences of injustice, both blacks and women have gained special insight into the scriptural thesis that God sides with the poor.

It is Latin American liberation theology, however, that has formed the most influential Catholic school. The document recently issued by the Latin American Bishop's Conference from its meeting at Puebla, Mexico, is a compromise piece, but it clearly sounds a call for liberation. That call means a firm identification with the poor. It also means naming the evil-doers who have made South America a land of dictators and repressors. In the blood of many martyrs, liberation theologians see a paradoxical sanguinity. If Latin Americans are willing to die for the truths their grass-roots church experiences and consciousness-raising reveal, there is hope for the rest of the Catholic world. The economic and political oppressions that afflict Latin America have mirror images all over the Southern Hemisphere, and behind most of them stand capitalist influences from the Northern Hemisphere. So the Latin American struggle is our own.

TRADITIONAL CATHOLIC TEACHING ON SOCIAL JUSTICE

Social justice has been on Pope John Paul II's mind from the beginning of his pontificate, as we shall see more directly when we deal with him in Appendix II. In part this interest reflects his pastoral experience in Poland, where a Communist regime forces Catholics to reflect on the socio-political features of their faith very carefully. In part it also reflects his need to respond to movements in Europe and Latin America that insist on the gospel's political impact. So long as John Paul II influences Catholic theology, then, the social dimension of traditional faith will likely be front and center.

In treating the materials of this chapter, we depart somewhat from a Rahnerian outline of current Catholic theology. Though Rahner has long stressed the historical character of human existence and long admitted its social side, politics and liberation have not bulked large on his horizon. That has provoked a sizeable reaction in some of his disciples, as we shall see below. He has responded to their criticism quite favorably, allowing that Christian visions such as his own do have to develop a theology of politics, and even signing protest statements, such as that which a group of German theologians issued on the eve (Fall 1978) of the Latin American bishops' meeting at Puebla to oppose manipulations by the right.

The reason systematic theologians such as Rahner did not pay much attention to social issues in the past was the tract division of the theology they inherited. If one worked in dogmatics or systematics, one paid little attention to biblical studies or moral theology, and vice versa. This division has broken down, as our survey of theological methodologies in the next chapter will show. Nonetheless, it had a shaping effect on theologians of Rahner's generation, making social justice the province of moralists. The moralists had considerable material on which to concentrate, for from Pope Leo XIII on Rome became interested in questions of labor, justice, and international order. The stimulus to this interest was historical: Europe was in the throes of various social changes. The upheavals of 1848, the year of Marx's *Communist Manifesto*, brought home to conservatives that the established order was in crisis, and by 1891 Leo, himself temperamentally quite conservative, had realized social justice bears heavily on Catholic faith. Since his *Rerum Novarum* of that year, papal theology has distinguished itself through a series of increasingly more visionary social statements.

David Hollenbach's recent *Claims in Conflict* focuses on the central issue organizing the series: the dignity of the human person. On the way to a creative dialogue with non-Catholic theories of human rights, Hollenbach provides a concise history of the recent Catholic tradition. For Leo XIII the watchword was, "Man precedes the State." In other words, political and legal institutions are good or evil by the standard of what they do to human beings. They exist for human persons, not vice versa. On the other hand, Leo opposed democratic theories of the state. Arguing from natural law tradition, which sees rights and duties built into human nature by God, he contested the notion that political power and moral values are the product of humans' free choice. Rather, there is an objective order that balances human voluntarism and moral restraint. Reading this position in the context of its times, one can see an effort to hold a middle ground between tyrannies of either the right or the left.

Rerum Novarum also took aim at economic abuses. By its time industrialism had shown the abuses to which it was liable, and many had grown aware of workers' oppression. Leo argued in defense of workers that systems that stripped them of dignity, for instance by paying wages that failed to allow a decent living, stood condemned as offspring of greed. The next innovator in Catholic social teaching, Pius XI, worked in a historical context dominated by three contemporary developments: the Great Depression, the consolidation of the Russian Revolution of 1917 into a functional Communist regime, and the rise of fascism in Italy and Germany. *Quadragesimo Anno,* issued in commemoration of the fortieth anniversary of *Rerum Novarum,* combined a reaffirmation of the dignity of the human person with a keen look at the economics of depression. Its principal protest was directed against vast disparities in human wealth, and it championed the proletariat. Though Pius rejected a Marxist-Leninist framework, in which the proletariat were counseled to class warfare, he condemned the capitalist tendency to reduce persons to their economic functions. The implications of the "Body of Christ" demanded that the worker be more than an interchangeable part of a huge machine. By this same conviction Pius opposed National Socialism. "Mit Brennender Sorge" (1937) rejected Nazism because it subordinated persons to idolatrous reifications of the state, the Aryan race, and Germany's going structures of power.

Deeply influenced by World War II, Pius XII made the central traditional tenet, the dignity of the human person, more explicit still. Developing natural law theory, which had the danger of seeming rather extrinsic and wooden, he taught that all forms of social life are essentially moral relationships. From that teaching it follows that decent social life—decent politics, economics, and culture—is impossible without conceiving of the state as a community of morally responsible citizens. That might have sounded utopian, had he not issued a balancing call for legal and institutional structures that could give such a community firm articulation. Moreover, Pius XII went into some detail on the specific rights that human dignity entails. His Christmas address of 1942, for instance, spoke of rights to maintain and develop one's bodily, intellectual, moral, and religious dimensions; the right to exercise religion through worship and charitable works; the right to marry and procreate;

the right to work; the right freely to choose one's state in life (e.g., the right to answer a religious vocation); the right to use material goods; the rights to exist, have a good name, and develop one's own culture and national character; and the right to have international treaties observed and natural law respected.

The next leap forward in Catholic social teaching came with John XXIII, whose relatively brief pontificate not only begot the influential encyclicals *Mater et Magistra* (1961) and *Pacem in Terris* (1963), but also provided an international gathering, the Second Vatican Council, that could imprint them on Catholic leaders' consciousness. The Johannine encyclicals sailed the human rights channel full speed ahead. Indeed, John responded to the growing strength of the Italian Communist Party by admitting that communist teachings could have "elements that are positive and deserving of approval." His encyclicals were more sophisticated than his predecessors' in other ways, too, acknowledging the complexity of both national and international social relationships. In fact, *Pacem in Terris* was a watershed in Catholic social teaching, because it applied the fundamental criterion, the welfare of the human person, to the various zones of social relationship systematically. From their humanistic center, civil, political, social, and economic rights form a web. Persons are so intrinsically social that this web constitutes much of their well-being.

During the Second Vatican Council the bishops assembled gave considerable attention to social justice. Two documents were special fruits of such attention, that on the church in the modern world and that on religious liberty. In situating the church in the modern world, the Council more clearly came to grips with the historicity of social situations than previous Catholic teaching had. Whereas the scholastic framework of the previous teaching had a tendency, from its roots in classicist thought, to abstract from temporality and change, the conciliar document faced change squarely. All specific situations in which justice is to be achieved both suffer the impress of the past and partake of current consciousness. Realizing this, contemporary human beings are tempted to relativism. The bishops want to avoid relativism, but they also want to sympathize with the confusions and difficulties rapid change brings. Concrete social morality often will be a matter of prudence and discernment. For instance, anyone trying to achieve justice through the political apparatus of a pluralistic Western society will face compromise every day. Anyone pondering the ethical implications of rapidly moving areas like biological or chemical research will have to think creatively.

The Council's statement on religious liberty both explicitated the implications of the current fluid situation for Catholic social doctrine and removed a blemish of the past tradition. The implications of social change boiled down to a vote for *development*. Catholic social teaching should change and grow. It has to recognize the empirical truths of new situations and advance its core convictions to illumine them. The blemish on past Catholic human rights doctrine was its restriction on religious liberty. Though that doctrine had nuance, outsiders had grounds for their impression that when Catholics were a minority in a given population, they spoke out loudly for the right to worship, educate their children in parochial schools, and decently to proselytize. When they were a majority, they wanted the special rights of an established religion and, consequently, a curtailment of the competition. For instance, in Spain the rights of Protestants were distinctly inferior to those of Catholics. The conciliar document made it clear that all persons have the right to form their religious consciences freely and express them publicly. Americans were especially proud of this doctrinal development, for their experience in a pluralistic situation, as argued elegantly by the Jesuit John Courtney Murray, was the strongest force provoking it. Murray had come under a cloud in the 1940s and been prohibited from teaching on church-state relations. The conciliar decree on religious liberty was his great vindication.

During the pontificate of Paul VI third-world peoples received special attention. In *Populorum Progressio* (1967) and *Octagesima Adveniens* (1971), Paul brought the historicity of social institutions to bear on the problem of underdevelopment. *Populorum Progressio* is subtle, sophisticated, and tentative, as the complexity of its problems demands. Development ought to occur on all levels, economic and spiritual, and it ought to take into account the worldwide community of nations. Thus, Christian conscience constrains rich nations to limit economic expansion that would, willy-nilly, depress or abuse poor nations. God gives the goods of the earth for all the earth's people. In many cases, the name of poorer people's justice will be development towards economic parity. *Octagesima Adveniens*, written to commemorate the eightieth anniversary of *Rerum Novarum*, acknowledges the conflicts developmental justice can encounter. In that regard, it offers a limited approval of Marxist and socialist tools of analysis, distinguishing them from their ideological or philosophical matrices. A stimulus to such detente was the Marxist-Christian dialogue that flourished in Europe in the 1960s.

The 1971 Synod of Bishops affirmed many of the principles in Paul's encyclicals, as well as their global horizon. Also, it offered a new version of the old criterion of the human person's dignity. When a society marginalizes a significant number of persons, injustice clearly obtains. Removing marginalization, or increasing participation, therefore offers a great tool, both theoretical and practical, for advancing social justice.

The recent Popes' social teachings have a new spokesman in John Paul II, as his encyclical *Redemptor Hominis* and his address to the Latin American bishops at Puebla (both of which we consider in Appendix

II) show. More compelling even than cogent social theory, though, has been the example of individuals and agencies that have put Catholic faith in the oneness of the human family into practice. Mother Teresa of Calcutta has deservedly received great attention for her self-sacrifice on behalf of India's most wretched poor, but she has been preceded over the centuries by hundreds of nurses and missionaries similarly dedicated. In the United States the relief agencies of many Catholic dioceses have distinguished themselves by their labors on behalf of the indigent, most recently on behalf of Vietnamese refugees. Indeed, the international character of Roman Catholicism makes its charities an effective reminder that we human billions share a single small and fragile planet. And whatever is done for starving Africans or Cambodians is an act pregnant with faith, for, as Rahner has shown, in the final analysis the love of neighbor and the love of God are one.

It remains, then, only to tally the strengths and weaknesses of the recent Popes' social doctrine. In our estimation, the strengths of the recent "gospel of peace and justice," as Joseph Gremillion has named Catholic social teaching since John XXIII, include the following: a world-wide viewpoint; independence of local political or economic party interests; and a consequent ability to criticize socialistic and capitalistic abuses equally. Catholic social justice tradition has kept the concrete life of individual human beings front and center, and often it has endeavored to speak a generalist language, translating its convictions to nonbelievers and founding them in the humanity all persons share.

Among weaknesses or lacks that remain we reckon, in agreement with Hollenbach, that Catholic social teaching could do more to suggest concrete ways of arbitrating social conflict. Hollenbach suggests three strategic priorities:

> The needs of the poor take priority over the wants of the rich. The freedom of the dominated takes priority over the liberty of the powerful. The partici-pation of marginalized groups takes priority over the preservation of an order which excludes them. [Hollenbach, p. 204]

Were these to win acceptance, the justice a Christian expects from arbi-tration would be close at hand.

Two further weaknesses are the tradition's slighting of ecological issues, and its silence about its own failings in justice. The slighting of ecology shows in Gremillion's "Overview": the references are passing, pro forma, and woefully inadequate to the abuses. Of the 138 pages, only 2.5 deal with "Environment and Human Settlements." This indi-cates the low rank ecology has had in even the most recent Catholic social teaching and it also suggests the cause: Catholic social thought has considered nature only in relation to humans' use of it.

The church's leadership's relative silence about its own failings in justice is a matter of ordinary human weakness, but also of insensitivity. The truism that any group's idealism is discredited by its contradictory practice has special acuteness when that idealism supposedly expresses divine revelation. Thus employers who closely represent the church (e.g., heads of Catholic schools and hospitals) and oppose collective bargaining or the formation of unions; church leaders who refuse to reverse the marginalization of women; and the lack of due process in proceedings against "suspect" theologians all vitiate the lofty social preaching. They and other blind spots cause more than cynical wonder whether the church's eloquence isn't a rather cheap voice *ad extra*—a rather easy preaching to the nations rather than the self.

POLITICAL THEOLOGY: EUROPE AND NORTH AMERICA

Largely from contact with Marxists, European theologians outside the Roman center have tried to open the Catholic tradition to radical social criticism. Frequently this opening has been rather cerebral, entailing (especially in Germany) heady discussions of hermeneutics (principles of interpretation), the sociology of knowledge, the utopian functions of imagination, and so forth. At its center, though, has been a commendable concern to accept the manifest truths in a Marxist critique of class antagonisms, ideologies, and false consciousness. For instance, it seems a fact, hidden only from ostriches, that one's position in a society shapes one's perceptions of its economics and politics. Thus, those who profit from the status quo tend to preserve it, and even to overlook its injustices. By contrast, those whom a status quo oppresses are primed to see injustice everywhere. Perhaps members of the John Birch Society exemplify the first stance; surely victims of racial or sexual discrimination exemplify the second.

Similarly, it takes no great historical or contemporary exposure to admit truth in the Marxist claim that religion can prop false consciences and unjust statuses quo. When religion is unreflective, or closely coincides with civil identity, it is slow to translate God's call into doing the truth in love. That slowness is partly understandable, as all human weakness is, and partly the surd, ugly tardiness we call sin. Colluding with the wealthy and the power bearers, religionists, Catholic Christians among them, have in some situations become tools of oppression. Admitting this, denying that it is a legitimate progeny of the gospel, and showing parallel abuses in Marxist regimes has advanced European Catholics into "political" theology. Many have accepted the Marxist challenge of making faith alleviate suffering and overturn systemic abuses. With at least implicit reliance on a theory of universal grace, they praise truth and goodness wherever they find them, caring more for the game than the players' uniforms.

Perhaps the most prominent European Catholic political theologian has been J. B. Metz, and his relationship to Rahner is interesting. He was Rahner's student, edited *Hearers of the Word* (Rahner's clearest anthropology), and remains a close friend. Yet "Baptist," as Rahner calls him, led the criticism of transcendental Thomism such as Rahner's, on the grounds that it neglected the importance of socio-political factors. Transcendental Thomism's strength lay in its analyses of individual consciousness. It was in good measure bringing Aquinas into dialogue with Kant and Hegel. But it did not move on from Hegel to Marx—to social factors and *praxis* (action, practice). The Frankfurt School of socio-philosophical analysis was a major influence on thinkers like Metz who felt these inadequacies. That school's often convoluted analyses of social consciousness and ideology provided them with sources of articulation. Rahner himself engaged in dialogues with Marxists, and admitted the need for a political broadening, but this movement seems to have occurred too late for him personally. He was so formed by reworking individual Christian consciousness in the context of Kant, Hegel, and Heidegger that the political dimension has remained an addendum. In his pupil Metz, however, it has become an effective focus of brotherly love.

Metz is not the clearest of theoreticians, and European Catholic political theology remains less than a lucid force. A link between it and North American political thought, though, is the work of some students of Bernard Lonergan. Matthew Lamb and Fred Lawrence, for instance, have been influenced both by European political hermeneutics and Lonergan's transcendental method. Their papers from the *Lonergan Workshop* show the rich potential of this dual influence. Lonergan's strengths include a clear cognitional theory, to ground the analysis of "horizons" in which political theology delights, and a strong empirical bent. While both he and his followers criticize empiricism (the view that only sensibly verifiable facts matter), they retain an Anglo-American temper and want close contact with experience. That has meant considerable work in economics, philosophy of science, and other disciplines. In effect, the Lonergan school calls for wholesale interdisciplinary collaboration, and its methodological depth provides good suggestions for how such collaboration might proceed. The result could be a more profound political science and theology, rooted in a religious analysis of human consciousness.

The theoretically minded wing of North American political theology therefore tends to read Marxist analyses with some critical distance. Insofar as those analyses often occur in an ideological framework, with less than lucid objectivity, they suggest the deficiencies of Marxist atheism. As a secularist's horizon can be pernicious, closing off God and the Spirit's farther reaches, so can a Marxist atheist's. By both experience and analysis, many Catholic thinkers in North America find human consciousness, especially human judgment and love, implying more. This finding may not appear especially political, but in fact it soon tends to be. For to answer questions of justice, the common good, the proper distribution of material resources, and the like, one must say what human beings are made for.

European partners to the Marxist-Christian dialogue realized this, so they concentrated on hope. Extending analyses of temporality, they became fascinated with the future. Insofar as both Marxists and biblically sensitive Christians consider the future open, they share a central conviction. Add their common instinct to imagine the future as a realm of greater justice, and they are at least cousins. When they further agree that we cannot sacrifice the present to the future, cannot be unjust today to secure justice tomorrow, they are brothers and sisters. For having an open future and a conscience set on justice now is a deep act of faith. It makes life's mystery such that honesty and love are the paths to a better tomorrow.

Some North American thinkers have also been drawn to sociology. When sociology is not a weak-minded mongering of the obvious (what Eric Severeid called "slow journalism"), it can give political theology considerable help. In the tradition of Max Weber and Emile Durkheim, North Americans such as Peter Berger and Robert Bellah have done stimulating studies of religious consciousness. Bellah adds a socialist political sympathy, Berger one more conservative, but either way, the stage on which they move has been sufficiently ecumenical to entice numerous Catholics. For instance, as we noted earlier, Avery Dulles joined Berger in the Hartford Appeal. The younger Jesuit sociologist John Coleman studied with Bellah and does political theology somewhat in his style.

Two publishing ventures by North American Catholics manifest other directions political theology has taken here. Orbis Books has done yeoman service in introducing Americans to third-world theologies. From Maryknollers' missionary contacts, Orbis has almost single-handedly translated the bulk of recent key Latin American, African, and Asian theologians. Their works reflect the break with colonialism many third-world peoples have recently accomplished, as well as their continuing struggles with Northern economic imperialism. Ecclesiologically, they imply missionary questions such as how to export the gospel without exporting Western culture, as well as the host of moral and infrachurch political questions that the "Third Church," based in the Southern Hemisphere, provokes.

The second publishing venture is a joint project involving the Jesuits' Woodstock Theological Center in Washington, D.C., and Paulist Press. Working with government officials, and drawing on interdisciplinary expertise, Woodstock has produced several works on justice and public policy that have an air of realism—of being in close touch with how government actually operates and what constraints actually obtain. Sometimes their oblique asides are as interesting as their explicit analyses. For instance, in introducing a volume on personal values in public policy, Maryland Senator Charles McC. Mathias tells how he was finally moved to support congressional representation for the people of the District of Columbia by a sense that it simply was right. That this consideration apparently was far down on his instinctive list, and even farther down on his colleagues', speaks volumes he may not have intended.

Political theology takes a less studious form among the many North American groups who go at it pragmatically. They often combine activism with a strong liturgical, contemplative, or community life, and frequently they target their efforts concretely. For example, Catholic Workers have long tried to render service to the urban poor. Establishing houses in the inner city, they have run soup kitchens, centers for discussion, and networks of neighborhood support. Drawing on Hispanic Catholicism, Cesar Chavez and leaders of the United Farm Workers have tried to bring justice to the fields where migrant workers toil. Other groups have been ad hoc collections of Christians in opposition—to the war in Vietnam, the denial of civil rights to blacks and women, the oppression of gays, or nuclear development. (Among the last one finds some of the strongest Catholic ecological awareness.) We shall consider black and feminist liberation theologies in the next sections. Here the summarizing point might be recent shifts in consciousness that have divided Catholics politically.

On one side are those who read the signs of the times as a call to across-the-board opposition. They interpret racism, sexism, environmental pollution, and militarism as an interconnected network. The common denominator is blinding self-service. Because it is profitable and advantageous, large groups of North Americans support systems that discriminate against minorities and women, continue to ravage the land, and keep the arms race building. The base form of this profit is financial: The status quo makes these people a comfortable living. Therefore, the gospel's message of peace and justice must be joined to the gospel's poverty. It is those who give up notions of the good financial life that are most likely to become radically Christian.

On the other side are many who doubt the church's competence to enter political battles and so want religion to be more private. Reacting to the turmoil of the sixties, they turned the volume down in the seventies. The wise among them know there are risks of being coopted, and the more impressive work at structural change. But many feel little kinship with radical Christians and relegate them to a past that failed.

For instance, that the Berrigans now inhabit the margins is for many proof of their inaptness. Unfortunately, what commitment to social justice *is* apt is a question many do not welcome. On the other hand, a noticeable number of Catholics would agree with exiled Russian novelist Alexsandr Solzhenitsyn's critique of Marxist-Leninism, including its rather militaristic approach to liberation. In their view, Christ came to slay evil and our times are a great warfare between darkness and light.

BLACK LIBERATION THEOLOGY

Among radical Catholics black theology continues to be a strong stimulus. Among conservatives it often conflicts with neighborhood interests. The fine documentary history of black theology recently edited by Gayraud Wilmore and James Cone shows what has happened since the heyday of Martin Luther King, Jr. It also shows how marginal black Catholics have been: Catholic statements comprise about 5 of the history's 625 pages—less than 1.5 percent. They include a judgment that an articulate black Catholic vanguard is presently emerging, but that seems largely a pious hope. The smallness of the black Catholic population, and the mainline character of most Catholic institutions, suggest that black Catholic theology is not likely to make radical impacts.

Consequently, it is the osmotic impact of Protestant and secularist black thought that has been, and probably will continue to be, the prime black political influence on Catholic theology. After pursuing civil rights, and then starting to realize the extent of structural racism, black theology has fanned out in several further directions. It has supported black power, criticized white religion as racist, shown some openness to dialogue with white theology seeking radical justice, reflected on the black church, confronted its own problems regarding women, and most recently allied itself with third-world thought, especially that of Africans. Such change in a fifteen-year period shows that black theology has been more than vital. What appear to be its current politico-theological perceptions?

Though black theologians naturally differ, they tend to agree that racism is a systemic evil, close to the bone of both white culture and white religion. From that they move in diverse directions, some separatist and some ecumenically pragmatic. Separatists prefer to be left alone, to control their own destinies. Ecumenical pragmatists work with anyone who can help them improve blacks' condition. Another set of movements is theoretical. There are black theologians influenced by Marxist analyses, and others who home to the Bible. The latter often read scripture as a text of liberation, and often have close ties to the black church. They point out that, historically, the black church has been one of the few places of black power, and one of the few places of black hope.

Admitting that such hope could turn other-worldly, they argue that it usually retained an acute sense of the present. Whether heard in a rural town or an urban ghetto, the biblical passage revealed the enemy. Black theologians of Marxist orientation underscore the economics of oppression, and also the psychology. They shout against pie in the sky religion, so they help the biblicists make a case for the primacy of praxis.

Related to the primacy of praxis is the primacy of the black community. For those held together by the church, the church is palpably social. Despite the problems such sociability can bring, which parallel the problems of the intense Jewish shtetl, its togetherness, its suffering shared, can make white church experience seem anemic. We know a white woman whose time in an interracial church in Harlem has left her unfit for white churches. When she was sick her community rallied round, and when she got better they all partied. Such genuine concern flowed out that for her "the church" has to be an intense fellowship. To show up on Sunday as a duty, hear a pale message and share a pale smile, is no Christianity she considers worth pursuing.

If ecumenical contacts we've had are representative, this small episode suggests another problem blacks have with white Christianity. In addition to the racism it frequently carries, white Christianity can seem to have little soul. At issue in such an impression is more than a clash between two neutral cultures. Insofar as Christianity entails being a people, and living for love, "soul" is not something indifferent. Rather, feeling and doing, singing and expressing, are of the essence. There is a warmth black religion knows, a warmth it develops if given half a chance, that most white churches have not known how to foster. When one ties this warmth to conjoint suffering, to sharing the troubles nobody outside knows, one has a pristine Christian cell. Whether they are conscious of it or not, many small black groups resemble nothing so much as first-century Christian churches.

Reflecting on black experience for a symposium on "Dilemmas of Pluralism: The Case of Religion in Modernity," Vincent Harding has advanced this shared suffering into an epistemological distinctiveness. From their experiences of downtroddenness, American blacks probably have the best understanding of Jesus' message that is available in their land. Just as Latin American theologians stress the importance of identifying with the poor, so black theologians of Harding's persuasion stress Jesus' solidarity with black poverty and discrimination. It was the poor to whom Jesus preached good news. It was the poor whom Jesus beatified. It is the poor, consequently, who are best positioned to understand many fundamental portions of Christianity. Primary among these is God's association with justice. If "divinity" means anything midst oppression and suffering, it means the redress of a present order that should not be. It should not be that some people throw away more food in a day than other people see in a week. It should not be that malnutrition virtually programs some children for failure by the time they are five. And, above all, it should not be that the skin one wears can determine one's destiny. Any God worth considering has to be the opposite, the enemy, of such evils.

Because they think "God" has deflected many of their people from working on this-worldly change, some black thinkers castigate religion. Most black theologians, though, go rather gently on even their people's superstitions. While they want religion to work social change, to be concerned for bodies as much as souls, they know the despair that is always close in the ghetto. This intuitive knowledge is confirmed by psychiatric studies: When internalized, racial inferiority often breaks out in destructive rage. How much crime, internecine prison violence, and infra-black cruelty this explains is hard to say, above all for white outsiders. What all indexes suggest, however, is that many blacks have found religion a psychic necessary.

If the choice is between possible illusion, by taking biblical myths as literally as if they were snapshots, and hopelessness, clearly possible illusion is preferable. The black mother of epic sterotype, long-suffering and fervently a believer, concretizes this creative response to impossible conditions. The resiliency Harvard psychiatrist Robert Coles found in the ghetto would have been impossible without her amazing grace. The male side of the coin is a more terrible tangle. Deprived of many of the symbols of male achievement, especially the basic one of a decent job, black males have faced overwhelming crises. The figures on unemployment for black youth today (often almost 50 percent) draw the base line. What future do those figures allow, and what do they say of American justice? Anyone hearing Catholic social teaching, or just unmuffled conscience, knows where the grapes of wrath are stored.

There are analogous descriptions and inferences embedded in the experience of Chicanos and Asian-Americans. The former have a hard time getting Hispanic bishops, the latter are so minor a Catholic number they are close to invisible theologically. Perhaps their most visible group has been the Vietnamese refugees. Some dioceses, especially in the Midwest, have been quite Christian to them.

To other such marginal peoples, as to the theological community generally, black theology reports on the effects of slavery. If American theological history had room for only a single symbol of our sin, beyond doubt it would be slavery. That may change in the future, if our playing with nuclear fire brings the unthinkable, but to the present black experience epitomizes how the New World has gone wrong, as it epitomizes Christian sin in Africa. Presuming to some special title, some errand in the wilderness or manifest destiny, European emigrants to the New World showed incredible ambitions. Mixed in, of course, were many noble hopes, and many short-sightednesses merely human. But there were core blindnesses with roots in the will that have drawn the pale face vulpine.

Though it would be convenient to turn aside and discourse on the Protestant ethic, or the bastardization of Calvinism that capitalism has wrought, the focus of this book suggests that Catholics attend to themselves and their own doctrine. The Spanish and French who threw Catholicism into the race for the New World did not greatly distinguish themselves from their Protestant competition. When the bishops of Latin America met at Puebla, they recognized indigenous peoples as the most abject of their continent's poor. When the upwardly mobile Catholics reached the boardrooms of power, they did not change discriminatory policies dramatically. No, the gospel of radical justice separates the "sheep" from the "goats" across denominational lines.

FEMINIST LIBERATION THEOLOGY

Black theology focuses on poverty and racism. Looking to God for relief, it reads the gospel as a social liberation. Feminist theology focuses on sexism. It reads the history of culture, non-Christian and Christian alike, as a long tale of women's bondage. In fact, since the rise of history, society after society has been patriarchal, in a pejorative sense. Women have not been equal to men, in opportunity, dignity, or power. What parity they had in matriarchal times, during neolithic agriculture and worship of the Mother, is lost by recorded memory. East and West, women historically have been subject—to fathers, then husbands, then sons. For a woman not to marry and produce sons was for her to live wretchedly on society's margins.

It is true that the rise of what we now consider the world religions somewhat ameliorated women's lot, but that is a relative judgment. The Buddha raised women's station in India (though aboriginal India may have treated women better than the India of his time), and the option of going to a Buddhist nunnery was a significant liberation. Nonetheless, women never received equal access to Buddhist power or honor. In East Asia the Tao had a feminine modality, but the prevailing Confucian mores can only be called misogynistic. Judaism rose from very patriarchal beginnings, in which a women was legally property. Talmudic Judaism made some provision for women's rights, but the morning prayer of the pious Jew still thanks God each day for not having made him female. Muhammad improved Arab women's lot significantly, in such areas as marriage, divorce, and inheritance. However, the Koran clearly subordinates women to men, and the tradition that followed regularly took the more subjugating reading.

Jesus' rather even-handed treatment of women and men therefore stands out from the usual practice of world religions. While it might be excessive to call him a feminist, since he did not explicitly reject contemporary Jewish views, he did implicitly overturn much prejudice. For a rabbi to consort freely with women was unthinkable in Jesus' time, as the disciples' reaction to his dialogue with the Samaritan woman (John 4) suggests. Unthinkable too was Jesus' view of marriage, in which the same stringency applied to both sexes. That astonished the disciples, as the Master's association with prostitutes astonished the Pharisees. The Son of Man, then, was Lord not just of the Sabbath. He also was Lord of the prevailing sexual mores: free to have friends, work cures, recognize faith regardless of gender. Pauline Christianity preserved some of this freedom, when it saw "in Christ" neither male nor female. Unfortunately, it also carried over strains of Jewish misogynism, especially when we count in the pastoral epistles. For them woman was the first to fall, a sex weaker and not wholly clean.

The fathers of the church, East and West, found asceticism and feminism incompatible. As was true for Buddhist monks, celibacy wrote woman out as a temptress. Tertullian, Jerome, Augustine, and Chrysostom all furnish misogynistic quotations. Augustine's own experiences with concubinage and Manicheanism seem to have rendered him unfit to appropriate Pauline egalitarianism. His equation of intercourse with the transmission of original sin was a disaster for women, as was his opinion that sexual pleasure has no end other than procreation. Chrysostom wrote fulminations against women that can only be called disgusting. At least on bad days they were for him storehouses of phlegm and spittle. That Chrysostom became a great authority in Eastern Christianity, Russian as well as Greek, did little to alleviate Orthodox women's oppression. In the West, where Augustine was the dominant figure until the later Middle Ages, women also fared badly. Medieval town law spoke of the husband's right to smash his wife's face in, should she oppose his sovereign volition. Aquinas did little for women, since he accepted the Aristotelian biology that made her a misbegotten male, and the Reformers' return to the Bible meant a return to pristine patriarchy. A few of the left-wing Reformation churches gave women equality, but the overall story, Protestant and Catholic alike, was of rampant sexism.

We have rehearsed this history because contemporary feminists have made it a running start for their liberation analyses. They note the biblical influences, the Gnostic influences (Gnostic opposition to matter and the body often focused on women), and promising roads that orthodoxy rejected. They also note the Fathers' spleen, the dark phenomenon of witch-hunting, Luther's offhand view that woman ought to "bear herself out," and the many current faces of Christian sexism. Among the Catholic feminists prominent in this work stand Rosemary Ruether,

Elisabeth Schüssler-Fiorenza, and Mary Daly. Schüssler-Fiorenza is a New Testament scholar who has retrieved roles and authorities women had in early Christianity and male scholarship has overlooked. At the beginnings, church order was not so rigid as it later became, and Paul's letters suggest that women led local churches. Similarly, the role of women such as Mary Magdalene shows how apostleship could have been nonsexist. Some feminists consider Schüssler-Fiorenza a reformer rather than a radical, but her self-description is "woman-identified."

Another "reformist" who bristles at the title is Rosemary Radford Ruether. Her original field was patristics, but she has broadened her historical studies to other temporal periods. Ruether combines considerable learning with a bent for radical politics, so her feminism is part of an organic socialistic vision. Ecological, communitarian, egalitarian, Christian, and free, her "church" would be very exciting. It would bite sizeable chunks from the established version, but each bit would be backed by good reasons. Ruether is too sophisticated historically, and too aware psychoanalytically, for establishmentarians to dismiss her easily. Indeed, her concern for justice and political commitment could teach them many of the lessons they most need.

In the beginning of her career Mary Daly was a Catholic theologian, but she has since renounced any Christian allegiance. The progression evident in her books—*The Church and the Second Sex, Beyond God the Father,* and *Gyn/Ecology*—is from reformist Christianity to militant feminism. We saw the beginnings of this change at Boston College in the late 1960s. Daly was denied tenure there, unjustly, and political rallies forced the administration to reverse its decision. Such treatment exemplified the thesis of her first book: Women are less than second-class citizens in Catholic history. Building on her studies of Tillich, Daly's second book tried to remove sexism from God. The sharpest angle in Catholic theology's bias, she astutely realized, is the maleness it has attributed to God. No matter that the high theologians admitted God is beyond sex, the popular tradition took "Father" seriously. Moving to a God who is active being, a verb more than a noun, she suggested, might cut out theology's apparent sanction of patriarchy. In retrospect, however, this theological suggestion was but a way-station.

Gyn/Ecology is a full-scale rehearsal of patriarchal religion's horrors. In chapters on Chinese foot-binding, Hindu widow-burning, African genital mutilation, Christian witch-destroying, and current gynecological practices, Daly shows how women have suffered. The language of the analytic portion of her text is highly self-conscious and punning. She is reflective enough to realize that the history she is telling suggests a new philosophy. So she would have women become "spinners," "witches," and "crones," retrieving those words' original possibilities. It is an impressive semantic exercise. Added to her empirical case studies of male savagery, it makes the work a milestone.

Unfortunately, these positive reviews are not the whole story. By its middle, *Gyn/Ecology* is more than excessive. By its end, it is too bitter to be borne. Of course, what one person is willing to bear may seem to another relatively light. Immersed in a tale of horrors, Daly probably thought no rhetoric too shrill. But there is a point beyond which righteous wrath throws the preacher off balance. In theory that point is where one stops loving unrestrictedly. After that there are people one need not regard, people outside one's pale. They do not have humanity like one's own, so they can be treated as another species. Erik Erikson describes this phenomenon as "pseudospeciation." Denying biology and common sense, it helped Greeks to consider foreigners *barbaroi*, Gentiles to pillory Jews, whites to treat blacks as primates.

The pseudospeciation in Daly's case is a reverse sexism. Men have so swollen in her imagination that they incarnate the enemy. This misanthropy, for all its historical title, runs aground on common sense. Men are almost half the race; infant boys are not responsible for the past; many women are happily heterosexual; despite all its problems, marriage still works quite often. No nicking the edges destroys the core accuracy of these observations. To sequester oneself in a misanthropic coven is to opt for a lot of illusion.

Daly's case shows how militant feminists have gone searching for a new religion. Actually, they have gone searching for an old religion, one that claims roots in pre-patriarchal times. This religion is nature-oriented and life-affirming. It entails a witchcraft, but one wholly positive. Ritualizing its convictions, new witches celebrate old mysteries close to the Mother. The Mother is Earth and Life, the mystery we all owe our being. Menstruation, intercourse, birth, and nursing are phenomena richly symbolic of her. Most covens work democratically, some admit males, and probably all are trying consciously to redress unhealthinesses that an excessively male, aggressive, phallic culture and religion have wrought.

Insofar as such witchcraft parts from Christ, rejecting his solutions to death and sin, we put qualifications on its acceptance. Nonetheless, it offers Christian liberation thought a great deal that is positive, especially through its emphasis on ecology. The liberation theologies we have seen, and the Latin American one we shall look at next, all neglect this ecological dimension. It is no accident they all also have recognized women's oppressions only tardily. Thus, a specifically feminist liberation school, sensitive to women's needs in all churches and cultures, is both a need and a benefit.

Finally, specifically Catholic foci of feminist liberation theology have been ordination and abortion. Non-ordination epitomizes how the Catholic church has denied women equal access to authority and service. Almost unanimously, feminists consider it a symbol of deep sexism. Abortion is more contested, for few Catholic feminists support it wholeheartedly. Most sympathize with women who, usually under great pressure, feel they must have an abortion, and many distinguish their religious ideal from politico-legal realities and vote prudentially for women's free choice. No Catholic feminists, however, are happy that their church gives so much occasion for thinking it misogynistic. All consider Catholic sexism a serious sin that smothers their tradition's best instincts.

POLITICAL THEOLOGY: LATIN AMERICA

The most logical nexus between this section and the preceding forces us to begin with some criticisms. Insofar as the final document of the Latin American bishops' Puebla meeting, whose topic was evangelization, represents liberation theology's official impact to date, feminists have little to cheer. The document does treat women's situation in both Latin American life and Christian evangelization (Nos. 834–849), and does note how they often suffer double oppression. Generally, "women have been pushed to the margins of society as the result of cultural atavisms—male predominance, unequal wages, deficient education, etc." The result is their "almost total absence from political, economic and social life." Specifically, there are the evils of women's sexual exploitation, through growing eroticism, pornography, and prostitution; there are also the economic evils of poor wages, noncompliance with laws designed for women's protection, abusive conditions for domestic employees, and so forth. Finally, the document has a sentence on the church's failings: "In the church itself there sometimes has been an undervaluation of women and minimal participation by them in pastoral initiatives."

Following this enumeration of negatives, the document asserts women's theological equality and dignity, using examples from scripture, above all that of Mary. Applying this to the present, the bishops speak of women making "a real contribution to the church's mission," but the next sentence shows their limited horizon: "The possibility of entrusting non-ordained ministries to women will open up new ways for them to participate in the church's life and mission." In other words, males will continue to hoard the power pieces. Jon Sobrino, an El Salvadorian theologian whose work on liberation Christology has made him very prominent, has written an illuminating commentary on the Puebla document that finds its center to be a firm identification with the poor. However, Sobrino says virtually nothing about the special poverty a majority of Latin Americans suffer because of their sex. It is left to Robert McAfee Brown, commenting on the significance of Puebla for North American Protestants, to make the hard observation that *machismo* has affected even the most progressive Latin American theologians. Bluntly, it has blinded them to women's inferior status in their culture and theology.

A second shortcoming of the Puebla document, again also applicable to Sobrino's commentary, is its neglect of ecological considerations. This criticism has little special edge, however, for among liberation theologians only feminists are consistently ecological. Others seem so concerned with social questions that things not directly bearing on the sufferings of the poor receive only scant attention. A last disappointment of Puebla is its weak ecumenism.

Failings such as these three mean that liberation theology must not seize all the Catholic attention. As David Tracy has shown, a fully adequate contemporary theology must pivot between the canonical Christian texts and the full range of human experience. If a theology slights half the race, makes little of Christians' need to overcome their divisions, and does not see nature's current throes, it is not the full understanding of faith we presently need.

We make these criticisms harshly, because the rest of our report is a paean. There is no other portion of the Catholic theological world that approaches Latin America's political depth and passion. Liberation theology has taken Europe's interest in Marx, joined it to the realities of the *barrios*, and forged a powerful insistence on liberational praxis. Since Gustavo Gutierrez' pioneering work, *A Theology of Liberation*, Latin America has led the illumination of Christian praxis. Biblical critics, such as José Miranda, have probed scripture's insistence on justice. Sobrino's Christology shows the primacy of *following* Jesus, and other thinkers, Protestant as well as Catholic, have illumined sin, grace, and the rest. A good introduction to all this is Robert McAfee Brown's *Theology in a New Key*.

What, then, does praxis imply? First, it has a theoretical implication. The Latin Americans are instinctively theoretical, due to both their own literary tradition and their ties to European philosophy. Thus, one finds many discussions of hermeneutics and ideology. Their upshot is usually the primacy of action over thought. North Americans know much of this from their own pragmatic tradition. William James, John Dewey, and C. S. Peirce all championed the primacy of doing. In simple terms, the argument is that only full engagement in a situation allows its full truth to emerge. True, we interact with situations, environments, and people just by thinking about them. We interact most richly, however, when we take our convictions to the trenches and find out how they feel, whether they work, what we will suffer for them. It is the difference between contemplating an appendectomy and undergoing it. The pain imagined and the pain actually felt differ instructively. So do imaginary poverty and the grinding reality, an imaginary imitation of Christ and carrying the cross step by step.

Second, praxis means letting realities speak, not doing theology *a priori* (from the head down). The Puebla document shows this thesis has not been fully accepted. Its doctrinal portions are quite *a priori* and fit its pastoral portions badly. Latin American theology has a special need to struggle with this problem, for the *a priori* comes naturally to the romance language mind. (In English-speaking countries, empiricism and common law tradition militate against it.) Still, all theologies need constantly to question whether they are elucidating basic faith—are clarifying lives Christians actually are living. Few have gazed so unblinking as those from Latin America.

For, third, the praxis of Christian faith in Latin America contends each day with massive evil. Not only is there staggering poverty. Perhaps worse, there is an economic injustice, caused considerably by Northern conglomerates, that grows decade by decade. An illustration is Brazil, touted as Latin America's industrial giant. Between 1960 and 1970, the top five percent of Brazilian income earners increased their share of the national wealth from 27.4 to 36.3 percent. During that same period the share of the bottom eighty percent decreased from 45.5 to 36.8 percent. When the top five percent of a country earn almost as much as the bottom eighty, justice cries out for revolution.

Brazilian leaders realize this, of course, as do leaders of other Latin American countries with similar economies. Consequently, they have developed a brutal regime, based on police surveillance and torture. "National Security" is the buzzword such Latin American regimes employ, as a blanket justification for their repressions. Because most of the opposition analyzes the politico-economic situation with Marxist tools, and aims at restoring the country to "the people," the dictators use "National Security" as vigilance against Communist revolutionaries. When the Somoza regime fell in Nicaragua, American television sent back mini-lessons on the rise and fall of a small National Security operation. Somoza and his family had shamelessly padded their own pockets. Yet they claimed to be protecting "the people" from teenage "revolutionaries" who wanted basic food and shelter. Northern interests had long propped Somoza, as they have long propped similar dictators. When he started to fall U.S. officials beat a hasty retreat, trying not to get splattered with his failure. That they already had years of blood on their hands seemed altogether secondary.

When commentators looked for women's presence at Puebla, they found one especially poignant clustering. Wives, mothers, and sisters who had had family members "disappear" joined to ask the conference's help. That people who oppose Latin American regimes "disappear," sometimes turning up weeks later mutilated, sometimes never resurfacing, is part of the southern landscape. Like the increasingly polluted cities, it is a constant psychic pressure. On the whole, church leaders have faced such pervasive evils courageously. Again and again, priests, nuns, dedicated laity, and bishops have spoken out strongly. It is another measure of the dictators' corruption that these appeals have not dented their operations. In countries massively Catholic and traditional, Christian leaders are imprisoned, tortured, and slain as enemies of the state. If the ancient notion that the blood of the martyrs is the seed of faith remains valid, Latin America has the brightest of paradoxical futures. Its martyrs now number into the hundreds and there is no sign when it will stop.

That the Puebla document should, despite foul play from the episcopal right, have emerged championing Latin America's poor is another sign of liberation theology's power. The light it carries, the good it encourages, the justice it makes plain are simply too godly to thwart. The link it forges between Jesus and the suffering is like the medievals' "golden chain." In the poor, love of God and love of neighbor take flesh brutalized. By identifying with the dispossessed, Latin Americans have recovered the Suffering Servant of the gospel. Like the legendary Veronica, who gave Jesus a cloth to wipe his face and received back an indelible portrait, they contemplate a haunting visage. The eyes are sad, the cheeks are hollow, but the chin is firmly set. As El Greco's painting of Veronica's cloth shows, the Christ is a suffering victor.

Identifying with the suffering Christ, as the poor give him his mystical body, has moved Latin Americans to pedagogical and ecclesial innovations. Pedagogically, Paulo Freire and others have focused on raising consciousness. This is familiar from women's groups, but its Latin American form is theological. Through greater political and economic awareness, Latin Americans lay the foundation of a new illuminative way. To understand the theology of injustice, they join it to Christ's sufferings. The ecclesial context for this pedagogy is their *comunidades de base*—"grass-roots" gatherings, such as Ernesto Cardenal's in Solentiname, in which members analyze together their experiences and the gospel. Together, raising consciousness and forming grass-roots communities offers the rest of the Christian world a stimulating model.

Though most do not realize it, other Christians, especially Northern Catholics, have a great stake in Latin American theology. For following Jesus, faith's politics, and God's identification with the poor, it is nonpareil. As Catholic economist Barbara Ward's recent *Progress for a Small Planet* shows, the economics of Latin America are replicated throughout the Southern Hemisphere. As Robert McAfee Brown's commentary on the Puebla document adds, President Carter has continued America's involvement in Latin American political theology, by ordering the CIA to put "activist" priests and nuns under surveillance ("lest he be confronted with another Iran-type situation"). Thus, we are in the Southern struggle right up to our bad conscience. In Iran we supported torture for economic profit. In Latin America we still do the same. The bottom line of liberation theology is that economic profit is a dirty word. It has visited structural violence, *violencia blanca*, on millions. That most liberation theologians consider counterviolence a last resort shows their deep Christianity. Suffering injustice with imaginative love, they try to slay the beast with recreative justice.

BIBLIOGRAPHY

Braxton, Edward K. "Black and Catholic—IX," *America*, 142/12 (March 29, 1980), 274–277.

Brown, Robert McAfee. *Theology in a New Key*. Philadelphia: Westminster, 1978.

Brown, Robert McAfee. "The Significance of Puebla for the Protestant Churches in North America," in J. Eagleson and P. Scharper, eds., *Puebla and Beyond*. Maryknoll, N.Y.: Orbis, 1979, 330–346.

Cardenal, Ernesto. *The Gospel in Solentiname*. Maryknoll, N.Y.: Orbis, 1978.

Coles, Robert. *Children of Crisis*. Boston: Little, Brown, 1964ff.

Daly, Mary. *Beyond God the Father*. Boston: Beacon, 1973.

Daly, Mary. *Gyn/Ecology*. Boston: Beacon, 1979.

Daly, Mary. *The Church and the Second Sex*. New York: Harper & Row, 1975.

Freire, Paulo. *Pedagogy of the Oppressed*. New York: Seabury, 1974.

Gremillion, Joseph. *The Gospel of Peace and Justice*. Maryknoll, N.Y.: Orbis, 1976.

Gutierrez, Gustavo. *A Theology of Liberation*. Maryknoll, N.Y.: Orbis, 1971.

Harding, Vincent. "Out of the Cauldron of Struggle: Black Religion and the Search for a New America," *Soundings*, LXI/3 (Fall 1978), 339–354.

Haughey, John C., ed. *Personal Values in Public Policy*. New York: Paulist, 1979.

Haughey, John C., ed. *The Faith That Does Justice*. New York: Paulist, 1977.

Hollenbach, David. *Claims in Conflict*. New York: Paulist, 1979.

Lamb, Matthew L. "The Production Process and Exponential Growth: A Study in Socio-Economics and Theology," in F. Lawrence, ed., *Lonergan Workshop, Volume I*. Missoula, Mont.: Scholars Press, 1978, 257–307.

Lawrence, Frederick. "Political Theology and 'The Longer Cycle of Decline,'" in F. Lawrence, ed., *Lonergan Workshop, Volume I*. Missoula, Mont.: Scholars Press, 1978, 223–255.

Metz, Johannes B. *Theology of the World*. New York: Herder and Herder, 1969.

Miranda, José. *Marx and the Bible*. Maryknoll, N.Y.: Orbis, 1974.

Rahner, Karl. "Reflections on the Unity of the Love of Neighbor and the Love of God," *Theological Investigations*, 6. Baltimore: Helicon, 1969, 231–249.

Ruether, Rosemary Radford. *New Woman New Earth*. New York: Seabury, 1975.

Ruether, Rosemary Radford, ed. *Religion and Sexism*. New York: Simon and Schuster, 1974.

Ruether, Rosemary Radford and McLaughlin, Eleanor, eds. *Women of Spirit*. New York: Simon and Schuster, 1979.

Schüssler-Fiorenza, Elisabeth. "Feminist Theology as a Critical Theology of Liberation," *Theological Studies*, 36 (1975), 605–626.

Schüssler-Fiorenza, Elisabeth. "Women in the Pre-Pauline and Pauline Churches," *Union Seminary Quarterly Review* 33 (1978), 153–166.

Schüssler-Fiorenza, Elisabeth. "You Are Not to Be Called Father," *Cross Currents*, XXIX/3 (Fall 1979), 301–323.

Sobrino, Jon. "The Significance of Puebla for the Catholic Church in Latin America," in J. Eagleson and P. Scharper, eds., *Puebla and Beyond*. Maryknoll, N.Y.: Orbis, 1979, 289–309.

Starhawk. *The Spiral Dance: A Rebirth of the Ancient Religion of the Great Goddess*. New York: Harper & Row, 1979.

Tracy, David. *Blessed Rage for Order*. New York: Seabury, 1975.

Torres, S. and Eagleson, J., eds. *Theology in the Americas*. Maryknoll, N.Y.: Orbis, 1976.

Ward, Barbara. *Progress for a Small Planet*. New York: Norton, 1979.

Wilmore, Gayraud and Cone, James, eds. *Black Theology: A Documentary History, 1966–1979*. Maryknoll, N.Y.: Orbis, 1979.

Recasting Catholic Theology   9

OVERVIEW

Having surveyed the principal topics of a contemporary Catholic theology, we turn to the question of how theology proceeds—its method. Great changes have occurred since World War II. One that epitomizes them is the difference between the "Roman theology" that ruled until Vatican II and the theologies of two giants of the past Catholic generation, Bernard Lonergan and Karl Rahner. Roman theology tried to impose a uniform system throughout the universal church. It was the heir of scholasticism, and it had the scholastic virtue of neatness. On the other hand, Roman theology strikes most of our contemporaries as ahistorical. Its ideal of uniformity reflects the prejudices of classicism, which thinks in terms of one uniform culture. Lonergan perceived the implications of modernity, which cracked the classicist mold. In a careful series of studies he reworked the scholastic synthesis, so as to make a new design rooted in human authenticity. This design stresses interdisciplinary cooperation, and Catholic theology has only begun to scratch the surface of its implications.

Karl Rahner responded to the complexity of modernity by going for faith's jugular. Under all our diversities, we face a simple obligation of saying yes or no to divine mystery. Our answer enfolds our destiny, and Rahner plays with its ingredients brilliantly. David Tracy, an erstwhile student of Lonergan, has fashioned a "revisionist theology" for the American scene. His work dialogues intensely with secular humanism, and it calls Catholic theology to become thoroughly critical. Rahner's mystagogy complements Tracy's critical thrust, as does Juan Luis Segundo's stress on praxis. Speaking for Latin American liberationists, he shows the reconception of theology that making praxis primary would entail.

TRADITIONAL ROMAN THEOLOGY

We have outlined the major ingredients of a contemporary Catholic theology. Both its doctrine of human nature and its doctrine of God have passed review. It is time, then, to turn to "theology" itself. Granted the foregoing view of Catholic faith's content, how ought one to conceive the process by which reflection renders such content ordered, intelligible, or persuasive? Further, what changes must Catholic theology make if it is to address a culture like the Western industrial, that often calls itself "post-Christian"? These are questions of theological "method," and contemporary Catholic scholars have not been loathe to face them. Influenced by the interest in hermeneutics that the humanities have incited since scholars such as Wilhelm Dilthey (1833–1911) tried to distinguish them from the natural sciences and by cultural change in general, contemporary theologians have rethought the theological enterprise. This chapter reports on their findings.

Of course, to enter the swirling waters of methodology entails several risks. For example, often these waters do not interest the general reader. It is professional theologians who get lathered about methodology, for methodology bears directly on their daily work. Others have to be shown its importance, usually in terms of what difference it can make to their own faith. In fact, we have placed our study of methodology at the end because the chances of showing its implications for faith seem better now than they would have been at the beginning. Also, it is a dictum of methodologists such as Bernard Lonergan that the best theories follow successful practice. In other words, one ought first to observe how good theologians instinctively do their work, and only later try to raise one's observations to the level of a formal set of procedural suggestions. An analogy from sport would be writing up one's instructions about how to shoot free throws after watching the five best free-throw shooters in the league. An analogy from the kitchen would be writing up one's instructions for a spinach soufflé after smacking one's lips over the five best chefs' work.

The theologians we treat in this chapter have all developed their methodological theories by observing recent Catholic practice. Though they differ in their conclusions, they agree that twentieth-century conditions have cast serious doubts about pre-Vatican II ways of theologizing. Were one to summarize those old ways in a single phrase, "Roman theology" would serve quite well. Prior to Vatican II, Catholic theology emanated from Rome. To be sure, there was considerable freedom in the provinces. German theologians spoke differently than French; American theologians manifested the conditions of the United States. But throughout the Catholic world the teaching office of the church, centered in Rome, set the tone and much of the content. Though that teaching office continues to function today, and though there are strong signs that Pope John Paul II wants to restore its control over Catholic theology, its old, pre-Vatican II cast has been thoroughly broken. Virtually no creative theology today considers the methods of Roman theology adequate to current realities.

So, what were those methods? In general, they were a legacy from scholasticism. The theology that emanated from the Curia in Rome thought of faith in propositional terms. From Augustine, Anselm, and others, it had the notion that theology is "faith seeking understanding." From the church councils and papal pronouncements it had a wealth of statements about different aspects of "faith." The task of the theologian was to understand such statements, such expressions of Christian faith. Breaking that down, some Roman theologians had recourse to Aquinas's notion of theology's two "ways." First, there was the way of discovery. This was a semi-historical study of how a doctrine arose and could be grounded in scripture and tradition. In Christology, for example, one could trace the successive definitions of Nicea, Chalcedon, and the other early councils, showing how, step by step, they filled in a picture of Jesus' twofold identity as human and divine.

Second, there was the way of teaching, in which one developed a somewhat deductive exposition of the materials themselves. In Christology this meant locating the core of Jesus' identity in the mystery of the hypostatic union. From the fact that the Word assumed flesh from Mary, and the hypothesis that the person of the Word gave Jesus his deepest identity and act of existence, one was able to structure the principal doctrines of Christology systematically.

For both the way of discovery and the way of teaching, magisterial authority was crucial. The traditional interpretation of the historical sources guided the Roman theologian's study of how a doctrine unfolded, and all systematic explanations of such a doctrine came under the arbitration of the magisterium, which asked whether they really did elucidate the traditional faith. By the time of Pope Pius XII (1939–1957), "dogmatic" theology, which was concerned with presenting the church's traditional teaching and operated along the lines of the way of discovery, had as its "most noble task" showing how the doctrine defined by the church was contained in the sources (scripture and tradition). By the time of the First Vatican Council (1869–1870), "systematic" theology, which was concerned with the way of teaching, was directed to seek the limited understanding of the divine mysteries which is available to human beings in analogies to things that we know naturally, and in the connections the mysteries have with one another and human destiny.

These two tasks—dogmatic and systematic theology—were the pride of Roman theology. Scriptural studies, historical studies, even moral theology and canon law had less prestige. So concerned was the magisterium with fidelity to past tradition, past conceptual content, that the dogmatic and systematic theologians who discoursed on Trinity, Incarnation, and Grace were the lions of the Roman forest. The division of their materials into "tracts" determined the courses at the core of Catholic seminarians' education, and a scholastic interpretation of their materials, usually that of Thomas Aquinas, reigned supreme. For instance, as late as 1964 Lonergan larded his Latin texts on Christology and trinitarian theology with references to Aquinas.

The advantages of Roman theology included unity and essentialism. Insofar as the Roman colleges, closely influenced by the Curia, wrote the texts and gave the model for church schools of theology throughout the world, Catholic theology spoke with a common voice. Priests and theologians everywhere had been exposed to a similar vision; the understanding of faith that most of the faithful received therefore was quite similar. By "essentialism" we mean a clear focus on the heart of the Christian matter. The treatises on Jesus, God, and Grace *are* the core of Catholic theology, whether one considers it historically or analytically. They represent the great themes the fathers, scholastics, and moderns all stressed. Equally, they represent the inner circle of faith's reality, faith's objective divinity and interpretation of human nature. Because Roman theology gave prestige to the dogmatic and systematic tracts that treated the cardinal mysteries, it helped the faithful keep the core of faith clear.

The disadvantages of Roman theology, however, were both many and serious. First, it purchased unity at the price of staying aloof from the cultural diversity of church members and the intellectual diversity of modern Western culture. To think that one uniform theology could fully serve both Africa and Italy was to ignore serious problems. Equally, to write off modern philosophy, science, and literature was to wall oneself in a corner. Prior to Vatican II, seminarians were discouraged from reading Marx, Darwin, Freud, and other giants of modern culture. Because these authors opposed traditional faith at many points, they were placed on the Index of forbidden writers. The idea that traditional faith itself might lack anything was half-heretical.

Second, part and parcel of this attitude was an ahistoricism. Where modern culture had taken historical change to heart, realizing that all species and cultures change, Roman theology clung to the classicist notion of culture, in which a single set of ideals, deduced from humanity's unchanging nature, reigned perennially. More and more rapidly, this separated Roman theology from contemporary realities. When we ourselves studied cosmology in the early sixties, our textbook, from the Gregorian University in Rome, still had theses on the passage of light through ether. Our text in philosophical anthropology, also from Rome, offered metaphysical arguments that evolution is impossible.

Finally, along with its ahistoricism Roman theology tended to be impersonal. By this we mean that its authority lay outside the individual theologian's personal consciousness. Though modern thought as a whole represented a great turning in to the personal subject, Roman theology argued at arms length by citing texts or papal pronouncements. What experience underlay those texts, or what practical impact they might have, was of little interest to Roman theologians. Their great passion, it now seems, was to defend church authority. If church authority conflicted with personal experience, it was personal experience that had to go.

Several of the assets and liabilities of Roman theology showed up recently in an article by Cardinal John Krol, Archbishop of Philadelphia. The article reprinted testimony he gave before the Senate Foreign Relations Committee in favor of SALT II. It shows, first, that Roman theology is far from dead. In cardinals such as John Krol, other members of the hierarchy, and a number of conservative clergy and laity, it is alive and kicking. Second, the article shows that Roman theology did not neglect moral issues. Though its core was the dogmatic and systematic tracts we mentioned, it developed a full moral theology which, especially in seminaries for diocesan priests, sometimes was more important than dogmatics. Third, Cardinal Krol exhibits much of the intelligence and courage that Roman theology developed. His analysis of SALT II builds on both traditional Just War Theory and the statements of recent popes, marshaling a strong case that not only nuclear war itself, but even using the threat of nuclear war as a deterrent, is immoral. Last, the cardinal's article is impressive, especially to outsiders, because it appears to present not the author's private views but the common position of the whole church (as expressed by its hierarchical leaders). In other words, it draws on the unity that Roman theology treasured. Sophisticated, analytic, moderate, it makes the reader recall the long history through which the Catholic church has learned how to live in the world, and the many times the church has championed life.

On the other hand, there is something in this article that sets a truly contemporary consciousness on edge. That that something is more methodological than substantial may begin to show how theological method does greatly influence theological form. For the cardinal completely identifies with Catholic tradition. There is no indication his personal mind, heart, soul, or strength has ever deviated or ever would deviate from the official line. We find something to admire in such a submergence of self, but also something to fear. When Cardinal Spellman, the late archbishop of New York who was in charge of Catholic military chaplains, vented his patriotism with the immortal words, "My country right or wrong," he showed what there is to fear.

Even when the submerged self does not work evils, such as the Nazi holocaust or the American slaughter at My Lai, both of which were replete with abdications of personal conscience through "obedience" to higher-ups, it smacks of something immoral, something affected and dishonest. Of course, an individual can freely, personally, affirm what the company or institution lays down as its official line. However, the history of institutions cautions that this happens rather rarely. More frequently, company men either don't know themselves or they work for their personal aims obliquely, clandestinely, using the corporate forms as a shield.

LONERGAN'S FUNCTIONAL SPECIALIZATIONS

Bernard Lonergan is the Catholic theologian who has most deeply explored methodology. Among his stimuli to this interest were early studies in mathematics, experiencing the inadequacies of Roman theology (by teaching dogmatic and systematic theology in Rome), and studying Aquinas, from whom he got a running start on the cognitional theory he developed brilliantly in his *Insight. Method in Theology*, which appeared fifteen years after *Insight*, made a smaller splash, as though Catholic theologians feared its far-ranging implications. Primary among those implications are the demise of an impersonal style and the necessity of interdisciplinary collaboration.

The vice in an impersonal style that condemns it to demise is inauthenticity. Potentially at least, the person who theologizes at arms length is inauthentic. For we only achieve genuine, admirable selfhood when our judgments and choices serve our self's transcendence. As Lonergan reads the human constitution, we must move from experience, through understanding, to judgment and decision. The implications of this reading are profound. First, it affirms the traditional Aristotelian conviction that knowledge begins with sensation. However, attentiveness should make human sensation more than just gazing. Thus, a student puzzling over solid geometry has to attend closely. So does a student working a microscope, or a literary critic reading a play. When we attend closely we pursue actively the images that serve understanding. Drawing its diagram carefully helps us grasp a geometric theorem. Reading a play slowly, out loud, helps us grasp its characters. That grasp is a step of self-transcendence animals never know.

Beyond knowing, however, there is judging: verifying that the rules do apply, the formula does explain. Insofar as judging demands more than understanding, because it affirms what is rather than what merely might be, it is a further step in self-transcendence. The wise person is judicious, knows the rules of evidence well. Still, there are persons who judge well and decide poorly. For instance, there are persons who affirm the surgeon general's correlation of smoking and lung cancer but continue puffing away. Similarly, there are politicians who admit the economy needs radical surgery but let themselves be deflected by reelection. So it is decision, rational love, that finally measures authenticity. Standing before God's throne, the self will finally be asked, "Did you do what you said? Did you act as you preached?"

If we allow judgment and decision to structure the self, they take us to mature religion. Mature religion is judgment that knows the contingency of all things created and so raises its sight to the creator. It is decisive love that does not stop at limited goods but reaches beyond unrestrictedly. Tutored by helpful and enriching symbols, supported by tradition and community, mature religion makes human time an adventure into mystery. Acknowledging consort with mystery to be its core vocation, the authentic personality is religious by dedication to honesty and love. It speaks the truth, loves the light, tries to build up community, because a core sense of ultimacy, of God, makes warm light or bright love the pearl of great price. This brings a clarity, an integrity, a rightness that tells us incontrovertibly what we have been made for. Christian conversion does not change such authenticity, it merely sublates honesty and love to a higher level. At that higher level it finds Jesus has defeated the inauthenticity that stalks us and incarnated honest loving. It finds he has made honest loving beautiful in ten thousand limbs and faces.

In great detail, Lonergan's method elaborates authenticity's background and implications programmatically. Its background includes predominently modernity's move from the static cultural ideals of classicism to historicity and pluralism. If one discerns "modernity" rightly, it encourages us to deeper interiority and personalism, and though many modern philosophers have not discerned history and pluralism rightly, and so have made them enemies of self-transcendence, that does not justify classicism. Cultures do change. Recently, for instance, psychology, sociology, and economics have altered our understanding of human nature. Moreover, religious authenticity can take diverse forms. The Spirit is not limited to classicist patterns. Therefore, theology above all has to come to grips with personal consciousness, for it is in personal consciousness that all such truths make their existential claims. If theology cannot develop working methods that root it incontrovertibly in honesty and love, it is less admirable than physical science or art. If the theologian cannot stand behind her work personally, her contemporaries will judge her inauthentic.

To be sure, there is the issue of accepting religious truths in faith. For the average person, who has neither the leisure nor the training to analyze religious truths personally, accepting them in faith is moral, valid, authentic insofar as the agency that teaches and promotes them itself appears to be authentic. If the agency is honest, loving, wise, and helpful, then taking its teachings to heart, giving them the benefit of the doubt, and expecting that they will enrich one's life is quite judicious.

For the professional theologian, who does have the leisure and training to analyze religious truths personally, intellectual integrity demands interpreting the data as best one can and remembering one's liabilities to error. For example, if either professional tasks or personal conscience makes papal infallibility something one has to study, one ought to treat it as just another objective problem. How did papal infallibility arise, historically? How cogent are the analytic arguments in its defense, the analytic arguments against it? When the answers emerge, one simply has to honor them. If history shows papal infallibility has a dubious lineage, so be it. If analysis shows papal infallibility makes good sense, so be it. Attentive experience, intelligent understanding, and sober judgment have reached their conclusions; rational love must embrace them, if the theological investigator is to remain authentic.

One's liability to error, which ought to beget humility, plays through these processes in two ways. First, it is a prime item in the sober review that precedes good judgment. Before we pass judgment, we ought to reconsider not only how the data constellate but also in what horizon, what "preunderstanding," we have set them. In stark honesty, we ought to consider how we wanted the investigation to turn out, what our own prejudices or predilections were. Neither the roaring liberal nor the conservative dinosaur is a good judge. A good judge settles outside of personal desires and views things dispassionately.

Second, our human liability to error has a face of contingency. We are all limited in what we can know. By deficiencies in education, intelligence, time and energy, as well as deficiencies in character, we grasp less than the full truth. This does not mean we must block all judgments and decisions, must wait for a never-never perfect day. It does mean we must recognize the slender character of all our conclusions and so make sure they do not puff themselves up.

A good historical description of the dynamics, checks, and balances of a Lonerganian theologian's consciousness occurs in Charles Davis's *A Question of Conscience.* In it Davis, who had been a leading Roman Catholic theologian, explains the process by which he came to break with his church. Explicitly, he sets his story in a Lonerganian framework. As a matter of authenticity, he had to reject Pope Paul VI's encyclical *Humanae Vitae,* and with that rejection he cast off convictions he considered essential to Catholic faith. Those who stress the humility that authenticity inculcates might reach the same conclusion as Davis regarding *Humanae Vitae,* and yet not read themselves out of the Catholic church. If they find in the church a core truth that meets a fallible person's need for God in Christ, they may accept a secondary function such as the papal magisterium as something that may, on judgment day, prove to have been wiser than they.

As we shall see in the next section, Karl Rahner's theological method can be read as a response to authenticity and limitation that stresses the central truth of divine mystery. Bernard Lonergan's methodological response is complementary. Where Rahner develops the limitations of the human person, in face of all he needs to know to pass religious judgment today, into a simplification to the essentials, Lonergan develops a program for interdisciplinary collaboration. The task is so complex, Rahner says, that personal religion has to get down to the bare, unavoidable core. The task is so complex, Lonergan says, that professional theology has to summon experts from all fields and find a way for them to collaborate. Using his own cognitional theory, Lonergan suggests the center of this collaboration be a patterning of eight "functional specialties."

The eight functional specialties are research, interpretation, history, dialectic, foundations, doctrines, systematics, and communications. Let us try to concretize their pattern by focusing on Christology, the core Christian doctrine. Research is the beginning of Christological investigation. It is going out to gather the texts, rounding up the evidence. Interpretation is the work of digging out how the evidence speaks, what the texts say. History makes what the texts say into a story. Placing what the texts report in the context of their times, it judges what Jesus and his followers likely said, did, thought, and experienced. Dialectic steps back and evaluates this history, determining whether it carries God's special light and will.

For those whose dialectical investigations bring them to affirm Christian history as God's revelation, there is a pivot, a conversion. Accepting such revelation as the most basic truth, they lay the foundation of an interpretation of human authenticity. Specifically, they take Jesus as their way, their truth, their life. On this foundation, they set the doctrinal edifice Christian faith has erected through the centuries. For instance, they explain the classical conciliar teachings about the Logos and Jesus' full humanity. It is systematics that works over such doctrines, trying to weld them into a synthetic vision. Finally, communications takes up the tasks of disseminating Christology popularly, through preaching, catechetics, the development of moral guidelines, and so forth.

Behind this eightfold, interlocking structure lies Lonergan's theory of consciousness. Each of the eight functional specialties expresses one of the four levels or foci he finds in human consciousness. The clearest way to put this is a diagram:

experience	1. research	8. communications
understanding	2. interpretation	7. systematics
judgment	3. history	6. doctrines
decision	4. dialectic	5. foundations

The movement (1–8) that we sketched above involves two exercises of consciousness's dynamics. Research through dialectic (1–4) is a progression from experience to decision. At the hinge between dialectic and foundations (4–5), an act of conversion makes the decision one's own, the foundation of one's personal theological edifice. In a second exercise (5–8), one builds this edifice. There the movement is a return from decision to experience in which the founding act of conversion picks up the doctrinal understanding and experiential data necessary if one is to proclaim faith in the world.

Lonergan would insist that this schema is simple-minded, for in actuality the functional specialties interrelate in manifold ways, as the four levels of consciousness do. But the schema has the utility of making it clear how theologians might begin to specify their different competencies and correlate them. It also has the utility of bringing theology into contact with nontheological disciplines, for much of the work implied in phase one (1–4) is prior to faith and could be carried out by anyone, non-Christian as well as Christian. Perhaps just this diagram will show why Lonergan's *Method in Theology* staggered the theological community. Its implications are so vast the community did not know what to make of it. When one adds the rich treatments of "the human good" and "meaning" that Lonergan provides as theological "background," *Method in Theology* becomes one of those rare books worth reading five times or more.

RAHNER'S USE OF MYSTERY

Karl Rahner and Bernard Lonergan were both born in 1904. They both were trained in the Society of Jesus, and they both became professors of dogmatic and systematic theology in Jesuit seminaries. Therefore, they both knew Roman theology to the marrow. All the more interesting, then, is the divergent way their theologies have cast off the Roman style. Where Lonergan is empirical and spare, Rahner is idealistic and full. Where Lonergan targets particular problems, Rahner implicates the whole. Much of this reflects ethnic differences. Lonergan is typically Anglo-American, Rahner typically German. Some of it reflects a difference in self-conception. Lonergan seems to have conceived his mission as a long-range address to scientific theologians that would help them converse with scientists of other disciplines. Rahner seems to have felt the times are urgent and the people's needs great. Therefore, he has hopped from topic to topic, as current debate and his perception of the church's needs have suggested, and has filled sixteen volumes with theological investigations.

The publication in 1978 of Rahner's *Foundations* broke this pattern. It was the most systematic work he had produced in two decades, and many read it as his capstone or summary statement on the whole. *Foundations* does not pretend to be that, but it does suggest Rahner's mature grasp of the basics. Moreover, its very appearance is significant: only a basic or first course in the Christian "idea" could lure Rahner to write a big book. Further still, Rahner defends the notion of a basic course methodologically. Currently there is a great need, he argues, for essential or primary statements about the Christian core. The main reason is the complexity we noted above. Life in Western society currently is so full of new ideas, so criss-crossed by change and reevaluation, that no individual ever possesses all the information a significant theological problem entails. For example, new studies in psychology and sociology raise numerous questions about the way we constitute a "world" or "lifestyle." Clearly such studies bear on Christian faith, which must express itself as a world view or behavioral path. A few scholars (John Bowker comes to mind) can plunge into new reports on the structuring of consciousness, but most theologians, and virtually all laypersons, have to make their crucial decisions about God, Jesus, and love with limited experience and limited study. Rahner wants to show that every life, no matter how circumscribed, carries with it all the essentials an authentic faith or humanity needs.

That is the reason he stresses mystery. The upshot of complexity is the upshot of deep philosophy or deep contemplative prayer: There is more than we can master. Cued by the faith of Jesus, Rahner generalizes the details of this "more" into their source and finds the basic motif of a mysterious God. Behind every existential item stands its mysterious source. Beyond every alluring experience stands a mysterious lover. If we go to the heavens, there is still more above our heads. If we go to the depths, there is more under our feet. To be is to imply mystery. Fullness alone explains any "is." To know, or love, or suffer is to ask this fullness to become significant, to explain you or me. Reading the good news of Jesus with a philosopher's eye, Rahner makes grace mystery's presence to all persons. Freely, beyond what "Creator" need have implied, God chose to become the horizon of human consciousness, the love of human love. Since that choice, God's inner Word has fanned the spark of light that makes us human. Since that choice, God's inner Spirit breathes the warm love that gives us a heart. "God" therefore is our sum and substance. In every direction, it is for him we grope.

Rahner's dependence on Jesus Christ keeps this interpretation of human experience Christian. Without the real life, death, and resurrection of Jesus grace would be a chimera. Even if we could conceive it, we would have to judge it merely a thought-project, a mental construct with no historical roots. Jesus gives universal grace historical roots. In his person, grace took flesh into divinity. In Nazareth, God's own inner life (specifically, the Word) drew a full humanity into such passionate, absorbing relation with the unbegotten primal Mystery that Jesus became a loving outreach to a divine Father. All that he was, his very identity, was filial.

That for Rahner Jesus' case is merely the extreme, perfect form of a universally human vocation shows how Jesus correlates grace, Christology, and anthropology. Believing in Jesus' good news, and accepting the traditional Christian view that Jesus is the God-Man, Rahner has probed human awareness and found a new meaning for the old scholastic notion of "obediential potency." An obediential potency is a capacity to be raised beyond one's given nature. Applied to the case at hand, it is human beings' capacity to receive divine life, to be raised by grace to share agape. In Jesus such an obediential potency found perfect actualization. In Jesus' sisters and brothers, it can find imperfect, but still wonderful, actualization as well.

Were we to put the rationale for such theologizing in a methodological thesis, Rahner's own "All theology is anthropology" could fit the bill. He gave birth to that dictum (or radically changed its original meaning from Feuerbach) to indicate the methodological pointer or background control that has guided most of his writing. When he approaches a theological problem, be it the meaning of the episcopate or the significance of Vatican II, Rahner looks to human nature. Human beings are spirits-in-the-world. They reach beyond their bodily, historical selves in search of a fulfilling more. That makes them listeners for a word of revelation, a sign from the more of where it can be found.

For those who believe Jesus is this sign, Christian history gives revelation its most specific (Rahner would say "categorical") channel. Consequently, theology is not merely a deduction of the truths human nature inclines us to expect. It is also an investigation of the free, singular things that have happened in a history that is open-ended, a time that could have unfolded differently. By playing back and forth between what has happened in Christian history and what human nature asks life to be, Rahner has orchestrated a brilliant series of theological études. The happenings of Christian history illumine our human constitution, while our human constitution in turn illumines the happenings of Christian history.

For example, the resurrection of Jesus gave rise to a developed eschatology. Using Jewish concepts, early Christians tried to imagine a final judgment, general resurrection of the dead, and consignment of sinners to hell. Taking this traditional imagery seriously, and using it to probe human consciousness, one can clarify the significance of human hope. Jesus' good news includes God's assurance that our hopes for justice and fulfillment are not vain. "Heaven" is a pledge that loving God and neighbor will bring us complete satisfaction. Further, as Marxist-Christian dialogue has emphasized, hope is essential if we are to labor to improve the world. We must believe things can change for the better. When Christians make the hopes they lay in God the foundation of this-worldly social action, they are as energetic as Marxists toward the future.

In ways like this, Christian history can illumine human nature. Conversely, studies of human nature can illumine Christian history and doctrine. In the case at hand, Rahner's studies have pruned traditional eschatological imagery. If we understand the projections of human consciousness, we realize that many of its scenarios are quite dubious. Thus, Christian depictions of cherubs and devils should not be taken literally. The surety of the good news does not extend to them. From Jesus we know that somehow things will be well. Somehow God will provide justice and fulfillment. What form this will take we have no way of knowing. God has sent no postcards. Dante and Milton are interesting but not guaranteed. Neither the lurid imagery of preachers nor the fanciful "prophecies" of Jehovah's Witnesses are entailed by Christian faith. We know little about the fate of Jonathan Edwards's "sinners in the hands of an angry God." Cosmic battle among principalities and powers is science fiction more than theology. Thus, theological anthropology dampens religious hysteria. Much religious imagery, including some in scripture, can only be taken very critically. It says more about the human psyche than about God's ways in the world.

Again and again, Rahner sets the below of historical facts and the above of human transcendence into creative friction. Beginning with apparently tangential doctrines, such as the Immaculate Conception or the Assumption, he circles around to the core issue: our openness for God. In this process doctrines gain a significance ordinary theology seldom accords them. As well, their severe limits emerge. For example, nothing in traditional Catholic doctrine compels us to believe anyone is damned. Traditional doctrine asserts hell is a real possibility. We can use our freedom to lose God and frustrate ourselves utterly. But we cannot know who is doing that now, or who has done it in the past. The Catholic teaching that no one knows his salvation surely means we all have to fear and tremble. The Catholic teaching that God gives all persons sufficient grace for salvation means we all have to relax and trust. It is possible God is so good that hell is empty. Maybe not even Judas Iscariot, Hitler, Stalin, or Ghengis Kahn is there. All we know, if our faith is strong, is that all human beings receive the eternal destiny they deserve.

As we hope this example suggests, the power of Rahner's theological method is its existential relevance. He is so well versed in the doctrinal tradition, and so sensitive to how we are made for mystery, that he consistently shows the significance a teaching or current event has for living faith today. Where other theologians get lost in concepts, Rahner itches to bring analysis back to the primordial mystery of salvation. Through all his difficult language and convoluted reasoning, this existential intent rules. And where does such an intent come from? The indications are it comes from prayer. Rahner's instinct for mystery has been honed by long intercourse in prayer. It is the passion of his life. Sober about human failings, and about fulfillment through worldly things, he has attuned his yearning to God. The result is a core simplicity. At the nub of his thousands of articles, an elementary option stands clear. By the warrant of Jesus Christ, Rahner has chosen to believe the mystery of human life a saving divine love. In ways beyond our comprehension, but congruous with our best intuitions, God has taken history into divinity. Now history takes place in God. It remains a concatenation of human things, but its aim and ultimacy derive from God. Thus, Karl Rahner finally is a "mystagogue"—a theologian constantly trying to show the presence of a God too good for most of us to accept.

TRACY'S REVISIONIST MODEL

David Tracy is a former student of Bernard Lonergan, and if the master has taken a giant step away from Roman theology, the student has taken at least two giant steps. From his work with Lonergan Tracy gained a solid commitment to both method and modernity. Method is the new watchword for systematic theologians, for only method offers them a way to handle the wealth of new information pressing in on their tasks. Modernity is the place where culture shifted from classicist ideals to historical and subjective ones. Many commentators say we live now in a "post-modern" age, meaning by that that Kant, Newton, and the other Enlightenment figures have become inadequate. Because of Marx, Darwin, Freud, and Einstein, we know more about economics, biology, psychology, and physics than the archetypal moderns did. Be that as it may, modernity forced theologians to come to grips with *critical* scholarship. The crux of the Enlightenment was the proposition that we human beings make much of our reality by our own judgments and decisions. David Tracy has accepted the challenge of rethinking Christian theology in the context of critical American thought.

More precisely, he has accepted the challenge of rethinking theology in the context of a contemporary university like the University of Chicago. Through dialogue with colleagues in the University of Chicago Divinity School like Langdon Gilkey, Schubert Ogden, Paul Ricoeur, and Norman Perrin, he developed the "revisionist" model of theology that his *Blessed Rage for Order* elaborates. The model begins with two main assumptions. First, Tracy assumes that the pluralism of current American theology can be enriching. There are Catholics, Protestants,

Orthodox, and Jews. There are phenomenologists, linguistic analysts, process thinkers, historians, Neo-Thomists, and more. Each represents a wealth of religious experience. None is without a valuable insight. Therefore a theologian's first reaction should be positive. How good that so many tools and insights surround me.

Second, however, the current pluralism does present serious problems. Unless the theologian takes special pains to clarify her assumptions, ways of proceeding, and the like, pluralism will become a great bog. Therefore Tracy plumps for methodological awareness. Each theologian ought to articulate an explicit method of inquiry and defend it publicly. Moreover, each ought to apply her method to the same materials: the symbols and texts of (a) our common human life and (b) Christianity. If Christian theology is to appropriate the riches of contemporary pluralism, it must apply methodological sophistication to the materials that comprise the core of reflecting on faith in Jesus. If theologians can say why they find these materials configuring as they do, they will be able to understand one another and argue profitably. One senses that Tracy's own experience of dialogue, as well as his orientation from Lonergan, has pushed him to this conviction. In the current context, Christian theology will best be ecumenical if it bends over backwards to specify its methodological options.

Equally interesting, however, are the primary sources Tracy stresses. The symbols and texts of Christianity are clear enough. In scripture and the decrees of the magisterium (councils, authoritative teachers, creeds, etc.), the Christian theologian has her best indication of canonical Christian faith. It is difficult to conceive Christian theology apart from these primary sources. Nonetheless, the symbols and texts are not a thin body. Scripture alone has many theologies; it is itself pluralistic. All the more, then, ought a theologian to specify how he approaches scripture (or a conciliar document, a papal pronouncement, etc.). The second primary source, our common human life, is even harder to handle. By insisting on it Tracy seems mainly to demand that theology be in dialogue with contemporary culture—that it assume the burden of making sense in terms of current human experience. Though he does not attribute this demand to Karl Rahner, he might have, for Rahner above all has tried to render traditional faith in terms of contemporary human experience.

To develop his program for a revisionist theology, Tracy chisels five theses. First is the base line we have been developing. The principal sources for Christian theology are Christian texts and common human experience (and language). Second, theology has to correlate what it finds in these two sources. In other words, it is not enough to study either Christian texts or common human experience alone. They must be set in dialogue or dialectic, so that they illumine one another mutually.

The second thesis is reminiscent of Rahner's use of anthropology and (Christian) history. It is also reminiscent of Tillich's "method of correlation," which insisted that theology dialogue with culture. From Gilkey and others who were formed by Tillich, the Niebuhrs, and other recent Protestant theologians of culture, Tracy accepts an "anthropology" that deals with more than the individual human consciousness. In principle, his notion of common human experience is open to whatever the social sciences or humanities, as well as theology itself, reveal about human nature. Therefore, his theology could have a substantial political component. *Blessed Rage for Order* does not emphasize this component, but neither does it exclude it.

The third thesis is that revisionist theology entails a phenomenology or careful description of the religious dimension that science, everyday experience, and everyday language all carry. We ourselves dabbled in such phenomenology in the second chapter, and it has frequently preoccupied Rahner, Tillich, and others. Indeed, correlating Christian tradition and contemporary experience almost automatically entails it. However, Tracy appears to want something more rigorous. For example, he refers to Stephen Toulmin's analysis of science, which shows the limits of the scientific horizon. Beyond those limits lie questions of ultimate meaning and value. They could point the astute scientist toward the legitimacy of religion.

The fourth thesis is that investigating Christian texts entails a strong commitment to history and hermeneutics. Many Catholic theologians already have made this commitment, but Roman theology continues to make others hold back. Post-modern consciousness takes it as a given that any statement is conditioned by its historical context. Current scholarship, which reflects this consciousness, makes no exception for religious scriptures. Rather, it assumes that they too share biases of their times. Theologians need not deny this assumption. The imprint of God they find in Christian texts does not destroy the human authors' imprint. For instance, Jesus spoke the Aramaic of an early first century Galilean. Nothing in his relation to the Father freed him from the grammatic and linguistic constraints such Aramaic imposed.

The connection with hermeneutics is that interpretation has to take a text's historical provenance seriously. In addition, however, contemporary hermeneutics has borrowed from literary criticism and approaches Christian texts with a sensitivity to their genres, rhetorics, uses of metaphor, and so forth. For David Tracy, Christian theology cannot hang back from such scholarly developments. It must employ the best tools of its time, confident that progress in understanding its sources will strengthen genuine faith.

Tracy's fifth and last thesis is that Christian theology should determine the truth status of its findings through a transcendental or metaphysical reflection. By this he means that Christian theology should retain its traditional commitment to ontology. Under the influence of historicism, phenomenology, and linguistic analysis, some contemporary theologians have bracketed ontology. In other words, they have given up the task of judging the objective truth, the hard reality, of Christian claims and contented themselves with description. Description has considerable value. It is useful indeed to know how early Christians worshiped or what meanings they read into phrases such as "Son of God." But traditionally Christian theology has been more than description. It has assumed that faith discloses genuine realities, a God and grace that are true. Consequently, it has accepted the respectability of thinking through the basic build of the world disclosed in Jesus' revelation.

For instance, if Jesus' God is the creator whom Genesis describes, then the world is radically contingent—radically sprung from nothingness. Similarly, if Paul's references to the Word's functions in creation are true, then the world holds together in God's self-expression. These assertions do not directly determine anything in the realm of sciences. They are no mandate to write physics one way or another. But they are intuitions of faith about the ultimate character of reality—about the origin and structure of being as such. By continuing theology's traditional commitment to being as such, Tracy maintains its commitment to faith's objectivity.

Blessed Rage for Order has a special significance for those who, like David Tracy, work in the context of the secular university. In the past generation, the secular university begot an entity called "religious studies." It represents an effort to acknowledge the importance religion has had in human history without accepting any particular religious faith. In other words, the religious studies scholar tends to bracket the question of her own faith-commitments and study Christianity as an objective phenomenon. *A priori*, she grants it no more status or truth than she grants a Hellenistic mystery religion or the *Federalist Papers* of the American constitutionalists. Tracy's revisionist theology attempts to take what is praiseworthy in religious studies and incorporate it into Christian theology. This leads, first, to a strong emphasis on rigorous scholarship. Theology can engage in no special pleading. It must study as carefully as the best of its secular analogues and reason as cogently. Second, there are portions of university theology that do not demand personal faith on the part of the theologian. Insofar as he is doing historical or exegetical work, the canons of history and exegesis are his first masters.

In Lonergan's terms, much Christian theology occurs in the first phase, before dialectics issues a personal commitment and begins to build foundations. That Tracy does not recur to Lonergan's schema and clarify his university brand of theology in its terms suggests he does not find it satisfactory. On the other hand, his commitment to

Christian texts shows that the "foundations" of his revisionist theology entail traditional faith. Further, under Tracy's commitment to common human experience lies the equivalent of Lonergan's authenticity. In asking theology to meet the scholarly standards of its contemporaries, he is asking it to make faith something today's men and women can affirm with no hedging.

Nonetheless, Tracy's slighting of divine mystery makes his theology more problematic than it need be. He acknowledges mystery but, by his own admission, does not have a good ear for its music. Consequently, his theology does not have Rahner's radical simplicity. For Rahner authenticity finally reposes in what we do about divine mystery. Divine mystery is the primordial fact, the base line of the human condition. Therefore, our response to divine mystery is the quintessence of our honesty and love. Christian texts finally say to common human experience, "Surrender. God is greater than our minds and hearts, even when they condemn us."

Neglecting mysticism marks Tracy's theology as academic. So does slighting praxis. Praxis will occupy us momentarily, when we deal with Segundo's methodology. Our last word here, though, ought to be positive. By asking theology to be thoroughly critical, David Tracy has made high university standards call it to grow.

SEGUNDO AND THE PLACE OF PRAXIS

Juan Luis Segundo is the liberation theologian who most fully addresses methodological problems. His *The Liberation of Theology* both attacks received notions of theological method and lays down the tasks that a theology pivoted on liberation now faces. In previous sections we have seen the emphasis liberation theology places on praxis. Combining its study of Marxist theory with its daily experiences of oppression, Latin American liberation theology has argued that praxis is the legitimate heir of the biblical prophets' concern with right religion. For the prophets, right religion above all was doing justice. The God of Amos and Isaiah wanted mercy, fair dealing, human compassion, not perfunctory sacrifice. A solid corps of eloquent theologians now says the Latin American equivalent is transforming societal structures that oppress millions. Doing justice on that continent means changing the "system." Segundo's volume rebounds from convictions such as these to cast a critical eye on Christian theology itself. If the Latin American situation shows the primacy of praxis, how must traditional theology change?

We have already noted Latin American liberation theologians' perhaps surprising interest in theory. By temperament or training, they tend to probe philosophical assumptions. For instance, Jon Sobrino begins his *Christology at the Crossroads* with a reprise of the assumptions of Karl Rahner, Wolfhart Pannenberg, and Jurgen Moltmann. In the cases of Rahner and Pannenberg, he finds a neglect of praxis—of the sociology and politics faith must inform. José Miranda's *Being and the Messiah* has a similar beginning. Before zeroing in on the Johannine texts that are his main concern, Miranda writes a prolegomenon on existentialist and atheistic thought. Thus, Segundo's interest in theory is not idiosyncratic. His Latin American colleagues find his interest in method fitting.

Segundo begins with "the hermeneutic circle." This is a tag that European reflection on interpretation has made famous. It emphasizes that no interpreter of a text or situation can step outside her relation to it. In the Christian case, there is no way an interpreter can divorce scripture from the subsequent history it generated. That history produced various readings of scripture, as interpreters with Hellenistic, medieval European, or Latin American sensitivities saw it through their different glasses. On the one hand, their different glasses led them to focus on different themes. For example, Latin Americans' concern with oppression recently led them to focus on justice—on *doing* the truth to social and political effect. On the other hand, interpreters have been constrained by the text itself to examine their own assumptions and values. In other words, the scriptural text has not been wholly captive to any generation's biases, for even the most opinionated readings have run into the stubborn fact that Jesus had a mind of his own. Consequently, the relation between text and reader has been circular. Again and again, it has bowed around to embrace them both.

The last century witnessed a rise in sociological awareness that bears on the hermeneutic circle. Comte and Marx were the pioneers, but since Emile Durkheim and Max Weber (early twentieth-century) sociology has had a full scholarly rationale. Indeed, it has taken on the air of a sober study of social consciousness, and frequently it has run into religion. Segundo thinks sociology is still immature. Analyzing social consciousness requires great sophistication, for one must join empirical information to subtle, unbiased interpretative techniques. Too often American sociology of religion has contented itself with questionnaires. Parsing numbers on church attendance, Bible reading, and the like, it has concluded with a whimper. On the other hand, dogma often has infiltrated continental sociology. Putting on tinted glasses, European scholars have read in both leftist and rightist convictions most people never suspected they had. Thus, sociologists of religion have a lot of hard work still ahead of them.

Third, past theology has shied away from politics, not recognizing that faith itself is a political option. When one makes a commitment to Jesus, politics is entailed inevitably. Any significant commitment to Jesus is a commitment to the twofold commandment. By the first portion of that commandment, no political regime can command one's total allegiance. By the second portion, social justice is a radical imperative. The early Christians sensed this and were quick to protest they had to obey God rather than men. They were slower to see that social customs such as slavery were incompatible with Christian views of human equality, but they did think of the church as a grouping without slave or free. Today, our current awarenesses ought to make the political implications of Christian faith quite plain. If following Jesus is to become full-bodied, it must become public action and witness.

We have interpreted Segundo's first three topics against the background of our previous chapters. They amount to an argument that theology has to broaden its hermeneutical, social, and political sensitivities. In his middle chapters, Segundo focuses on "ideology." Ideology is a term with Marxist overtones, and traditional theology has received it coolly. Usually it means the distorting preconceptions a group uses to protect its vested interests. For example, capitalist ideology has included the notion that the poor are lazy. Looking at a slum, capitalists have pointed to the lethargic men hanging around the corner bar and sermonized, "No wonder they live in hovels." When the slum lord turns preacher, you can suspect ideology.

However, turnabout is fair exchange. By their ideological heavy-handedness, Marxists have sinned egregiously. In the 1940s the Soviet agronomist T. D. Lysenko became infamous because he repudiated Mendelian genetics on the basis of Marxist "orthodoxy." To the present-day Chinese Communists subordinate art (ballet, for instance) to political propaganda. These cases have in common the ideological conviction that Marxist theory is more important than facts or creativity. In the Marxist treasury the paramount value is advancing the revolution. Frequently that has twisted Marxist history, science, and art. During the 1960s Americans caught some Marxist fallout. Waving Mao's red book, various groups spouted an incredible blend of jargon, cant, and outrage.

There are theologians who pretend to be above the ideological fray, but Segundo will have none of that. Not only is Catholic history full of ideological distortions, ideology continues in Catholic theology today. The conciliar definitions of dogma came from passionate fights against what were perceived as threats to salvation. The case of Galileo was an ideological debate, and the witch hunts were a tragedy. Even today Roman theology has strong vested interests. It was slow to allow free biblical research, and it still harasses theologians who depart from the time-honored formulas.

However, Segundo would have a good ideology lodge deeper, below these mutual accusations. Stripped of its vicious connotations, "ideology" might signify the commitment or point of view that any text, author, or institution assumes. In fact, simply to have a position, to be definite about something important, is to have an ideology. Agreeing with this, one of the bishops at Puebla challenged his colleagues: "Let him who is without an ideology cast the first stone." The Bible surely has an ideology. For Segundo it is a preference for the poor. God does not approve all regimes or moralities indiscriminately. Some are good and some are evil. Why, in fact, did Jesus die, if not for the conflict between his ideology and that of the prevailing establishment? What Catholic theology now must do is recognize its ideologies and see whether they are compatible with Jesus the liberator. If they prop the oppression of Jesus' constituency, they obviously are not Christian.

Segundo himself has an ideology, which gives him his agenda. His book would undermine critics of liberation theology at their foundations. Critics who stand to lose power or money if a just social order comes to Latin America are dismissed easily. That group includes many North Americans, which reminds us again that we have a stake in Segundo's work with church critics. The issue can also be losing money or power in the church. The church sits alongside the other institutions of established society, so bishops hobnob with bankers and politicians. The church is in the world, so its leaders learn many of the world's ways. Raising money, they run into high society, or even organized crime. Seeking advantage, they play golf with politicos and advertising moguls. It is hard to countenance a theology that attacks the people with whom you golf. Since getting along with such people seems essential to the church's welfare, many hierarchs try to blunt liberation theology.

Of course, they are not the whole of liberation theology's opposition. Another group criticizes its reading of the gospel on violence. For this group, the gospel has little to do with politics. Above all, it opposes violence. Did not Jesus say those who live by the sword perish by the sword? Did he not go to his death nonviolently? These questions are telling, and they have forced liberation theologians to meditate on violence deeply. Still, true to its methodological bias, liberation theology has best understood violence by stressing praxis.

If one begins from the experiences of the oppressed, one finds violence to be systematic. The soldiers and torturers may be far away, but there is maldistribution of resources, unemployment, unsanitary housing, a lack of medical attention, and so forth. As the encyclicals of the recent Popes have taught, human beings have a right to these goods and services. Society exists to furnish them. The invisible violence (*violencia blanca*) of disordered social systems wrecks thousands of lives every day. Do traditionalist theologians want to make Jesus a defender of this wreckage?

It is desirable, of course, that change come with minimal hurt. Ideally, not even dictators would suffer a blow. But what does one do when a regime refuses to grant the minimal civil rights by which peaceful change might occur? How is one to defend the legions of suffering when there are no free elections, no free speech, no right to free assembly? Like a raging cancer, unjust political regimes sap the lives of millions. Is it un-christian to apply the political equivalent of chemotherapy or surgery? Do the rights of the vicious few weigh more heavily than the rights of the suffering many?

Were Catholic theology to turn methodically to praxis, questions such as these would shape its Christology, ecclesiology, and treatises on grace. They would make it obvious that cloistering in either curial or academic chambers disserves Jesus' gospel. Jesus' gospel was good news to the downtrodden. For Juan Luis Segundo, the downtrodden write theology's next moves.

CODA

Roman theology and the four later theological methods we have surveyed are not wholly discordant. On many points they do not so much disagree as place different emphases. Further, they share a great reverence for Christian revelation. The truth that faith discloses is for all of them a primary treasure. By implication, therefore, theology is a privileged undertaking. Roman theology especially stresses the grave beauty of tradition, but the other theologies also realize that they would serve poor fare indeed were their message merely of their own devising. The same is true of almost all other serious theologians. They seek no innovation for its own sake. Whatever novelty they bring forth is in the service of clarifying "that which was from the beginning" (1 John 1:1).

Thus, whether it stresses papal authority, the dynamics of authentic consciousness, religious mystery, critical rigor, or evangelical praxis, a contemporary Catholic theology of depth aims simply at reviewing, renewing, reexpressing the original deposit of faith. It is the considerable achievement of current Catholic theology to have regained the primitive Christian realization that the original deposit of faith finally is Jesus himself. Jesus is the living metaphor of revelation; he is faith's personal motive and model. The history of Christian theology is the story of how the Christian generations have understood Jesus' message and work, while constructive Christian theology is considering how Jesus configures the human vocation. Theological methods are as good as the profit they derive from such history, the aid they offer such construction.

BIBLIOGRAPHY

Bowker, John. *The Sense of God.* Oxford, England: Clarendon Press, 1973.
Carr, Anne. *The Theological Method of Karl Rahner.* Missoula, Mont.: Scholars Press, 1977.

Davis, Charles. *A Question of Conscience.* New York: Harper & Row, 1967.

Dilthey, Wilhelm. *Pattern and Meaning in History.* New York: Harper & Row, 1961.

Hennelley, Alfred. "Theological Method: Southern Exposure," *Theological Studies* 38/4 (December 1977), 709–735.

Krol, Cardinal John. "SALT II and the American Bishops," *America* 142/9 (March 8, 1980), 183–185.

Lonergan, Bernard. *Insight.* New York: Philosophical Library, 1957.

Lonergan, Bernard. *Method in Theology.* New York: Herder and Herder, 1972.

McShane, Philip, ed. *Foundations of Theology.* Notre Dame, Ind.: University of Notre Dame Press, 1972.

Ogden, Schubert. "Theology and Religious Studies," *Journal of the American Academy of Religion* XLVI/1 (March 1978), 3–17.

Rahner, Karl. *Foundations of Christian Faith.* New York: Seabury, 1978.

Roberts, Louis. *The Achievement of Karl Rahner.* New York: Herder and Herder, 1967.

Segundo, Juan Luis. *The Liberation of Theology.* Maryknoll, N.Y.: Orbis, 1976.

Tillich, Paul. *Systematic Theology.* Chicago: University of Chicago Press, 1967.

Tracy, David. *Blessed Rage for Order.* New York: Seabury, 1975.

Tracy, David. *The Achievement of Bernard Lonergan.* New York: Herder and Herder, 1970.

Conclusion 10

OVERVIEW

Our conclusion focuses on personal theologizing and a short formula of Christian faith. Collecting the emphases developed in the last chapter, we try to apply them to the average Christian's situation, so as to make theology part of his vocation. This means broadening or democratizing the traditional notion that theology is "faith seeking understanding." Essentially, it makes an "amateur" theology: reviewing daily experience with an eye of faith. Daily experience asks faith for cogent interpretation. Conversely, faith asks daily experience for examples and instances. Karl Rahner has pioneered the use of "short formulas" that put the Catholic substance of such instances in a nutshell. Having exposed how "everyman" can be an amateur theologian, we suggest the core content with which amateur theology deals.

PERSONAL THEOLOGIZING

The previous chapter described contemporary theology in terms of methodological emphases on history, authenticity, mystery, criticism, and praxis. They are major angles today's theologians bring to received Christian doctrine. Of course, past theologians were aware of these angles. Nonetheless, the classicist ideal of a single system, controlled by Rome, blunted them.

With an appropriation of history has come pluralism. In academic theology, Catholics now write from a variety of viewpoints. With an acceptance of modernity's turn to the subject has come a stress on authenticity. Increasingly, Catholic theologians are loathe to put forward doctrines they cannot fully accredit personally. For instance, current psychology makes theologians find traditional Christology problematic. Schillebeeckx, Schoonenberg, and others are in trouble for their reservations, and the resolution of these troubles will say much about future Catholic theology's authenticity.

History and authenticity have led Lonergan to stress interdisciplinary collaboration. To handle the new diversity, theologians must specialize; to keep theology from fragmenting, they must make their specialties communicate. A more personal way to handle diversity is to rivet onto God's mystery. The fact of mystery is something the most rigorous criticism cannot erode. Finally, the political facts of life have forced current theology to examine faith's praxis. What doing flows from this thinking? More fundamentally, what doing flows into this thinking? If liberation theology becomes part of future Catholicism's landscape, praxis will loom large.

We have summarized these recent shifts because they have analogues in personal theologizing. Insofar as faith guides a person's life, new approaches have personal implications. We shall indicate some such implications momentarily, but first let us justify the notion of personal or amateur theologizing itself. The notion is that every Christian ought to love seeking her faith's understanding. "Amateur" implies a work of love, and the tradition relates amateur theology to the Spirit. When faith manifests the Spirit, we notice a love of authentic religion. That is, the Spirit fosters a love of understanding God, of getting a better hold on Jesus, of seeing the twofold command more clearly. She is behind the savor we find in ruminating a scriptural passage or discussing grace.

At first this can seem pious, even affected. Before long, however, it is sober and unobjectionable. For we humans do need to consider our lives under this aspect of eternity. The wisdom Erikson puts at the end of the life cycle does beckon us earlier on. Many feel it in adolescence, when a teacher or a book first cracks open their minds. They see what education could be, and they suffer ever after. The love of wisdom may seem muted in middle age, but it reasserts itself regularly. When money troubles arise, or children are contrary, or parents die, we are rocked back to ruminate. The same when we feel backbiting on the job or learn another marriage has shattered. Indeed, by the time the children have left the warren they may find us sententious—all too ready to philosophize. The theologian would have us be ready to theologize— to brighten the eye of our faith. Aristotle thought a person needs fifty years before he can discourse on ethics well. The Spirit seems to think fifty years ought to make one ripe for the mystery of God.

By the fact that we have faith, intelligence, and time, we are ripe for at least amateur theology. If we have accepted Jesus' extraordinary humanity, we have staked out the first mile of a Christian way. If that way is to go farther, we have to develop what we first accepted. The tacit crisis in many Christians' faith is its underdevelopment. They have done little with theology since they left catechism class, and they wonder why faith seems childish. Granted, they ought to get adult fare in the Sunday sermon or the diocesan newspaper. But often they do not, so their religious childishness is their own problem. They are individuals with capable minds and free wills. Why can they not take responsibility for developing their faith, as they take responsibility for developing their financial security? The summer schools overflow with good theology workshops. The periodical rack groans. The problem, then, is not a lack of fare but a lack of appetite.

Still, it is not hard to sharpen appetite. Even unease can be an aperitif. Just as most workers feel underemployed, so people generally feel under-challenged and bored. This reflects their poor education. If they knew their minds and hearts, they could find a week's experience material for a lifetime of study. Amateur theology can be the process of turning ordinary experience into material for deep study. Assuming faith in Jesus, it tries to regard the world as a child of grace. In other words, the amateur theologian explicitly compares her experiences with those of Jesus, testing Jesus' proposition that God shares our time lovingly. The process itself is open-ended. One can delve into Jesus or human experience for years and never glimpse the end. Therefore, the light must come more from the doing than from the ending. Simply making Jesus and one's present time dialectical usually produces a flame.

It also draws a hermeneutic circle. Taking Jesus as God's human paradigm, amateur theology probes both good times and bad. Consider, for instance, school times. When we actually are learning, we never question the value of school. Learning has a rightness that is self-justify-ing. Thus, one grows in mastering accounting. Both the mathematics and the business it involves develop intelligence. There are further questions, such as where to use one's accounting knowledge, but even if we answer them badly our knowledge itself is good. To understand is to use time well.

Similarly, to fail to understand is to seem to use time badly. This may be deceptive, since significant understanding can demand an incubation period of confusion, but let us assume it is not. Let us assume given materials for study are unintelligible. Because of poor teaching or sloppy texts, many students run into this situation. In our case, it occurred with canon law. Though the teacher and the text offered principles, they fell into no coherent order. This was utterly frustrating, and we found relief only through what Lonergan calls an "inverse insight." One day we realized there was nothing to understand. Canon law has no coherent system, no explanatory connection to ontology, theology, or political science. The only thing to do was to memorize it. That was painful, but at least we were no longer seeking something nowhere to be found.

From a good learning experience the amateur theologian can better appreciate what it means that God is light in whom there is no darkness at all (1 John 1:5). From a bad learning experience she can learn that unintelligibility is not mystery. Canon law, for instance, would only be mysterious if it held a fullness of understanding one could grasp at a higher level.

So far our examples have been speculative, but practical examples serve equally well. A good personal relationship carries overtones of communion. If things go well with a friend or lover, we grow a full set of affective ties. They illumine the scriptural conviction that human beings should not be alone, give weight to the scriptural adage that a brother helped by a brother is like a strong city. If the passion is profound, they may even bring to mind "love is strong as death." Of course, a good personal relationship will bring none of these to mind if one never has read scripture. The revelation pole in the amateur theologian's consciousness must be high enough to attract some attention. On the other hand, the experiential pole grows higher when we can add data of revelation.

In a bad personal relationship, the data might be labeled "sin," "creaturehood," or "redemptive suffering." We can reach for security when we are hurt, be tempted never to risk love again. Wrapped like a porcupine, we would make ourselves all sharp quills. When the pain goes down, though, faith suggests we reconsider the life of a porcupine. You don't see much when your head is tucked under your tail. You don't feel much when your skin is all sharp quills.

So, how did Jesus bear himself toward the world? How did he respond to misunderstanding, deception, and betrayal? Even if Jesus' example seems beyond us, the honesty to face it is a spiritual healing. In time, we may be able to imitate Jesus' large-heartedness. And, the logic of such imitation is intriguing. Those who imitate Jesus wager they will gain light and peace. For instance, the saints wagered they would find the center of things, the still point of the turning world. Winning, they said they learned more by trying to stand toward human beings as Jesus did than by either withdrawing or joining the stream. Ultimately, of course, the saints did not trouble themselves much with logic. Ultimately they simply fell in love with Christ. But along the way Christ intrigued them. There is no good reason he cannot intrigue us similarly.

Amateur theology, then, is simply reflective Christian living. It goes to scripture, tradition, or current theologians simply to sharpen its perceptions of faith. The faith is primary, the reflection secondary. Living in face of mystery, amateur theologians use whatever helps them understand it more. The medievals were convinced theology could disclose an objective order. The amateur theologian shares this conviction, for he reflects hoping to understand. The moderns sensed much "reality" stems from our own interpretations. The amateur theologian shares this sense, too, for she wants faith to show her what interpretations yield the most light. When she hears faith answer, "The interpretations that are most loving," the Spirit plucks at her heartstrings. Amateur theology is but love's exegesis of time.

A SHORT FORMULA OF CHRISTIAN FAITH

Our description of personal or amateur theologizing assumes that reflection can find profit in both good experiences and bad. For faith God holds all times, so no time need be lost. That is the ideal, but it can seem inhuman. Most of us have to struggle to believe our times come from God, especially the destructive ones. What "profit" can parents find in the death of a tiny infant? What "growth" justifies a sundering divorce? To make times of war come from God is to risk obscenity. Surely a mature faith must be more critical.

Indeed it must, but at the end of all criticism the mystery still remains. In short form, Christian faith is a loving response to mystery, based on the story of Jesus Christ. Since mystery embraces our whole lives, it entails sin and evil, as well as grace. The loving response of faith does not demand closing our eyes to sin and evil. It does not demand denying the anger, hurt, or diminution they bring. Half the world suffers real diminution, real loss, through poverty and its after-effects. All the world experiences things that should not be, things that rightly cause anger. Christian faith should take these realities seriously. In fidelity to conscience, it cannot whiten black deeds. In fidelity to history, it cannot forget Jesus suffered evil unto death. The deepest liberation is from evil and death. There would be no absolute savior were there no mortal sin.

Despite this unblinking realism, Christian faith still finds life's mystery good. Where sin abounded grace abounds the more. Where evil twisted the spirit into knots, good remained what the spirit was made for. If there is a mystery of evil, so is there a mystery of good. If it is a puzzle that an aged person should have to die, it is more a puzzle that a child should be born. Because of Jesus, Christian faith makes all these equations unbalanced. It says, better to have lived than never to have been born. Better to have loved and been hurt than never to have loved at all. Better even to have done evil than not to have been free. Joining its contemplation of Jesus to its contemplation of experience, Christian faith struggles to live out such confessions.

An articulate theology can aid confession immensely, but finally it is a choice we each face at heart. Rahner's theory of anonymous Christianity reminds us that Jesus clarifies a universal condition. All persons live amidst mystery. All come to know both evil and good. So all have to choose, to interpret their time. Even if they affirm an established tradition, the affirmation is a matter of personal choice. We cannot abdicate responsibility for our time's deepest issue. We cannot transfer to others our yes or no to God. At the stillest hour, we can only follow Jesus or hold back, only commend our spirits trustingly or refuse to go gentle.

The advantage of short formulas is their condensation of endless implications. If Christian faith is saying yes to mystery in virtue of Jesus Christ, a thousand collateral issues fall into the shade. To be sure, the "yes" must be active, practical. It must be the deed of our life, the synthesis of our love. Not those who say "Lord, Lord" but those who do his will please God. Not those who talk about the twofold commandment but those who really pray and serve fulfill the law and the prophets. Still, Jesus makes the task blessedly plain. We are given time in order to learn our lives' gravity. Theologically, their gravity is an image of the Trinity. Our weightiest product, our fullest humanity, reflects the fathomless Father, the expressive Son, and the gathering Spirit of love.

Philosophically, our reflection of God engages a reality with four primary zones. Nature, society, self, and divinity are the four irreducible factors of a human being's world. Therefore, the Christian's response to mystery relates her to all these factors. To deny nature or society is almost as distorting as denying God. Even to undervalue one of the four factors is to warp one's response to mystery. For instance, our bodies give us a basis in matter which faith denies at its peril. From sacraments to relaxation, nature impresses itself.

So too with society. A church is as inevitable as a tribe. There are no independent human beings. All of us have mothers, fathers, and collaborators. Similarly there are no Christians who have not received from the church and do not owe recompense. When they try to pay it, they learn what the relation between society and self ought to be. Society ought to enhance the individuality of its members. Conversely, the members ought to find their fullest selves in social relation. When a given local society does not know this, and so crushes individuality, the individual can rightly stay away. But even staying away shows her what ideally would obtain. The church is emptier than it ought to be, and many individual lives lack an important luster.

Thus, the subthemes of the main commitment unfold soberly. Though grace abounds more than sin, sin is by no means meager. Though peace is inseparable from the Spirit of grace, it can lodge on the very rock bottom. Christian faith does not promise a sinless life, nor a life where peace is unthreatened. It has nothing to do with financial success, and little to do with status. It has everything to do with the self's definition, its absolute relation to God. Is God a mystery worth loving? Does time hint a parental care? Believers say yes to these questions—true believers on the basis of experience.

For Karl Rahner's mature theology, mystery-grace-Jesus are the Christian nub. The common, foundational reality is mystery. The goodness faith finds comes from grace, God's love. The sign and paradigm of God's love is Jesus. If one begins with the deepest common denominator, the theological word is "mystery." To be human is to have a reflective consciousness that plunges into life's too-fullness. Hindu, Hottentot, or Hamite, the human being is the animal that asks why. Asking why is responding to mystery. At core we *are* responses to mystery, embodied questionings. A child is born and we ask why love becomes so wrinkled and wiggly. A government collapses and we ask why human beings still haven't learned to cooperate. We turn a page and a biblical image transposes such asking. Creatures should not expect full understanding. Full understanding depends on full responsibility, full initiation. No creature has full responsibility, so no creature has full understanding. For there to be full understanding there must be a creator. If there is not a creator, creation is casual. Both our minds and creation repudiate that. A casual, senseless creation gives our minds no reason to be. It does not square with scientists learning to make nuclear fission, psychiatrists learning how to heal sick spirits. Mystery, then, is a fullness, not a void. It is more than we can handle, not less.

That is an argument of common sense, raised slightly by Christian philosophy. Ultimately, it comes from a second naiveté: Tulips spring from bulbs, tides from wind and moon. If something is "there," there is a cause. If something changes, there is a reason. We may not be able to grasp it fully, but a single experience of understanding proves it must exist. Grace buttresses this reasoning. Shoring the mind, it tips the scale against absurdity. Though the mind is limited, discovery after discovery proves it can investigate the world successfully. The mind has to be patient, come to know its limitations, but they do not make the world an idiot's tale. When Heisenberg formulated indeterminancy, he helped set physicists' limitations. Obviously, though, he did not say physicists' cannot know, waste their time. His own theory claimed to be a knowing. Its validity says he used time well.

Similarly, grace shores the heart. The surd that really unravels human beings is moral evil. Physical evil—earthquakes and cancers—is as logical as statistical probability. Moral evil makes no sense, violates constitutional laws. We are the species who can violate our own constitutional law. We can see the good and not do it, specify the evil and take it home. Partly from finitude, which makes us fallible, and partly from disorder, which has no intelligible cause, we can frustrate our inmost calling. Such frustration writes a tragi-comedy. Our inhumanity tells heaven it did bad work. The irony of knowing and not doing makes us blush and then smile. Grace urges the blush and blesses the smile. Against God's invitation, mystery's largess, we are ingrates who do well to blush often. But when we accept the humiliating truth, it becomes a liberating humility. Graciously, God forgives our sin. With her there are new beginnings. So our pretense to sufficiency becomes funny, our drones and struts vaudevillian.

Most societies have understood tragedy, and many have glimpsed irony. Deep comedy, though, is a child of grace. For grace finally is divinization, humanity's complete success. Taken into God's own life, our time ends discretely. Death is a leap, a final saltus, beyond the happiest extrapolation. That saltus makes human time a *divina commedia*, a play or puppetry. Too subtly for our sensing, God makes creation elevation. The mystery we move in is an amniotic fluid. From death a new, glorified existence is born. The delivery room is so oxygenated that "heavenly" life is most intense and most fulfilling. It is like the life of the resurrected Christ.

Jesus, then, anchors all Christian talk about mystery and grace. Without his resurrection, there would be no comedy. Similarly, there would be no shoring against life's evil. And, historically, there would be no Christianity. Christianity depends on the resurrection of Jesus. It is the memory of God's eschatological act, the burgeoning of time's core revelation. Because of the resurrection Jesus' followers preserved the story of his painful death, remembered his wonderful teaching. Because of the resurrection, they created liturgies. Many theologians were kids enthralled by liturgies. In prolix treatises, they have spun out the liturgies' wisdom. In short formulas, they have condensed grace's power. The power and wisdom is Christ.

BIBLIOGRAPHY

Burrell, David. *Exercises in Religious Understanding.* Notre Dame, Ind.: University of Notre Dame Press, 1974.
O'Donovan, Leo, ed. *A World of Grace.* New York: Seabury, 1980.
Rahner, Karl, and Vorgrimler, Herbert. *Theological Dictionary.* New York: Herder and Herder, 1965.
Rahner, Karl. "Brief Creedal Statements," in his *Foundations of Christian Faith* (New York: Seabury, 1978), 448–460.
Stoeckle, Bernard, ed. *The Concise Dictionary of Christian Ethics.* New York: Seabury, 1979.

Appendix I. A Brief History of Catholic Theology

OVERVIEW

Our treatment has four subdivisions. The formative period of Catholic theology was the first five centuries or so, when scripture and the fathers predominated. Against the background of contemporary Judaism, Jesus introduced several striking innovations. Reflecting on Jesus, the apostolic age produced the New Testament. Joined to the Hebrew Bible, it is Catholic theology's charter. The early apologists began the task of translating this charter into Hellenistic categories. As heresies arose, bishop-theologians and episcopal councils developed Catholic doctrine by reaction.

Greek theologians dominated the formative period, but Latins dominated the medieval. By the time of Peter Abelard (1079–1142), the West had Aristotelian categories and theological reasoning had gained greater precision. Aristotelianism found its great Christian interpreter in Thomas Aquinas, with whom scholasticism reached full flower. Unfortunately, by Luther's time scholasticism had greatly wilted. Put off by nominalism (word games), Luther went back to the Bible. Responding to the Reformers, Catholic theology regrouped at the Council of Trent. The doctrines and disciplines hammered out there shaped Catholic faith to the twentieth century. From the seventeenth century, however, Catholic theology was in decline. Slow to accept modern science, and bitterly opposed to modern philosophy, its luminaries were few. At the turn of this century, though, the giant awakened. After World War II it began moving, and there seems no stopping it now.

SCRIPTURE AND THE FATHERS

Catholic theology begins in the Hebrew Bible. There was no inevitable connection between Abraham and a church centered in Rome, but after the fact one can trace definite lines. For Jesus and the first Christians, "scripture" was the Hebrew Bible, above all the Pentateuch. Reading scripture they found a transcendent God. Unlike the Canaanite baals, Yahweh stood beyond nature. He was the Lord, the source of all creation. Human beings could commune with him, but their sin made communion difficult. Were God to judge harshly, none would survive. Still, God had chosen Israel as his people. The covenant pledged his presence, and the Hebrew Bible witnesses to Israel's search. Its focus was history. Unlike an Eastern Absolute, Yahweh participated in human time. As a result, Jewish religion was singularly concrete. It was what you did, how you lived, whether you fulfilled the Law that determined your righteousness. What you thought was secondary.

Jesus worked several transformations on these themes. First, he turned Lord into Father. Second, without denying sin he spoke more of God's love. If one would repent and believe the gospel, God's love would make her whole. Third, Jesus told God's people they were in crisis. He brought the hour of judgment and opportunity. The great image Jesus used to drive the crisis home was the Kingdom. Momentarily, God would oust Satan, and establish a new eon of justice. The way to enter the Kingdom was faith. Accepting the gospel, one had only to keep its twofold commandment. Ever since Jesus' preaching, Catholic theology has made love of God and neighbor the crux of authenticity.

The writers of the New Testament shifted faith from the Kingdom to Jesus. Thus, the proclaimer became the proclaimed. As early as Paul, they separated Jesus from ordinary humanity. In virtue of his cross and resurrection, he became the saving Lord. When they first sought to describe Jesus' status, the New Testament authors seized upon Jewish notions. First, they tried "Messiah" on for size. Jesus was the anointed deliverer Judaism had long sought, though his deliverance was not political but spiritual. Second they considered Son and Word. Word, like Spirit, was an aspect of Yahweh that Jesus seemed to manifest. Thus, Jesus was like a son who expresses a father, like a divine Word become flesh. By the end of the first century, when Johannine theology had matured, Jesus had a solid preexistence. When God made the world, the Logos was with him. By faith, followers of Jesus could join the Logos' "body." Thereby, the Incarnation continued in the church. The church expressed divine life in word and sacrament. Its missionaries continued Jesus' proclamation of the gospel.

The early apologists of the generations after the New Testament writers had a twofold task. When Christians became numerous enough to provoke notice, the apologists began a "political" defense of their faith. Primarily, they tried to show Christianity was neither immoral nor subversive. Jews had won a grudging respect for their high morality and Christians argued that they deserved the same. Far from being subversive, they were Caesar's most solid subjects, so long as he did not ask them to call him Lord. The second task was more philosophical. Educated Christians lived in a Hellenistic milieu. Hellenism lay great stress on philosophy. Though the schools that dominated the early Christian years were inferior to those of Plato and Aristotle, the love of wisdom remained a high ideal. With the mystery religions come from the East, it focused a great longing for truth that could save. The apologists therefore translated Christianity as a philosophy—a saving truth, God's own wisdom. Jesus not only fulfilled Jewish prophecy, he fulfilled Plato and Aristotle. His church had a knowledge *(gnosis)* more saving than the mystery religions'.

Justin Martyr (ca. 100–165) related all human illumination to the divine Logos. Clement of Alexandria (ca. 150–215) expanded Justin's approach, trying to show how Christian revelation and sacramental life were a rich humanism. Origen (ca. 185–254) made Clement's efforts flower, writing voluminous scriptural commentaries remarkable for their allegorical interpretation. These commentaries and other Alexandrine efforts showed Christians could be intellectuals. Without denying the need for practical charity, they developed Christian *theoria* (contemplation). For classical philosophy *theoria* was the highest human activity, the best reflection of God. Though Origen came under a cloud for seeming to subordinate the Son to the Father, his brilliant use of Platonic philosophy gave Christian theology its first great speculative consolidation.

This consolidation was important because Arianism, the most potent early heresy, relied on hard reasoning. Arius (ca. 250–336) tried to solve the mystery of the Trinity and concluded the Logos was not substantially the same as the Father. Many church leaders instinctively rejected this conclusion, but only those competent philosophically could meet Arius's challenge head-on. It was not sufficient to repeat biblical descriptions, because the Bible did not focus on the question of substance. So when Athanasius (ca. 296–373), leader of the "orthodox" party, considered meeting Arius on his own grounds, the foundational issue was whether Christian doctrine could develop beyond biblical categories. Backing Athanasius' decision that it could, the bishops at Nicaea (325) proclaimed that the Son *is* of the same substance as the Father. Thereby, they backed the implicit proposition that the church is competent to apply scriptural faith to new situations in new language. Later theology has shown that the problems of focusing such competence and determining whether a given development is indeed faithful to the New Testament can be very weighty. Nonetheless, by its conciliar responses to such early challenges as Arius's, the church endorsed theological reasoning and doctrinal development.

The other challenges of the early centuries helped round out a theological core. In Christological controversies, bishop-theologians developed the orthodox view that Jesus was truly human and truly divine, one person in two natures. The ultimate mystery of Jesus' identity lay beyond human grasp, but he was both like us in all things save sin and the eternal Word. An important notion that this Christology sanctioned was the *theotokos*. To concretize its belief that the Word took flesh from Mary, orthodoxy labeled her the "God-bearer." Not only did this label summarize the mystery of the Incarnation, it also established Mary's singular place in Christian salvation. Indeed, all her other titles derive from her dignity as the mother of God. Eastern Christianity has greatly reverenced the *theotokos*, and greatly contemplated the Incarnation. Its later controversy about icons probably would not have arisen except for the *theotokos*, for the most influential icons showed God's Mother. When the Emperor Leo III (717–740) attacked icons, calling them an impediment to the conversion of Jews and Muslims (who thought their use idolatrous), those who defended icons pointed not only to their consonance with the Incarnation, but also to the centuries through which the faithful had prayed before images of Jesus and his Mother.

The Western fathers were not so influential in conciliar decisions as the Eastern, but they produced significant theological reflections. Indeed, Augustine (354–430) finally became the greatest figure of the patristic age. He used Platonic philosophy to speculate on the Trinity, and took the Roman Empire's decay as an occasion to ponder the theology of history. In his *Confessions* Augustine sounded like a modern—autobiographic, personal, existential. In his controversies with Pelagius, who seemed to deny salvation's gratuity, Augustine ventured into the deep waters of predestination. Principally, he sought to establish God's utter priority in human salvation. But the complexity of the question, and his less than complete lucidity, sowed seeds for the tedious discussions of grace and freedom that distressed theologians in the sixteenth and seventeenth centuries. Another Westerner, Pope Leo I, made the fifth century the time when Rome consolidated its influence. When his "Tome" was accepted by the Council of Chalcedon (451) as a standard of Christological orthodoxy, Rome's magisterial primacy was set.

Other great theologians of the patristic age include the Cappadocians and Jerome. The Eastern Cappadocians—Basil, Gregory of Nyssa, and Gregory Nazianzen—dominated the Council of Constantinople (381), which dealt Arianism more doctrinal blows. These three bishops combined speculative acumen with great concern for the spiritual life—so much so that Basil gave Eastern monasticism its primary rule. Jerome (ca. 342–420) was a Westerner who lived a monk's life at Bethlehem and made his greatest impact through scriptural translation and commentary. His Latin Vulgate version of the Bible became the common text in the West, and his choleric observations of the contemporary scene make him a vivid stop on the patristic tour. With Athanasius, who was intrigued by Antony's desert experiences, and Basil, Jerome pushed monasticism to the Christian fore.

From the patristic age, then, Christian theology received a considerable clarification of the original, New Testament faith. This age reverenced scripture, but its experience of church life showed the need for greater precision in both doctrine and morality. The fathers mainly used Greek categories in their systematic speculations, and they struggled, not always successfully, for a balanced view of the flesh in their morality. Overall, their theology had the vitality of intelligent pastors trying to explain faith on all fronts. It may strike us as time-bound and misogynistic, but it was wonderfully alive.

MEDIEVAL THEOLOGY

The East never lost the patristic conception of theology. Until the capture of Constantinople by the Turks in 1453, it continued to enjoy the cultural unity of the old empire. This supported a strong bias against innovation. What one found in scripture, the seven ecumenical councils (II Nicea in 787 is the last on the Eastern list), and the fathers constituted *paradosis:* "tradition." The East was loathe to change tradition. The bad aspect of this was a tendency to stagnation. The good aspect was a sense of unity with past ages. Nonetheless, Eastern interests shifted significantly. Kallistos Ware has noted four major changes. From 325 to 381 doctrinal discussion centered on the Trinity. From 431 to 681 it focused on Christology. The iconoclast controversy dominated the years 726–843. The years 858–1453 featured polemics against the West and mystical theology. John Damascene (ca. 675–749), St. Symeon the New Theologian (949–1022), and St. Gregory Palamas (1296–1359) were the luminaries of later Eastern theology who provided it originality and systematization without departing from its fusion of thought and life.

Catholic theology ought to consider Eastern developments part of its own store, for before the division of 1054 there was one church, however strained, and after 1054 theological differences remained relatively minor. Still, Roman Catholicism developed its distinctive character in the West, above all in medieval scholasticism. Where the Eastern mind tended to be speculative, Roman law impressed the Western mind deeply. As early as Tertullian (ca. 160–220) moral questions dominated the West, for sin and salvation were its chief theological interests. To be sure, Augustine was a great speculative power, and he remained the scholastics' chief tutor, but even Augustine worried sin and salvation considerably.

During their slowly widening estrangement, the Eastern and Western church zones shared several controversies. The monothelite controversy about Christ's wills and the iconoclast controversy are primary examples. Popes involved themselves in these originally Eastern issues, but not always to the benefit of church unity. In the *filioque* controversy the West ran afoul of the East's traditionalism, for the Western proposition that the Spirit proceeds from the Son as well as the Father was not explicit in the Nicene Creed. The filioque was the major doctrinal divergence between East and West, but several disciplinary divergences also developed. Thus, the East protested some of the privileges the Popes had assumed, the rise of compulsory celibacy for the clergy, the West's denying priests the power to administer confirmation, the Western doctrine of purgatory, and other relatively minor issues. The main fault in them all was their innovation.

In the ninth century Western theologians debated the nature of the eucharist, and also aspects of predestination. Charlemagne had brought some unity to the Western tribes, and monastic schools began laying the foundations of a new theological intellectualism. Anselm (1033–1109) sprang from this foundation, and he clarified the importance of reason. For example, his notion that theology is faith in search of *understanding* spotlighted reason, as did his inquiries about the rationale of the Incarnation and the proof of God's existence. With Peter Abelard (1079–1142) dialectical argument took center stage. By laying out reasons for and against a theological proposition, Abelard contributed to the scholastic *questio*: the interrogation of evidential grounds and supposedly probative reasonings.

Bernard of Clairvaux (1090–1153) was Abelard's polar opposite, his mystical bent running directly counter to Abelard's rationalism. In fact, Abelard and Bernard symbolize the two poles medieval theology struggled to reconcile. Peter Lombard (1100–1160) did later medievals the favor of collecting traditional opinions on various doctrinal points, and many later giants commented on his *Sentences*.

In the background of the theology of the Middle Ages stand the medieval university and papacy. Theology was queen of the sciences, but by no means the only intellectual interest. The medieval university assumed Christian culture, but under that umbrella considerable secular study went on. The West had received Aristotle, largely through Arabic interpreters, and with him came a new power of argument. For both philosophy and natural science, Aristotle became the starting point. The medieval papacy had ongoing struggles with various imperial centers, as church and state battled for supremacy. This battle stimulated canon law, which tried to detail church powers. Some church powers concerned sanctification, so from the twelfth century there was considerable interest in the sacraments. Penance and matrimony slowly entered the sacramental ranks, and by 1439 they were on the list of seven sacraments proposed to the Greeks.

The two schools that contested theological influence in the thirteenth century were the Franciscan and the Dominican. Both orders had arisen as innovations on traditional Benedictine monasticism, to give greater mobility. The early Franciscans stressed poverty, the early Dominicans preaching. In the university they tended to stress love and understanding respectively. Bonaventure, the most prominent Franciscan, continued the Augustinian emphasis on love, will, and mystical union. The roots of this Augustinianism were in Plato, for whom knowledge was the soul's vision.

Aquinas, the most influential Dominican, opted for Aristotle's more realistic epistemology, which made understanding an active cooperation of senses and intellect. With this in hand, he had the tool to probe faith's intelligibility more lucidly than any of his predecessors had. Indeed, Aquinas's great achievement was to integrate reason with revelation and construct a full overview, a "summa." Because of its balance, he came to represent "official" Catholic theology.

Aquinas did not merely apply Aristotle to Christian faith. Though he admired much in the "Philosopher," Aquinas changed Aristotle's metaphysics. Aristotle had stressed individual beings, noting that their intelligibility derived from their form and considering form their essential act. Aquinas stressed existence, the act of being, from which he could show God to be the inmost reality of all that is. The difference in these two metaphysics stems from Aquinas's Christian view of creation. If God makes all beings from nothing, the "is" of each is a divine gift. Further, Aquinas moved beyond Aristotle's anthropology, conceiving human destiny as the beatific vision of the trinitarian God. Beyond "nature," then, Aquinas saw a new order wholly dependent on God's gratuity. He clarified what nature could know and do by itself but he knew that in the concrete human beings are fallen into sin and solicited by grace.

Indeed, Aquinas read scripture to say that human sin provoked the Incarnation. The Word took flesh to redeem a fallen race. Therefore, Adam's transgression was a "happy fault." Nothing showed God's goodness more than the cure worked through Jesus. On the cross Jesus redeemed us by his love and obedience. That the Father would give up the Son for our sakes shows how great is the Father's love for us. We now struggle to outgrow our selfishness and respond with obedient love.

Overall, the mark of Aquinas's theology is its balance. Reason and revelation, nature and grace, interlock carefully. Scripture plays an important part, as does tradition, but reasoning too receives respect. Faith enables reason to understand more of the divine mysteries than it would alone, but even without faith reason can perceive vestiges of God. The world is God's creation, so all of it speaks of the divine truth. We may miss many overtones, but in itself the divine work is a fullness of intelligence. Thus, even in heaven reason will remain active. The vision of God that beatifies is a sublime act of understanding. It does not remove God's mystery, but it does give limited intellects all the happiness they can bear.

Shortly after his death Aquinas came under suspicion because of his Aristotelianism and rationality. Advocates of Augustine and the Fathers branded the Thomist synthesis insufficiently "Christian." They had support from mystical theologians, whose philosophical inspiration often was Neo-Platonic. Aquinas seemed too dry, too logical, compared to the concrete imagery of scripture, the vivid rhetoric of Augustine. In fact, Aquinas never intended to supplant either. He knew scripture inside out, and he reverenced Augustine as his great teacher. But he was convinced theology serves a useful purpose when it concentrates on understanding. To be sure, theoretical theology is not the theology to preach popularly. Equally, it is not the language for prayer. But it answers a need as legitimate as the needs of preaching or prayer: the mind's need to understand. Aquinas himself likely was a mystic, and he wrote hymns for the liturgy. Before him the Victorines had joined contemplation with theology, and after him the Rhineland mystics did. Thus, medieval theology was far from divorcing the mystical and the intellectual. In Aquinas, though, the intellectual gained its greatest medieval depth.

The problem modernity has with the high medievals is not their lack of piety or depth. In their own way, the medievals resemble the Fathers, for they seldom forget that the God of their discourse demands wholehearted love. But from the end of the thirteenth century scholasticism declined. The logic that had served three centuries well now had no giants to call master, so it became master itself. The result was that theology became arid, deductive, lifeless. Diversely, the forerunners of the Lutheran Reformation, such as Wycliffe in England, Hus in Bohemia, and Groote in the Netherlands, made the fourteenth century a search for new vitality. That century suffered both the Black Plague and the greatest church disarray—the "Babylonian Captivity" of the Popes in Avignon. Thus, the spirit aborning was a search for personal meaning and ecclesiastical reform. It generated controversies about the eucharist and the nature of the church, and received back heavy-handed persecution by church authorities. Regretably, the thirteenth century scholastic

synthesis was tarred by this faithlessness. It could have helped the classical Protestant Reformers of the sixteenth century keep faith and reason
together.

THE COUNTER-REFORMATION

The fifteenth century witnessed a Renaissance in Italy that soon
spread to the rest of Europe. This movement entailed both a rediscovery
of classical Greek and Roman culture and a new personalist mood. Educated Europeans like Erasmus (1469–1536), who led the Renaissance in
Northern Europe, found the church failing their humanistic ideals. Far
from being a mother and teacher, it was a grievous burden. Erasmus'
scholarship helped Christendom recover the New Testament and opened
theology to historical research. There was little impressive scholasticism
to renovate the fifteenth century, so when the sixteenth-century Reformation dawned the times were ripe for upheaval. Politically, culturally,
and religiously, the going Roman system seemed to be rotten. Martin
Luther was the prophetic figure who put the axe to the roots.

Luther observed the roots first hand during a visit to Rome in 1510.
Returned home and assigned to teach biblical studies, he discovered a
new message. Personally, Luther had for some time suffered scruples
about his religious observance and found it hard to gain peace of soul.
When he grasped Paul's teaching that justification comes through faith
rather than works, it seemed a personal message. Though he could never
be sure his own observance pleased God, Paul told him God justifies
apart from human merit. This was hardly a novel doctrine, for commentators on Paul, including Augustine and Aquinas, had exposed this meaning plainly. Indeed, the Council of Orange (529) had defined the gratuity
of salvation unmistakably, using Augustinian language. Thus, it was
Luther's personal investment, and the works-orientation of his time,
rather than a lacuna in the tradition, that set the torch of Reformation
burning.

The personal investment took scriptural garb. Luther had found his
key Christian doctrine in Romans. The New Testament was the only
place where Christ, that doctrine's cause, could be found unalloyed.
Therefore, to *sola fide* (by faith alone) one had to add *sola scriptura* (by
scripture alone). Scripture alone deserved the total allegiance due God's
Word. Tradition, at least as interpreted by prevailing church leaders,
was not trustworthy. Unless scripture ruled the church, the church
was not God's household. Thus, faithful interpretation of scripture became a matter of private conscience. Luther joined the emerging personalism to his scriptural findings and pushed forward the concrete "I."
A person must stand behind his commitments. No one can say yes or
no for him. Before God, faith is a matter of individual responsibility.

Social convention, including church law, is something secondary. It testifies to Luther's influence that a majority of Americans now take these tenets for granted.

Luther's theses—both the 95 of 1517 and those he developed later—set the agenda for Reformation times. Other reformers developed his notions of faith, scripture, grace, and the church, while the Catholic opposition had to meet his terms. In John Calvin (1509–1564) the Reformation gained a first-rate exegete and dogmatician, who put its main tenets into systematic form. However, Calvin discoursed more deeply on human depravity, the sovereignty of God, and predestination than Luther had. The Catholic counter-reformers thought both Luther and Calvin had lost a traditional balance. On the relation of sin and grace, they found the Reformers too pessimistic. Granted that Adam's sin separated humanity from God, it did not vitiate human nature. In this the Catholics could claim Aquinas, who made grace nature's healing and perfecting, not its substitute.

On the relation between scripture and tradition, the counter-reformers again tried to redress what they considered an imbalance. Granted the importance of scripture, it was historical fact that scripture had always been interpreted by the church. The canon that determined what books belonged in "scripture," and the explanation of its faith, had fallen to the magisterium. Indeed, what was the function of bishops and councils, if not to determine scriptural revelation's true sense?

The counter-reformers continued this balancing act on the question of faith and merit. It was true that salvation is gratuitous, a gift of God's bounty in Christ. Thus, no fulfillment of the law forced heaven to open. Nonetheless, God wanted good morality (which Luther did not deny), and faith not issuing good morality was suspect. Whether such "morality" or "works" was identical with keeping church laws was secondary. The counter-reformers could agree there had been abuses in the "system" of masses and indulgences. Too many Christians did think that mere attendance at Mass, or crass alms giving, gained them heaven. But this was something to clean up, not cause for tearing the whole down.

Moreover, there was scriptural evidence (Hebrews) for the Mass's sacrificial character which Luther, in his insistence on its memorial character, underplayed. There also was good reason behind indulgences, for Christians formed a communion, an organic whole, such that the good deeds of one redounded to the benefit of all. As the saints served common Christians good example, so common Christians could share in the saints' merits. Not that saints could save other Christians by themselves, apart from Christ. They ought never be more prominent than Jesus. But one Christian reached out to all, even those in purgatory and heaven. Few later writers have judged this Catholic defense of indulgences satisfactory, but at least it shows they had roots other than simple greed.

The official, conciliar form of the Catholic response was the twenty-five sessions of the Council of Trent (1545–1563). Beset by political troubles, the Council was frequently in recess, but slowly it hammered out doctrinal and disciplinary reforms. Benjamin Drewery has summarized the doctrinal topics under three heads: Scripture and Tradition, Justification, and the Sacraments.

The Council's hallmark was a reassertion of church authority. Pointedly, it made the Catholic church the sole legitimate interpreter of scripture. While this position had hermeneutical merits, since all texts stand in a history of interpretation and none springs from heaven directly, it neglected the unique character of the New Testament, which was the church's own founding book. On justification the Council disputed the Reformers' notion that righteousness is merely imputed to believers because of Christ. Rather, original sin really is removed, though after baptism concupiscence or the "tinder of sin" *(fomes peccati)* remains. Justification leads on to sanctification or inner renewal, for the grace that makes one righteous presses further to make one holy. Finally, the Council denied the teaching of some Protestants that true believers know their own salvation with certainty, and it insisted on the validity of works and merit.

Concerning the sacraments, the seventh session (1547) first stressed their necessity: "All true righteousness either begins or is increased or is restored through the sacraments." Jesus instituted all seven sacraments, and they confer grace objectively *(ex opere operato)*, not merely through the recipient's faith. The eucharist is the preeminent sacrament, in which Christ really is present, body and soul, humanity and divinity. The Mass represents the sacrifice of Calvary and is efficacious for the remission of sins. The traditional requirement that mortal sins be confessed to a priest is to continue.

Thus, the doctrines of Trent served to distinguish Catholicism from Protestantism. By Trent's close reconciliation with Protestants seemed impossible, so its decrees, with their corresponding anathemas, became a sort of boundary line. Summarily, the Council repudiated the Reformers' main charge that the Roman church had become discontinuous with early Christian faith. Rather, it justified the main lines of Christian evolution, often reading sixteenth-century structures back into New Testament times.

After Trent polemics became the order of the day. The prince of Catholic polemicists was Robert Bellarmine (1542–1621), a Jesuit cardinal. Jesuits had served as theologians at the Council of Trent, and throughout the counter-reformation they were the papacy's main arm. Bellarmine, though, was moderate in his interpretations of Trent, and in his temporal claims for the papacy. He realized through the Galileo controversy (1616 ff.) that the church would have to accommodate to new scientific knowledge. On the central issue of justification, Bellarmine stressed God's cooperating grace, which allowed the believer to become responsible for her good deeds and so merit heavenly rewards.

Grace also was the key issue in the Jansenist controversy, an infra-Catholic affair of the mid-seventeenth century. In brief the Jansenists thought human nature so weak its only hope for salvation lay in Christ's grace. This seemed to endanger human freedom and merit, so papal theologians succeeded in getting it condemned in the 1650s and 1660s. The great Jansenist propagandist was Blaise Pascal (1623–1662), whose *Provincial Letters* satirized the Jesuits and popularized the notion that they defended human freedom excessively. Behind the Jesuits' stance was the theory of Luis Molina, hammered out in the "De Auxiliis" controversy (ca. 1597–1607) between Jesuits and Dominicans, that God bestows grace in light of his foreknowing who will freely cooperate with it.

The seventeenth century also witnessed a controversy about Quietism, the view that one does well to abandon human freedom and depend totally on God. This position originated with Miguel Molinos (ca. 1640–1697) and was condemned by Innocent XI in 1687 because it seemed to make God the author of sinful acts. A leader in the fight to condemn Quietism was Bishop Jacques Bossuet (1627–1704), a great preacher of the day. Bossuet defended the Roman church as the true guardian of Christian tradition, but he opposed the ramifications of papal power.

In a nutshell, the Counter-Reformation settled few of Protestants' grievances and determined many subsequent Catholic characteristics. Rome became the guardian of tradition, and the Roman system became something to be defended tooth and nail. Rome stressed the outward things of church life—hierarchy, magisterium, works, sacramental rituals—because Protestants emphasized inward personal experience and faith. Scripture took on "Protestant" overtones, as did any stress on the lay vocation.

Further, the Reformation controversies hardened the perennial Western tendency to concentrate on the moral aspects of Christian life and neglect the ontological. The debates about justification entailed ontology, for they had to take up how divinity and humanity interacted, but they were at least one step removed from the Greek view of grace, which was divinization. With divinization went a clear focus on the Trinity, the source and substance of "uncreated" grace, and a contemplative attitude toward the sacraments. Thus, the justification controversies advanced Western legalism and distanced both Catholics and Protestants still further from Eastern orthodoxy.

MODERNITY

The last four centuries have been a time of increasingly rapid cultural change. By 1800 contact with non-European cultures, Newtonian science, new philosophies, the divisions of the Western church, and a repugance induced by religious wars had left traditional theology besieged. In the nineteenth century Darwin and Marx changed social thought, while in the twentieth century Freud and Einstein revolved accepted views of the psyche and the universe. The dominant influences on modern Catholic theology, then, have been the massive changes in Western culture to which it has had to react.

First, changes in philosophy and physical science severely challenged traditional belief. From Descartes to Hegel, Catholicism's old balance of faith and reason came under fierce philosophical attack. Hume, Locke, Kant, and Hegel, who fired the most powerful salvos, agreed "revelation" was a dubious proposition. They had appropriated a new subjectivity that made revelation seem wooden, heteronomous. How could a heavenly knowledge come into human senses and brains? Catholic theology has struggled with modern subjectivity since Luther, first bitterly attacking it and lately trying to appropriate its manifest truths. Except for Cardinal Newman (1801–1890), successful appropriations date only from the last sixty years or so.

The scientific theories of Galileo, Copernicus, and Newton overthrew the geocentric universe. For many believers, this entailed a traumatic ousting from a privileged place in the heavens. Insofar as the new astronomy and physics conflicted with biblical accounts, "revelation" again came into question. Those who accepted the new science but wanted to remain religious tended to attenuate faith to Deism—a clock-maker God who merely got the universe ticking. Although Stanley Jaki, a historian of science with traditional Catholic commitments, has argued passionately that modern science in fact has relied upon a realistic epistemology quite compatible with Christian faith, most eminent modern scientists have not expressed themselves in traditional theological terms. Publicly, then, the appearance was that science and religion collided. As with its philosophical collisions, Catholic theology has only responded positively in the past few generations.

Second, the past three centuries have produced massive social changes, history both speeding up and expanding. The American and French revolutions dramatically altered European consciousness, but Catholic thought tended more to fear their anarchic possibilities than to support their outreach for justice and freedom. Marxist theory made such progress after the Russian Revolution of 1917 that the Catholic fears of socialism developed in the nineteenth century seemed well warranted. We noted the Catholic response after Leo XIII, which lately has become a full counter-program for social justice, but until John XXIII that response seemed rather hedged and unapplied.

The expansion of consciousness that foreign discoveries entailed altered world history itself. For instance, when one laid the traditional historical schema developed by Augustine, and retained to Bossuet, beside Voltaire's new general account (1756), "sacred history" seemed provincial indeed. New information about China, India, and other nations made laughable the notion that salvation runs only through Jerusalem and Rome.

The most eminent figure of eighteenth-century Catholic theology was Alphonsus Liguori (1696–1787), who concentrated on morality. His work moved in the wake of the earlier debates about human freedom, seeking a middle ground between laxism and rigorism. The result was an influential "equiprobabilism": An opinion or proposed course of action is licit if it is as probably correct as the alternatives.

During the nineteenth century Roman authority hardened and largely turned its back on modernity. The First Vatican Council (1869–1870) capped a consolidation of papal power with its decress on infallibility, but already in 1864 Pius IX had condemned eighty propositions that represented "errors" of mid-century Europe. The last proposition that he condemned supported progress, liberalism, and civilization as then understood. Collectively, these notions amounted to what we might call "secularism." Pius was especially aggrieved that traditional Italian politics were encroaching on Catholic education, and that Europe in general was trying to make Christian religion just another ingredient in a pluralistic culture based on tolerance.

The Catholic theologian of the nineteenth century most praised today is Newman, whose conversion from Anglicanism forced him to contend with his times' most pressing problems. Above all, Newman had to contend with historical consciousness, which was making deep impacts on Protestant biblical and doctrinal theology. As critical history revealed the time-conditioned quality of both scripture and past formulas of faith, it easily imported *historicism*—the relativistic view that all times change and we with them. This was anathema to a church championing "tradition," which it understood in terms of Vincent of Lerins' (ca. 425) "everywhere, always, and by all." Newman's achievement was to show how doctrines could develop, not so much changing their original thrust as unfolding their implications under the impact of later times.

Such development was central to "modernists" efforts to update Catholic faith, but Pius X's antimodernist decree *Lamentabili* (1907) specifically condemned Loisy's version, seeming to enforce a uniform faith untouched by history. Similarly, Pius's oath against modernism (1910) rejected "the false invention of the evolution of dogmas." This denial of history was bound to founder, but it kept the "manual" scholasticism of the nineteenth century in the driver's seat another forty years.

The philosophical and theological manuals prescribed for Catholic seminaries were a model of abstract precision. They lined up biblical proof texts, gave "adversaries'" positions in a sentence or two, and then chopped-off syllogistic arguments for the thesis in question. Completely lost were the history of the question, its relation to living faith, and its intellectual complexity. Yves Congar and Gerald McCool have shown that manual scholasticism was not the only theological force of the nineteenth and early twentieth centuries, but it did disastrously narrow traditional theological understanding.

Pius XII's *Humani Generis* (1950) was the last great gasp of Roman conservatism. From the early years of the twentieth century Catholic studies in the history of faith and doctrine had implied that the manualists' aridity was a sorry aberration. In works on liturgical practice, patristic thought, medieval scholasticism, and biblical criticism, Europeans unearthed a past richness the manualists little suspected. The liturgical movement finally broke through with reforms of the Easter liturgy and holy week in the 1950s; the biblical movement got a charter for scholarship in Pius XII's *Divino Afflante Spiritu* (1943); and under the leadership of Henri de Lubac and Jean Daniélou patristic studies flowered in France after World War II.

Dogmatic theology was under a tighter rein, but the efforts of philosophers (for instance, Pierre Scheuer, Joseph Maréchal, Max Scheler, Maurice Blondel, Jacques Maritain, and Etienne Gilson) to reconcile Aquinas and modern thought began to bear fruit after the war. Rahner and Lonergan are probably their most eminent yield, but Schillebeeckx, Küng, and others also have their roots there.

Were one to try to epitomize the recent burst of creativity in Catholic thought, most of it sanctioned by Vatican II, key words would be "history" and "pluralism." Finally appropriating modernity, Catholic theology has entered the battles over interpretation that modernity entails. Because we human beings are temporal and change, none of our institutions is static. Equally, none of our understandings is static, for we always understand "from where we are." The first postulate from these verities is sophistication: One has to know the circumstances of the text she is studying, and also the circumstances of her own study. When history forms a scholar's critical consciousness, it forces hermeneutical obligations.

Because of the complexity that historical sensitivity finds in Catholic theology of the past, many theologians are willing to accept pluralism in the present. Factually, Catholicism never has been monolithic. It has always varied in worship and belief, from place to place and time to time. The several Catholic liturgies, many schools of spirituality, and many theological schools all testify to a past multiplicity. As new regional areas, such as Latin America, Asia, and Africa, enter the theological scene, we should expect more multiplicity in the future. Indeed, we should welcome it, for different regional experiences, like different philosophical outlooks, help display the fullness of Christ.

To be sure, multiplicity can become chaotic, if theologians fail to find a common center. But few Catholic theologians deny the centrality of Jesus, and in a world-historical horizon that gives them great commonality. Making Jesus the decisive interpretation of human reality separates Christian from atheists, Buddhists, Muslims, agnostics, and the like. It makes Christians' sense of life different, because the horizon in which one sets experiences shapes their meaning. For instance, suffering is different if one sets it against Christ's cross rather than the Buddha's first noble truth ("All life is suffering"). To choose Christ, then, is to choose a band of brothers and sisters who have chosen similarly. Their unity is far more important than their differences.

We believe this unity should be the fulcrum of future ecumenical theology, and a prime hermeneutic in infra-Catholic discussions of orthodoxy. If a theologian confesses Christ's decisiveness, her basic plank is solid. Sophisticated existentialists, such as Rahner, have shown how such decisiveness implicitly entails Christ's divinity. Sophisticated methodologists, such as Lonergan, have distinguished the various horizons—mythic, commonsensical, theoretic, and so forth—which vary a statement's significance. They show the benefits of modernity's having forced philosophers to study consciousness intricately.

In Catholic theology, "intentionality analysis" now tries to make such studies bear on the religious self's different levels and moods. The end of intentionality analysis is not yet in sight, so the present is no time for heavy-handed determinations of what a traditional proposition *must* mean. Such determinations will only cause future embarrassment. The mystery at the core of human being has myriad forms of expression. As Aquinas noted, "It is not the property of the wise person to care about names." The wise person cares about realities. Fortunately, current Catholic theology cares passionately about the reality of a truly divine, incomprehensible God and the reality of the humanization Christ offers. That is good ground for forecasting its future with hope.

BIBLIOGRAPHY

Chadwick, Owen. *The Secularization of the European Mind in the Nineteenth Century.* New York: Cambridge University Press, 1975.
Congar, Yves M-J. *A History of Theology.* Garden City, N.Y.: Doubleday, 1968.
Drewery, Benjamin. "The Council of Trent," in Hubert Cunliffe-Jones, ed., *A History of Christian Doctrine.* Philadelphia: Fortress, 1980, 403–409.
Jaki, Stanley L. *The Road of Science and the Ways to God.* Chicago: University of Chicago Press, 1978.

McCool, Gerald. *Catholic Theology in the Nineteenth Century*. New York: Seabury, 1977.

Neuner, Josef and Roos, Heinrich, eds. *The Teaching of the Catholic Church*. Staten Island, N.Y.: Alba House, 1967.

Pelikan, Jaroslav. *The Christian Tradition*, 1–3. Chicago: University of Chicago Press, 1971, 1974, 1978.

Rahner, Karl. "A Basic Interpretation of Vatican II," *Theological Studies*, 40/4 (December 1979), 716–727.

Rahner, Karl. "Theology," in K. Rahner, *et al.*, eds., *Sacramentum Mundi*, 6. New York: Herder and Herder, 1970, 233–246.

Schoof, Mark. *Breakthrough: Beginnings of the New Catholic Theology*. Dublin: Gill and Macmillan, 1970.

Ware, Kallistos. "Christian Theology in the East 600–1453," in Hubert Cunliffe-Jones, ed., *A History of Christian Doctrine*. Philadelphia: Fortress, 1980, 181–225.

Appendix II. John Paul II as Theologian

OVERVIEW

Pope John Paul II surely will mark the next era of Catholic theology decisively, so we offer a brief estimate of his theological mind. The Pope wrote extensively before his election, and scholars are beginning to evaluate those writings. Obviously, the experiences John Paul II has as Pope can change his perception, but the early years of his pontificate reveal a consistent theological mind. To describe it, we focus on his major encyclical, *Redemptor Hominis,* and one specimen of local applications, his speech in Puebla opening CELAM III. They suggest a vigorous social teaching, but a doctrinal grasp neither so contemporary nor so profound as our times require.

BACKGROUND AND REDEMPTOR HOMINIS

In the first years of his papacy, John Paul II established himself as a very powerful personality. His trips to Mexico and the United States drew great crowds, while his personal interest in the cases of Küng, Schillebeeckx, and the Dutch church signaled that, unlike Paul VI, he would try to control theological trends. The Pope arrived with the reputation of being an intellectual. He spoke many languages and had written voluminously. Among his obvious interests were contemporary views of human nature. He had Vatican II documents at his fingertips, and he explicitly aligned himself with Paul VI. Because of his vigor, theologians quickly took special notice. For example, Richard McCormick, the distinguished moral theologian, structured his 1979 "Notes" for *Theological Studies* around three themes of the Pope's speeches in the U.S.: the dignity of the human person, the need to stand by hard-line pronouncements on such issues as divorce, and concern for community-dividing problems such as nuclear energy and warfare.

On matters such as these, the Pope spoke as a universal pastor. His vigor soon made theologians ask what weight such pastoral utterances carried. When the Curia moved against Schillebeeckx and Küng, academic theologians returned to questions of heresy, academic freedom, and the relation of theological research to pastoral application. These questions could be useful, for vigorous theology always wonders about its own fundamental nature. However, limits in the Pope's own theology started to make liberals fear that his magisterium might soon become burdensome. Therefore, those interested in Catholic theology did well to study the Pope's own words carefully.

Representative works in which John Paul's pre-papal thought may be found include *The Acting Person, Fruitful and Responsible Love*, and *Sign of Contradiction. The Acting Person* is an anthropological investigation, more philosophical than theological, whose main debts are to the Catholic phenomenologist Max Scheler, the Aristotelian-Thomist tradition, and Vatican II. The basic thesis is that voluntary action is the human spirit's most distinctive feature and acting with others its fulfillment. *Fruitful and Responsible Love* is an address Cardinal Wojtyla gave to an international congress in Milan (July 1978) commemorating the tenth anniversary of the encyclical *Humanae Vitae*. It shows tender regard for conjugal love and reaffirms the encyclical's ban on artificial contraception as a violation of such love. *Sign of Contradiction* represents a lenten retreat that Wojtyla preached before Pope Paul VI and members of the Curia in 1976. It opposes the Christian view of humanity to the godless "Anti-Word" of modern secularists and shows a piety nourished on scripture and papal documents.

Here, though, we concentrate on John Paul II's first encyclical,

Redemptor Hominis, taking it as perhaps the most important early expression of his papal theology. It addresses the universal church and presumably was intended as an overture to his pontificate. Then, to help particularize *Redemptor Hominis,* we set in counterpoint to it John Paul II's address at the opening of the Latin American bishops' meeting in Puebla, where the Pope tried to focus his universal care to a local church. The encyclical was dated March 4, 1979, and the Opening Address was given January 29, 1979.

Redemptor Hominis opens with the powerful sentence, "The Redeemer of Man, Jesus Christ, is the center of the universe and of history." Presumably, then, the Pope would endorse a version of Rahner's "absolute savior." Moreover, both the title and the content show John Paul II's anthropological interests. It is what Christ has done for humanity that John Paul first notes. With the approach of the year 2000, the Pope wants to reaffirm Jesus' historical significance and the wisdom two millennia of faith have developed. He faces 2000 relying on Christ, and in continuity with John Paul I, Paul VI, and John XXIII. Thus we see a leader describing himself as the heir of Vatican II. John Paul praises his predecessors, affirms the collegiality and evangelization they stressed, and commits himself to their ecumenism.

After such orientational remarks, the encyclical takes up its titular theme, the mystery of the redemption. Redemption occurs within the mystery of Christ, imports a new creation, and reflects the Trinity. Its human dimension focuses above all on love: "Man cannot live without love." If human beings want to see their full dignity, they must look from Christ's love and truth. If the church would discern its own mission, it must look from Christ's love and truth. The Vatican II documents on non-Christian religions and religious freedom make clear what we will see: "what is in man," the riches of humanity all cultures carry.

Next John Paul deals with modern social conditions. His overriding criterion, as that of all recent Popes, is the dignity of the human person. For the church believes Jesus meets every individual, touches all persons everywhere. Modern culture, however, makes human beings afraid of their own works. Their technology threatens devastation and denaturing. Therefore, it demands a greater moral development. "The essential meaning of this 'kingship' and 'dominion' of man over the visible world, which the Creator himself gave man for his task, consists in the priority of ethics over technology, in the primacy of the person over things, and in the supremacy of spirit over matter." Applied to world economics and politics, these convictions have written most of the recent popes' social encyclicals. John Paul II reaffirms their concern about great disparities in wealth and power that fly in the face of human unity. Equally, he reaffirms his predecessors' commitment to peace. The work of justice is peace; its sign is human rights.

The last major section of *Redemptor Hominis* deals with "The Church's Mission and Man's Destiny." Human destiny stands clear in Christ, who offers divine life. The church is responsible for the truth that nourishes divine life, and must oppose the falsehoods, such as modern materialism, which threaten it. John Paul's ecclesiology reflects Vatican II's document on the church, *Lumen Gentium*, and he praises theology that serves the magisterium. Theology may admit "a certain pluralism of methodology," but "the work cannot . . . depart from the fundamental unity in the teaching of faith and morals which is that work's end. Accordingly, close collaboration by theology with the magisterium is indispensible." The conflicts that various competencies in the church may suffer will lessen if all genuinely serve the truth.

The church carries out its mission sacramentally, and the encyclical singles out the eucharist and penance for brief discussion. Here its theology is rather traditional, and its concern for liturgical propriety manifest. The Mass should follow approved rules; penance should retain individual confession of sins. More generally, members of the church should remain faithful to their sacramental vocations. Priests should recall the indelible character ordination "stamps on their souls," and treasure their celibacy. In such ways do Christians find true freedom. The encyclical concludes with reflections on Mary, "The Mother in Whom We Trust," and prayers for her support. She shows the mystery of redemption in a special way, and helps us link ourselves to its center, Christ Jesus.

PUEBLA ADDRESS AND CRITIQUE

John Paul II took the occasion of CELAM III to address the episcopate of Latin America, no doubt for several reasons. The heavily Catholic population of Latin America figures prominently in future church demography; the divisions of the episcopal conference over liberation theology had attracted world wide notice; and John Paul is a pastor who takes all his flock seriously.

At Puebla the topic was evangelization, so the Pope cast his thoughts toward missionizing Latin America. His first concern was to remind the bishops they must teach Christ's truth, watch over purity of doctrine. Pure doctrine radiates from a solid Christology, one which is not silent about Christ's divinity. Christ's redemption is more than social improvement, and it never resorts to violence. John Paul's second theological topic was ecclesiology, and he reminded his hearers of an earlier resolve: "In the first address of my pontificate, I stressed my desire to be faithful to Vatican II, and my resolve to focus my greatest concern on the area of ecclesiology." *Lumen Gentium* is the Vatican II text to which the bishops should go for his ecclesiology. It shows that evangelization is "the essential mission, the specific vocation, the innermost identity of the church." However, there can be no authentic evangelization without sincere respect for the sacred magisterium, where one finds not the word of human beings but the authentic word of God.

Third, John Paul turned to anthropology. The primary truth about human beings is their need for God, which atheistic humanism denies. (There are echoes here of the Pope's experiences as a pastor in Communist Poland.) The bishops' own unity should show how Christians commune, and their defense and promotion of human dignity should give their concern for Christian truth social form. The Pope quotes Matthew 25 (the classical text on serving Christ by serving those in need), condemns great disparities in wealth, stands up for fundamental rights (to be born, to life, to responsible procreation, to work, to peace, to freedom, to social justice, and to participate "in making decisions that affect peoples and nations"), and condemns forms of "collective violence" such as racial discrimination and physical or psychological torture. Full liberation is freeing human beings from everything that oppresses them, but especially from sin and the evil one. Thus, John Paul II goes out of his way to remind the bishops of the recent Popes' social teachings, and he identifies the church with the oppressed eloquently.

The priority foci the Pope lists in conclusion are the family, priestly and religious vocations, and young people. The family is under assault: "Think of the campaigns advocating divorce, the use of contraceptives, and abortion, which destroy society." Priestly and religious vocations show the vitality and maturity of a community, for "lay vocations, indispensible as they are, cannot be a satisfactory compensation." And young people clearly are the hope of the future, the energy Latin America will need.

Like *Redemptor Hominis*, then, the Opening Address brims with pastoral concern. The Pope's faith, ardent and strong, pours out in every direction. Christology, ecclesiology, and anthropology are its recurring theological accents, and its style is to quote profusely, especially from scripture and Vatican II documents, but also from recent papal documents. In Christology the stress is redemption—the Jesus who saves. In ecclesiology the stress is the church's mission to continue the redemptive process, serving humanity the truth it most needs. In anthropology there is a twofold emphasis: the human person's constitution for God and social justice.

These traditional themes become contemporary through the Pope's references to current problems. In Christology he is distressed by trends that seem to reduce Jesus merely to human status, or to make him a political liberator. In ecclesiology he stresses the magisterium's duty to guard doctrine, and the church's mission to enlighten the world. This mission demands religious freedom of civil governments; of Church members it demands cheerful sacrifice. In anthropology the pope refers to atheism and materialism, which falsify human nature. Socially, both capitalism and Marxism miss the mark. The one denies that the goods of the earth are for all the earth's people, the other crushes individuals for the benefit of the state. Morally, current libertarianism, especially in things sexual, leads many astray, while the arms race and abuses of the natural environment threaten the whole species' future.

Clearly, then, the Pope is a passionate defender not only of Christian tradition but also of beleaguered humanity. His heart goes out to the poor, to victims of political oppression, to those misled by false philosophies. He wants the church to champion human rights, improve the lot of the marginalized, and continue to provide the wisdom of the gospel. Summarily, he argues persuasively that only the gospel points human beings in the right direction, gives them their fulfilling straight and narrow. When human nature is not open to divine truth and love, it closes upon itself disastrously. This frustrates the individual, stains the social fabric. All manner of violence and suffering ensue. Believing that humanity cannot be humane without the redemption of Jesus, the Pope dovetails his compassion for humanity with his commitment to Christ.

If we turn now to negative criticism, we do not mean it to outweigh the positive merits of John Paul II's theology laid out thus far. Rather, we mean our negative criticism to balance the uncritical commentaries that have abounded, and to exemplify the role a theology not under direct magisterial pressure might play.

The first negative reaction a critical theologian might feel when ruminating about John Paul's encyclical or Opening Address is that the style remains "Roman." We discussed Roman theology in our chapter on methodology, and we assume that discussion here. The Pope somehow remains extrinsic, more sensitive to tradition than to a problem's inner analysis. This is somewhat peculiar, for John Paul has studied phenomenologists, such as Max Scheler and Maurice Merleau-Ponty, who put modernity's demands for inner analysis and authenticity powerfully. Yet John Paul's theology is not modern, let alone contemporary. It seems innocent of historicity, hermeneutics, intentionality analysis, and the other categories post-modernity has introduced.

Hypothesizing about this peculiarity, an analogue to some believing scientists comes to mind. Occasionally academic circles witness a sophisticated physical scientist plumping for almost fundamentalist religion. John Paul II's theology is not fundamentalist, but it is not sophisticated to the level his intellectualism would lead one to expect. Rather, it is as though he has not allowed his philosophical and literary studies to impinge on his traditional faith. That faith has been too valuable, too clearly the core of survival in communist Poland, to be subjected fully to critical scrutiny. So he does not get inside the atheist's critique, or the materialist's program, to see the valid grievances they bear traditional religion. So he appears not to see the deep reform Catholic religion and theology must pursue, if they are to be authentic today. Tags like "atheistic," "materialistic," and "capitalist" go bail for hard religious analysis. Faith is argued with little reference to its current experiential complexity.

Relatedly, there is little self-criticism. The church John Paul describes, reflects upon, exhorts, is quick to confess neither its past failures nor its present inadequacies. John Paul would not deny that the church is a body of sinners, but he little relates that sinfulness to the history of Latin America, the secularization of Western culture, or the sundering of Christian unity. The ideal of what the church ought to be, what it is in God's heavenly counsels, absorbs most of his attention. The reality of what the church was during the religious wars, the Inquisition, or the witch hunts is left for critical outsiders to retrieve, as is the reality of too many boring parishes, paranoid bishops, and dilettante clergy. It would be better if the Pope, or the episcopal magisterium generally, were the church's first critics. That would be more authentic, more convincing to post-moderns sensitive to Sartre's *mauvais foi* (bad faith).

For there is advantage to power-holders in the status quo—advantage that the most convincing power-holders guard against publicly. For instance, one does not have to accept full-scale Marxist class analysis to point out that current rules of access to church power serve only straight celibate males, who cannot be more than ten percent of the natural population. Thus, current rules of access to church power obviously benefit only a small minority. The Pope ought to know to know this, deal with it openly, and so engage the difficult task of upgrading church theology to satisfy a current conscience refined by faith's Spirit. That would pressure theology to move inside, away from quotations of scripture and references to papal documents. It is fine to quote and refer, but unconvincing unless they serve an argument internally lucid, convincing in terms of experience and profound religious analysis.

Thus, the Pope's pastoral concerns, which somewhat justify his broad brush and lack of intense self-criticism, themselves reveal the need for a free, uncoopted theology. Unless there are Catholics who can say, "the emperor has no clothes," the church will be incredible to many of the most sensitive. Similarly, unless there is a personal theology that shows how divine mystery, decisively clarified in Jesus, is the fundamental reality, and how the twofold commandment is the simple human imperative, few moderns will account magisterial rhetoric stirring. The magisterial pot has rich fare, but who can digest its complexity? With all due respect, we wish John Paul would study Karl Rahner.

BIBLIOGRAPHY

Curran, Charles. "Heresy and Error," *America,* 142/8 (March 1, 1980), 164–166.

Elizondo, Virgilio. "The Pope's Opening Address: Introduction and Commentary," in J. Eagleson and P. Scharper, eds., *Puebla and Beyond.* Maryknoll, N.Y.: Orbis, 1979, 47–55.

Fitzmyer, Joseph. "John Paul II, Academic Freedom and the Magisterium," *America,* 141 (1979), 247–249.

John Paul II (Karol Wojtyla), *Fruitful and Responsible Love.* New York: Seabury, 1979.

John Paul II. *John Paul II in Mexico: His Collected Speeches.* New York: Collins, 1979.

John Paul II (Karol Wojtyla). *Love and Responsibility.* New York: Farrar, Straus & Giroux, 1980.

John Paul II. "Opening Address at the Puebla Conference," in J. Eagleson and P. Scharper, eds., *Puebla and Beyond.* Maryknoll, N.Y.: Orbis, 1979, 57–71.

John Paul II. "Redemptor Hominis," *The National Catholic Reporter* (March 23, 1979), 13–20.

John Paul II (Karol Wojtyla), *Sign of Contradiction.* New York: Seabury, 1979.

John Paul II (Karol Wojtyla). *The Acting Person.* Boston: Reidel, 1979.

John Paul II (Karol Wojtyla). *Sources of Renewal: The Implementation of Vatican II.* San Francisco: Harper & Row, 1980.

McCormick, Richard A. "Notes on Moral Theology: 1979," *Theological Studies,* 41/1 (March 1980), 98–150.

Whale, John, et al. *The Man Who Leads the Church: An Assessment of Pope John Paul II.* San Francisco: Harper & Row, 1980.

Wilder, A. "Community of Persons in the Thought of Karol Wojtyla," *Angelicum,* 56 (1979), 211–244.

Index